Isaac Babel and the Self-Invention of Odessan Modernism

Isaac Babel and the Self-Invention of Odessan Modernism

Rebecca Jane Stanton

NORTHWESTERN UNIVERSITY PRESS / EVANSTON, ILLINOIS

Northwestern University Press
www.nupress.northwestern.edu

This book has been published with the support of the Andrew W. Mellon
Foundation.

The Harriman Institute, Columbia University, sponsors the Studies of the Harriman
Institute in the belief that their publication contributes to scholarly research and
public understanding. In this way the Institute, while not necessarily endorsing
their conclusions, is pleased to make available the results of some of the research
conducted under its auspices.

Printed in the United States of America

10 9 8 7 6 5 4 3 2 1

Library of Congress Cataloging-in-Publication Data

Stanton, Rebecca Jane, 1972–
    Isaac Babel and the self-invention of Odessan modernism / Rebecca Jane
Stanton.
        p. cm. — (Northwestern University Press Studies in Russian literature and
theory)
    Includes bibliographical references and index.
    ISBN 978-0-8101-2832-3 (cloth : alk. paper)
    1. Babel', I. (Isaak), 1894–1940—Criticism and interpretation. 2. Kataev,
Valentin, 1897–1986—Criticism and interpretation. 3. Olesha, I͡Uriĭ Karlovich,
1899–1960—Criticism and interpretation. 4. Russian literature—20th century—
History and criticism. 5. Russian literature—Ukraine—Odesa—History and
criticism. 6. Modernism (Literature)—Russia (Federation). 7. Odesa (Ukraine)—
In literature. I. Title. II. Series: Studies in Russian literature and theory.
PG3476.B2Z799 2012
891.7342—dc23

                                                                    2012002271

For Edward Tayler, who taught me to read

Contents

Acknowledgments

I am hugely indebted to the many people and institutions whose help and support have made this book possible. The research and writing of it were supported in part by a postdoctoral fellowship at Harvard University's Davis Center for Russian and Eurasian Studies, and a Title VIII Combined Research and Language Training fellowship from the American Council of Teachers of Russian. An indispensable special assistant professor leave from Barnard College allowed me to travel to Harvard and Odessa to take up those fellowships and work on the project without distractions. Numerous smaller grants from Barnard have supported both my research and my study of Ukrainian, which is rightfully assuming increasing importance in post-Soviet Odessa. A PepsiCo Research Fellowship and a publication grant from Columbia University's Harriman Institute for Russian, Eurasian, and Eastern European Studies helped to fund my research in Odessa and the indexing and proofreading of this book, respectively. I am enormously grateful for the generosity of each of these institutions, without which the book could not have been completed.

Numerous people read all or part of the manuscript and offered helpful suggestions at various stages of its gestation. At the dissertation stage, Cathy Popkin, Catharine Theimer Nepomnyashchy, Mark von Hagen, Jeremy Dauber, and the late Robert Maguire gave me a sympathetic reading and a great deal of sound advice. I owe Cathy Nepomnyashchy profound thanks for reading and critiquing it again a couple of incarnations later, and more generally for her unflagging support and encouragement as my department chair during my years at Barnard. Julie Buckler provided wisdom and reassurance at crucial moments. Kevin Platt very generously read and offered invaluable, thoughtful suggestions on an early draft. Taras Kosnarsky read the penultimate draft with extraordinary care and offered comments that were both inspired and meticulous. Three anonymous reviewers for Northwestern University Press also provided detailed comments that helped me improve the manuscript significantly. The contributions of all these readers have enriched the book immensely; any remaining flaws, on the other hand, are all my own work.

I am deeply grateful to Mike Levine at Northwestern University Press for his apparently inexhaustible patience and kindness in shepherding this first-time author through the process of submitting a manuscript, and to the many others at NUP whose efforts went into making the book a physical reality, especially the project editor, Anne Gendler, and my indexer, Kirsten Painter. Ron Meyer at the Harriman Institute has also been unfailingly helpful and kind. For stimulating conversations, advice, corrections, references, and other less tangible expressions of scholarly fraternity, I would like to thank Thomas Seifrid, Gabriella Safran, Monika Greenleaf, Keith (Kalman) Weiser, Philip Hollander, Andrew Hicks, Douglas Greenfield, Jared Ingersoll, Justin Weir, Sasha Senderovich, Jonathan Bolton, and John Hope; my fellow members of the "Odessa cabal," especially Patricia Herlihy, Tanya Richardson, and Jarrod Tanny; my library comrade-in-arms, Mona El-Ghobashy; and my wonderful colleagues at Barnard and Columbia. My students, both graduate and undergraduate, are a never-ending source of inspiration, whose often unexpected insights into Babel and Olesha over the years have helped me rethink and refine my argument.

Early versions of material that became portions of chapters 1 and 2 appeared in the following articles: "Isaak Babel's Great Credibility Caper," in *Australian Slavonic and East European Studies* 15, nos. 1–2 (2001); "Identity Crisis: The Literary Cult and Culture of Odessa in the Early Twentieth Century," in *Symposium: A Quarterly Journal in Modern Foreign Literatures* 57 (2003); and "From 'Underground' to 'In the Basement': How Odessa Replaced Petersburg as Capital of the Russian Literary Imagination," in *American Contributions to the 14th International Congress of Slavists, Vol. 2: Literature,* ed. David M. Bethea (Bloomington: Slavica, 2008). I am grateful to the respective editors of those volumes for giving space to my ideas, and to their publishers for permission to include parts of that material here.

On a personal note, I owe special thanks to Edward Tayler and Nikolai Kachanov, two great teachers whose examples have inspired me for many years; to my ever-supportive parents, Frances and Basil Stanton, who made my education their top priority long before I did; and to my beloved husband, Chris Snyder, who did *not* devotedly type up my manuscript like the academic spouses of yore, but who has done—and put up with—just about everything else. Thank you.

Note on Translation and Transliteration

Throughout my text, I give quotations from Russian (and other foreign-language) works in English translation. Unless otherwise specified, all translations into English are my own. For Russian names, in the notes and bibliography, I have used the Library of Congress transliteration system, without diacritical marks. In the body of the text, I have modified the Library of Congress system in proper names only, by ignoring hard and soft signs and replacing *–ii* with *–y* (Gorky, not Gor'kii); by substituting *–ye, –yu,* and *–ya* for *–ie, –iu,* and *–ia* where I felt this would assist pronunciation (Yury, not Iurii); and in general, by giving all personal names in their most familiar English forms (Isaac Babel, not Isaak Babel'). Ellipses are mine, except where specifically noted.

Isaac Babel and the Self-Invention of Odessan Modernism

Stories That Come True

THIS IS A BOOK about stories that come true.

Stories can "come true" in a variety of ways, and these self-substantiating (or self-instantiating) stories belong to a variety of genres: there are popular myths that prove more enduring than scientific efforts to debunk them, clever lies that effectively alter the fabric of reality to accommodate a wished-for circumstance, or—as in many a narrated life—metaphorical confessions and creative testimonies that mask or even obliterate the memory of "what really happened." There are also official versions, stories told by the powers that be with the explicit intention of remaking "reality" in a form deemed more suitable for public consumption. Russian literature is especially rich in stories that come true, being a place in which the boundaries between the printed page and everyday life, between textual and physical worlds, have proved particularly porous: one might think, in this context, of the way walking tours of "Dostoevsky's Petersburg" take in both the dwelling places of the writer himself and sites frequented by the characters of *Crime and Punishment;* or the way Pushkin's narrator in *Eugene Onegin* appears to share certain autobiographical experiences with the poem's hero and others with its author, allowing him to act as a kind of "bridge" between the virtual world of the novel and the real world in which it was written.

These last are not idle examples; they are selected not only for their prominence in relation to the Russian literary canon but for the clues they yield about the kind of literary terrain in which this "crossing over" between fictional and real worlds can take place. The first of these is a terrain in the literal sense: the geographical place which, accumulating over time a set of mythical, historical, and literary signifiers unique to it, becomes a kind of palimpsest whose narrative can be reshaped and elaborated but never erased.[1] Not all such places are cities—haunted forests and sacred mountaintops also, surely, figure in the mythical landscapes which writers, in their literary mapping, both record and create—but the city, itself a "poem" in the etymological meaning of "thing created," is the literary place par excellence, and the one that seems most thoroughly to inscribe itself on literary works (which in turn reinscribe themselves on it).

The city with the most fully elaborated text in Russian literature is, of course, St. Petersburg, designated by Dostoevsky's narrator in *Notes from Underground* as "the most abstract and intentional city on earth" and by Yuri Lotman as a city "devoid of history,"[2] an ideally empty signifier destined to be filled up by successive generations of writers. As Julie Buckler puts it:

> St. Petersburg has been comprehensively mapped in terms of the literary mythology created by Pushkin, Gogol, Dostoevsky, Blok, Bely, Akhmatova, and Mandelstam, and by scholars who tease out allusions and influences within this select group of authors and texts. . . . This second literary-canonical Petersburg insistently *inscribes itself upon human subjects and transforms them into textlike bearers of cultural legacy.*[3]

The implication—Buckler is summing up here a set of arguments advanced by numerous writers and critics over more than a century—is that to live and breathe in St. Petersburg is to be enmeshed in a canon of Petersburg narratives from which one cannot escape, and that to tell stories in Petersburg is an endeavor fraught with the weight of stories already told. The territory of St. Petersburg belongs to Hermann, Raskolnikov, Akaky Akakievich, and countless other fictional personae who, so to speak, "outrank" the mere flesh-and-blood occupants of their storied stamping grounds: in Petersburg, the real feels virtual, and the virtual real. Any literary work produced—or set—in the spaces haunted by such ghosts is immediately absorbed into the cumulative "Petersburg text," and proceeds to inscribe itself in turn on the denizens of this "most abstract and intentional" city.

Isaac Babel, in his 1916 essay "Odessa," suggests that St. Petersburg exerts a sinister literary force which inexorably overwhelms any author hapless enough to enter its sphere of influence:

> Do you remember the life-giving, bright sun in Gogol, a man who came from Ukraine? Though such descriptions are there, they are an episode. . . . Petersburg vanquished Poltava. Akaky Akakievich shyly but with horrifying authority rubbed out Gritsko, and Father Matvey finished the business that Taras started.[4]

Babel proposes to offer resistance to the "mysterious, heavy fog of Petersburg," counteracting it with a "real, joyful, clear depiction of the sun"—a meteorological talisman he has brought with him from Odessa. As Babel is eager to point out, the Odessa city-text is largely defined in opposition to that of Petersburg, much as Petersburg's own city-text is (according to Toporov) "largely constructed as a mythologized anti-model of Moscow."[5] These three cities—Moscow, Petersburg, and Odessa—are the most mythologized in Russian literature, so much so that they are named by Vladimir Jabotinsky among "the few cities which create their own type of people. In all Russia before the war there were only three such cities: Moscow, St. Petersburg, and Odessa."[6] To use Buckler's formulation, these are the three cities whose accumulated texts are rich and compelling enough to "inscribe [themselves] on human subjects."

Considering this process of inscription, in which the text appears to write the person rather than the other way around, brings us to the second literary terrain that particularly lends itself to breaches of the boundary between "truth" and "fiction": the human subject, or, as we more usually refer to it, the self. It is a curious fact that stories about the self seem to command, purely by virtue of their recourse to the first-person singular, greater credulity from the reader than stories written in the third person. This general observation holds true, as we shall see, even in the case of stories that quite openly declare themselves as fictional; and it constitutes a kind of "loophole" in the ordinary contract between the writer and reader of fiction, whereby the fictional text "specifically, [though] not always explicitly, excludes the intention to deceive."[7] In fiction, the reader's disbelief is suspended in exchange for the tacit assurance that the story is *not* true (so that the reader is only playing at believing it, and real life is unaffected by the transaction). The presence of the first-person singular undermines that contract (the promise of the author not to deceive, and of the reader not to be deceived) by introducing a trace of the "autobiographical pact," a rival contract identified by Philippe Lejeune which "opposes the fictional pact." Lejeune explains:

> A person presenting you with a novel (even if it is inspired by his life) does not ask you to believe as fact that which he is recounting, but simply to play at believing it. The autobiographer, on the other hand, promises you that what he is going to tell you is true, or, at least, that he believes it to be true. He comports himself like a historian or a journalist, with the difference that the subject upon which he promises to give reliable information is himself.[8]

Lejeune is talking about narratives that explicitly identify themselves as autobiographies, but a long history of hue and cry occasioned by obviously fictional texts that, as it were, "trigger" autobiographical reading through their use of first-person narrative demonstrates that the autobiographical pact can be invoked *alongside* the fictional pact, setting up a condition of paradox that favors the movement of narrative material between the realms of "truth" and "fiction." It is a loophole that authors (or authorial personae) with a particular interest in transgressing the boundary between those two seemingly mutually exclusive realms have been quick to exploit.

Authors and readers instinctively understand the relative truth-weight of material governed by the "fictional" and "autobiographical" pacts: thus, in the example of Pushkin's *Eugene Onegin,* the narrator's first-person intrusions into the text feel closer to "reality" than do his third-person accounts of the doings of Eugene and Tatiana, and something of this feeling surely underlies both our appreciation of the narrator's gift for witty play (which strikes us as emanating more or less directly from the poet's own personality) and the contemporary criticism leveled in the *Moscow Telegraph* that "the Poet . . . simply wanted to have a frame into which he could insert his opinions, scenes, heartfelt epigrams and madrigals to friends."[9] The implication of either response is that, for good or ill, Pushkin's poem serves not merely as a pleasing fiction about patently imaginary events but as the expression of something real about the poet himself. It is not my intent here to essay an analysis of Pushkin's text; rather, I wish to suggest some of the directions from which an author with the ambition to make his stories "come true" might begin to mount an assault on the wall dividing "fiction" from "truth," virtuality from reality.

ODESSAN SELVES: THE WRITERS OF THE "SOUTH-WEST"

A cluster of such writers emerged, in the immediate post-Revolutionary period, from one of Jabotinsky's "cities which create their own type of people" (and his hometown): the Black Sea port of Odessa. Referred to by some scholars as the "Odessa school" and by others (following Viktor Shklovsky, the first to assert the aesthetic affinity of the group) as "the Southwestern school," "the Southwestern group," or simply "South-West," this group comprised a dozen or so writers born near the turn of the twentieth century, including the writers to whom this study is chiefly devoted: Isaac Babel (1894–1940), Yury Olesha (1899–1960), and Valentin Kataev (1897–1986). Other names frequently mentioned in connection with the group are those of the humorist duo Ilya Ilf (pseudonym of Ilya Fainzilberg, 1897–1937) and Evgeny Petrov (pseudonym of Evgeny Kataev, 1903–1942); the poet Eduard Bagritsky (pseudonym of Eduard Dziubin, 1895–1934), from whose collection of verses "South-West" the group takes one of its names; Bagritsky's fellow Constructivist poets Ilya Selvinsky (1899–1968) and Vera Inber (1890–1972); and a collection of less celebrated writers including Lev Nikulin (1891–1967), Vladimir Narbut (1888–1938), Sergei Bondarin (1903–1976), Georgy Shengeli (1894–1956), and Lev Slavin

(1896–1984). Finally, though not born in Odessa, the Moscow-born writer Konstantin Paustovsky (1892–1968) went to significant lengths to identify himself with the Odessa group and contributed substantially to their collective mythos. Coming of age around the time of the Russian Revolution, these writers became fellow travelers in the literal as well as in the literary sense, migrating from marginal Odessa to metropolitan Moscow in the early 1920s. Far from severing their Odessan roots, this relocation appears if anything to have strengthened them, as a group including Babel, Kataev, Ilf, Petrov, and Olesha ended up working together in Moscow on the railway workers' periodical *The Whistle* (*Gudok*), "exchang[ing] the warmth of the poets' collective for the comradeship of a newspaper office."[10] It was here that the young Odessan writers began to make names for themselves, and to earn a collective reputation that Shklovsky would later cement—for good or ill—in "South-West" ("Iugo-zapad," 1933), his article exploring the formal and thematic correspondences among their works.

Shklovsky would close his article by insisting: "This is a literature, and not just material for memoirs."[11] Yet it is precisely the memoiristic aspects of the Odessan literature that underpin Shklovsky's reading, and subsequent readings, of this literature as a collective phenomenon.[12] A striking proportion of the Odessans' literary output is couched in memoiristic or confessional modes of narration, including both fictional first-person narratives in which the narrator seems to share the sensibilities of the implied author (such as Olesha's *Envy* and Babel's *Odessa Tales*), and the more overtly autobiographical (though still generically ambiguous) works with which my analysis will be chiefly concerned. In both cases, a version of Lejeune's "autobiographical pact" appears to operate in tandem with the "fictional pact" to which it is theoretically opposed. Elena Karakina, in her lyrical study of the group, *On the Trail of the "South-West"* (*Po sledam "Iugo-Zapada,"* 2004), notes:

> Autobiographicity [*avtobiografichnost'*], incidentally, is one of the characteristic features of the Odessa school. The authors of the "South-West" loved to write from the first person, and the lyric hero experienced the same situations as the writer himself. *In this was expressed the character of the city,* where the life of the soul is not set up in opposition to the life of the body, and *where literature naturally, smoothly, and harmoniously flows into life, and life into literature.*[13]

This "autobiographicity"—the "self-invention" alluded to in the title of my book—is, as Karakina's language suggests, intimately connected both to the "South-West" writers' self-identification as Odessans, as "textlike bearers of cultural legacy" inscribed with the Odessa city-text, and to their preoccupation with crossing over, or even dissolving altogether, the border between fiction and reality.

The fictionalized "selves" projected by Odessa writers in such generically ambiguous works as Babel's childhood tales and Kataev's *My Diamond Crown*, along with the reminiscing narrators of Olesha's *No Day Without a Line* and Paustovsky's *Story of a Life*, coalesced—with the assistance of Shklovsky's article and the writers' own social relationships—to produce a powerful impression of a collective personality. In addition, the insistent self-identification of these narrative personae with the city of Odessa anchored this collective personality in a specific, and highly symbolic, place, connecting the personal myth of the Odessa writers to the literary and cultural mythology of Odessa. This mythology, like that of Petersburg, had begun to accrue from the very founding of the city, and the "Odessa text" in canonical Russian literature was over a century old by the time the writers of the "South-West" group caught Shklovsky's professional attention. The innovation of Babel et al. was to take ownership of this text, originally produced by the exoticizing gaze of nineteenth-century Russian authors, by locating their autobiographical experience within it; this allowed them to take up a ready-made place in the Russian canon, fashioned by metropolitan Russian writers, but validated by the biographical data of the Odessa writers themselves. In essence, the Odessans reversed the direction of colonization, staging a successful invasion of mainstream Russian literature using the tools left for them by "invading" Russian writers over the course of the preceding century. In a gesture that would become characteristic of Odessan modernism, they used autobiographical discourse to make stories—in this case, the stories about Odessa—come true.

LITERATURE INTO LIFE, LIFE INTO LITERATURE

Though Shklovsky and later critics have been at pains to identify thematic and stylistic commonalities among the Odessa writers, there can be little doubt that biography played a crucial role in their reception. The parallels among their lives, as well as the apparently genuine bonds of friendship that brought them together, hold enormous appeal for the reader's imagination, especially in Russia, where literary reminiscences (*Vospominaniia o . . .*) constitute a thriving genre. The biographical coincidences in particular are striking, and lend credence to the widespread perception of Odessa as a kind of combination melting pot and crucible, a miraculous incubator of motley talent or (in the words of one critic) a "literary cradle."[14] As I show in chapter 1, Odessa society encompassed a wide range of nationalities, languages, and political orientations, and these differences were reflected in the early biographies of the Odessa writers. While the confluence of their careers in the 1920s may be largely attributed to the relationships they formed with one another in various collective settings during the Revolutionary and Civil War years, this confluence is nonetheless remarkable given the wide divergences in their backgrounds. Indeed, the very choice of Russian as their language of composition was, for many of the Odessans, a significant aesthetic and political statement: Babel could have written, had he wished to, in Yiddish or possibly Hebrew—*did* write, if one believes his own claims, some early stories in French; Olesha might have written in Polish, Shengeli in Georgian.[15] Bagritsky and Ilf also chose to become "Russian," not "Jewish," writers—a decision that, almost anywhere but Odessa, would have seemed too obvious to be considered a choice at all. But Odessa's "literary cradle" fostered modern Hebrew and Yiddish literature, and Russophone Zionist writers like Vladimir Jabotinsky, in addition to the resolutely Russian Odessa school. For many of the Odessans, "signing on" to the Russian literary tradition was not the only option within their power to choose, but it offered a chance to be admitted to an established canon, on the one hand, and to participate in something utterly new—Revolutionary Soviet literature—on the other.[16]

In the choice of Russian, accompanied for most of the Odessans by a physical movement from Odessa to Moscow, one can discern a drama of desire. Whatever may have fueled this desire—whether pure aesthetic preference, Revolutionary zeal, or some version of the postcolonial aspirations seen in other empires—it drew the Odessans from the margins to the metropolis. It also united them under the standard of a common ambition, and, perhaps most importantly, it made them the bearers of a common nostalgia. The fact that their fraternity also rehearsed a favorite theme of early Soviet narratives—the triumph of shared ideas over differences in social background—cannot have been lost on the Odessans. Indeed, the early careers of Babel, Olesha, and Kataev—the three writers on whom the present study focuses—might almost have been invented to illustrate the concept.

In childhood these three writers were separated by ethnic, class, religious, and ideological boundaries: Babel's parents were bourgeois urban Jews; Olesha's, Polish Catholic monarchists; and Kataev's, according to his Soviet biographers, were culturally correct ethnic Russians who instilled a proper love of approved literary classics (and disdain for suspect ones) in their elder son.[17] Yet their lives in the immediate post-Revolutionary years proceeded in near-perfect parallel: both Babel and Olesha volunteered for the Red Army (in Olesha's case, causing a break with his parents, who subsequently fled to Poland) and spent the Civil War years engaged in journalistic-propagandistic activities on its behalf. Kataev also saw active duty in the Red Army, although apparently not before serving a brief stint with its opponents and serving time in prison for "counterrevolutionary activities" (a detail that "soon disappeared from his official biography").[18] It was during this period that Olesha's and Kataev's literary interests brought them into physical, as well as ideological, proximity. In the later 1910s, an assortment of Odessans, including both Olesha and Kataev, as well as Ilf and Bagritsky, gathered in the "Green Lamp" and "Poets' Collective" literary societies; in 1921, Babel joined all four of the above-mentioned writers on the staff of the Odessa paper *The Seaman* (*Moriak*), under the editorship of Konstantin Paustovsky.[19] Paustovsky, though a native Muscovite, is often counted (including by himself) as a member of the Odessa group, thanks to his fervent embrace in the 1920s of the Odessan writers and their city; his accounts of this period are an important contribution to the Odessa literature.[20]

When the turbulent Civil War years yielded to the comparative calm and literary renaissance of the New Economic Policy (NEP) period, the former crew of the *Seaman* gradually reconstituted itself in Moscow, where Kataev, Ilf, Petrov, Babel, Olesha, and Bagritsky worked alongside Mikhail Bulgakov on the staff of *The Whistle*. Their most fruitful writing years came in Moscow in the 1920s and early 1930s, with only Kataev continuing in physical, political, and artistic health long enough to make any significant contribution thereafter—although his establishment, in the mid-1960s, of a "Mauvist school" (from the French *mauvais*, bad) of writing encoded deliberate reminders of other Odessan writers, as I shall discuss in chapter 4. The remainder of the Odessans fared, on average, less splendidly than Kataev, with lives cut short by war, illness, or political disfavor. However, they left their readers with a vibrant, though small, body of literature, and with a collective mythology that attracted the attention of a succession of critics.

The first of these, as already noted, was Viktor Shklovsky, who promoted the Odessa writers as a group in his 1933 article "South-West." Shklovsky's article sets out to define the literary contribution of the "South-western literary school, whose tradition has not yet been clarified."[21] This "literary school" consists, Shklovsky makes clear, specifically of Odessa writers—"'The South-West' is, geographically speaking, Odessa" (470)—but in adopting the "South-West" designation for what might more accurately be termed an "Odessa school," Shklovsky takes his cue from Bagritsky, whose 1928 collection of poems had been published under this title. The "South-West" label chosen by Shklovsky and Bagritsky is suggestive, evoking yet revising the historical axes along which Russian-Ukrainian cultural relations had been organized, such as the division of Rus' into a north ("Great" Russia) and a south ("Little Russia," or Ukraine), and the Russian imperial annexation of right-bank Ukraine, formerly Poland's "Eastern borderlands," as its own "Southwestern land" (*Iugo-zapadnyi krai*). By removing the "*krai*" and retaining the "South-West," Shklovsky and Bagritsky manage to extricate the name from its imperial usage while salvaging one of its major imperial connotations, the rightful *Russian*-ness of the region and literature under discussion—a point Shklovsky underlines, insisting that "the South-Western school is a school of Russian literature, realized on Ukrainian territory" (470).[22]

The more distant echoes of "Southern Rus'" contained in the name "South-West" evoke a slightly different set of connotations, again one that locates the "South-West" firmly in Russian cultural space, but this time through an explicitly literary connection. Shklovsky refers the reader to the first half of the nineteenth century when Ukrainian figures, eager to reunite southern and northern Rus' (and thus to reclaim their privileged place in the historical Russian state), played an especially active role in shaping the culture of "Great Russia." Like Babel in the 1916 "Odessa" essay, Shklovsky points to Gogol as a forerunner of the Odessans—a writer who traded on the exotic appeal of his native culture to make Ukrainian "local color" a feature of metropolitan Russian literature, and rose to become that literature's preeminent "national poet." Whereas Babel argues that Russian literature assimilated Gogol, obliterating his light and color in the damp and fog of St. Petersburg, Shklovsky sees him in the context of a movement:

> Gogol was not alone. At the same time we have the works of Grebenka, earlier we have the works of Narezhny and Kapnist, later we have the works of Nestor Kukolnik and, in music, Glinka, who created Russian national music on Ukrainian motifs. (470)

Both arguments seek to cast the Odessa writers as an important source of renewal for Russian literature, at a moment when it is once again in need of redefinition; but while Babel, feeling a personal imperative to get out from under Gogol's overcoat once and for all, tries to cast Gogol's invasion of Russian literature as an eventual failure, Shklovsky seizes on him as the standard-bearer of an earlier "school of Russian literature, realized on Ukrainian territory."

The term "South-West," then, revives what Shklovsky calls the "complicated question" of Ukrainian-Russian literary relations; reminds the reader of Ukraine's double place in Russian history, as the southern half of ancient Rus' and as the Empire's southwestern frontier; and establishes a precedent for the "invasion" and reshaping of Russian literature by writers from the south that Shklovsky is describing and advocating here. At the same time, it strips these historical allusions of their original ethnic, religious, national, and imperial connotations, as it were sanitizing them for the new Soviet context. Perhaps mindful of the political hazards involved in singling out a regional school from the supposed unity of Soviet literature, Shklovsky is careful (but, as official reaction to his article would show, not careful enough) to avoid simple regionalism, instead founding his argument

11

for a "South-West" movement on the more orthodox ground of "social relations":

> Of course, literary schools are not defined by geography. But the social rela-
> tions obtaining at a particular geographical point at a particular moment in
> time are unique, and here one must take into account geography as well. (470)

For Shklovsky, the key point about the geography of Odessa—which
"explains much" about its unique social relations and cultural profile—is
that it is a port city, specifically a Russian port on Ukrainian soil. He invokes
a comparison to ancient Alexandria, a Greek port on Egyptian soil—and,
though Shklovsky does not state this explicitly, a city whose ethnically and so-
cially diverse population, attracted by the bustling trade economy, included
not only the autochthonous Egyptians and immigrant Greeks, but also the
world's largest Jewish community. Extrapolating from Shklovsky's reference
to Alexandria, a center of both Hellenic and Jewish culture and (crucially) a
space of encounter between the two, the reader can infer that Odessa owes
its status as "the center of a new literary school" to its cosmopolitan mix
of ethnicities and social classes, and to its sizable Jewish intelligentsia—a
group that had had little previous opportunity to make a significant mark on
Russian literature. Like Gogol (Shklovsky implies), the Odessa writers bring
with them from the south an abundance of local color, humor, and above
all good stories; but they also bring a modern, cosmopolitan, postnational,
and democratic sensibility that well befits the literature of the young post-
Revolutionary state.[23]

The "South-West" appellation also, of course, encodes a reference
to "the West," and it is here that Shklovsky's argument runs into obvious
political danger.[24] (The article as a whole is unusually disjointed and aphoristic, suggesting that the writer was inhibited by the political difficulty of
advancing the argument he wanted to make.) Shklovsky sees the chief contribution of the "South-West" group as being their "knack, the knack of the
Levantine and of the European, for creating a narrative poem [*siuzhetnaia
poema*]" (474). He contends that plot (*siuzhet*) made its way into Russian
poetry from the West, and that the advent of Futurist poetics banished plot
while declining to replace it with an alternative ordering device, such as
meter (471). In the post-Futurist era, therefore, Russian literature is due
for a new injection of plot, and it is here that the writers of the South-West,
with their "Alexandrian," "Mediterranean" sensibility, come in:

> The attempt of the Acmeists to create a perceptible world, to overcome
> "verses made out of verses," under the influence of the Futurists became a
> struggle for a new thematics. . . .

The Odessan Levantines—people belonging to the Mediterranean culture—were, of course, Westernizers. Moving toward a new thematics, they tried to appropriate it via the West. (472)

Though official response to his article would deem otherwise, Shklovsky is actually arguing here *against* both "formalism" (in its Stalinist sense of dedication to form over content) and Westernism in literature. He applauds the Odessans' restoration of plot to Russian literature, and their successful evolution of authentic Russian versions of the heroes and stories they initially "tried to appropriate via the West." They may have "looked at [Till] Eulenspiegel in order to see themselves" (472), but what "the mirror of Eulenspiegel reflected and made visible" was "the contrabandists of Odessa, who then came back to us as Babel's Benya Krik, as Vera Inber's Vaska-Svist, as Ilf and Petrov's Ostap Bender, as the heroes of Selvinsky's verses" (472).

Of all the possible "thematics . . . from the West" Shklovsky could have thought to use as an example, Till Eulenspiegel—neither particularly celebrated nor particularly Mediterranean—might seem like an odd choice, but as usual Shklovsky is onto something: the ethical trickster of medieval German folklore (who, not coincidentally, enjoyed a renewed popularity in early twentieth-century Russian culture, including a 1916 ballet starring Vaslav Nijinsky) is as much a forebear of the idiosyncratic rogues who populate the stories of Babel, Olesha, and Ilf and Petrov as were the real-life smugglers and gangsters who plied their trade in the port of Odessa. Eulenspiegel's signature accessory, the mirror, also suggests something of the "looking-glass logic" that pervades the atmosphere of Odessan fiction. Finally, the canonical prankster's mobility across linguistic and cultural boundaries makes him an apt analogue for the Odessan writers themselves, as well as for their fictional protagonists. As I shall argue in the next chapter, the Eulenspiegel-esque figure of the "Odessa rogue" would play a key role in both the character and the fate of Odessan modernism.

Shklovsky's interest in the colorful characters of Southwestern literature, however, centers less on the mischievous personality of these characters than on the role they play as prime movers of their own narrative plots; endlessly inventive and constantly on the move, they make things happen around them, perpetually creating story. The necessity—keenly felt in the Soviet literary world in 1933—of restoring plot-driven narrative to the center of the literary stage demands that the Southwesterners work as a "school," with a correspondingly amplified influence on the course of Russian literature: "The Southwestern school will have a very great influence on the subsequent narrative [*siuzhetnyi*] period of Russian literature. This is a literature, and not just material for memoirs" (475). Shklovsky's insistence on a distinction between "literature" and "memoir," as well as his focus on literary *plot* (*siuzhet*, a favorite topic of Shklovsky's previous theoretical writings) as the area in which the Odessans are to make a contribution, invite us to consider the collectivity of the Odessa writers on the level of form, not just of content.

Shklovsky's reference to "memoirs" here is, however, telling, for two reasons: first, the extent to which the Odessans' own predilection for autobiographical discourse has affected subsequent scholarship on the Odessa school, and second, the nature of Shklovsky's own interest in the school. In fact, Shklovsky's perception of the "Southwestern school" was influenced at least as much by biographical as by literary considerations. According to Mikhail Slonimsky, Shklovsky first met the Odessan writers in 1923 or 1924, while working on a parent publication of *The Whistle*, which employed Babel, Olesha, Kataev, Ilf, and Petrov.[25] He had, then, known them for ten years before penning the article that inducted the "school" into literary history. If this by itself were not "material for memoirs," Shklovsky's wife, Serafima Gustavovna Suok, had previously been married to Vladimir Narbut, an Odessan; and her two sisters, Lidia and Olga, were married to Eduard Bagritsky and Yury Olesha, respectively. In fact, after Olesha's death, his widow, Olga Suok, would work with her brother-in-law Shklovsky to produce the edition of his previously unpublished, fragmentary writings that appeared under the title *No Day Without a Line* (*Ni dnia bez strochki*) in 1965. It seems safe to say that Shklovsky's professional interest in the "Southwestern school" was rooted as much in "memoirs" as in "literature." In fact, as we shall see, Shklovsky's article on the Odessa writers was one of many stories about them that passed from life into literature and back into life again. It is another example of the characteristic feature of Odessan modernism, the story that comes true.

This particular story, which Shklovsky had borrowed from his own life, "came true" in a very different way from what its narrator had expected: the "very great influence" that he predicted for the Southwestern school materialized in the form of political peril and vituperation. The "South-West" article appeared in print mere days before the January 1933 plenary session of the Central Committee of the Communist Party and Central Control Commission, the first of many political meetings that year at which new formulae binding art and literature to the service of the Party and Soviet unity were developed, along with provisions for "purging" unwanted elements. In this context, Shklovsky's efforts to institutionalize a regional school in Soviet literature appeared "depraved" and "harmful," and immediately attracted a torrent of condemnation from more orthodox critics, who were mindful of the incipient formulation of Socialist Realism. In addition to singling out a Southwestern "school"—viewed as an attack on the unity of Soviet literature just when plans were underway for the first All-Union Congress of Soviet

14

Writers the following year—Shklovsky's article dared to imply that Soviet men of letters could derive inspiration from the West rather than from their common Soviet heritage.[26]

The rhetoric against Shklovsky escalated, casting him as a "class enemy" and, by February 25, forcing him to recant his position in a letter to the editors of *Literaturnaia gazeta* (which, however, was not published until April 29). At this point, according to A. Iu. Galushkin, "the discussion about 'South-West' transmuted into a broad 'Discussion of Formalism,' which continued to the end of the year," reaching beyond literature into the realms of musical, theatrical, and visual art, and pitting the concept of Formalism against that of Socialist Realism.[27] While it would be overstating the case to see in Shklovsky's article the single mis-aimed snowball that would eventually lead to an avalanche of cultural purges under Stalin, it is sobering to think that in seeking to elevate the status of the "Southwestern school" in Russian literature, Shklovsky may inadvertently have hastened its decline. Under the circumstances, the question of any such "school" in Soviet letters was not broached again in official criticism until the 1960s, when it was cautiously reopened in the context of new studies of Olesha and Ilf and Petrov by critics who carefully avoided the use of such terms as "Western influence."

In "the West" itself, critics for a long time dispensed with the distinction drawn by Shklovsky—however halfheartedly—between "fiction" and "memoirs," and his disclaimer that "it is, of course, wrong to set up one group of writers against another on biographical grounds" found no echo in non-Soviet commentaries on the writers of the "South-West." Rather, many critics—disarmed in part by the Odessans' apparent compliance with the "autobiographical pact," and perhaps also in part by a widespread understanding of Soviet disfavor (into which most of the Odessa writers would eventually fall) as a badge of literary honor—until comparatively recently were inclined to trust statements made by these writers (or even by their fictional narrators) about themselves, their compatriots, their origins, their aspirations, and their craft. The tendency to accept at face value the apparently autobiographical statements of Isaac Babel in particular has been, until relatively recently, a hallmark of Western scholarship on writers of the Odessa school.

Given the biographical considerations underlying Shklovsky's choice of aesthetic object on the one hand, and the autobiographical leanings of the Odessans themselves on the other, it is perhaps hardly surprising that subsequent scholarship on this group of writers has often failed to observe a clear distinction between biography ("material for memoirs") and aesthetics (the stuff of "literature"). Some critics focusing on individual Odessa writers have interpreted the biographical data as a corroboration of their Odessa-based works, which are thereby taken to be strictly autobiographical. Meanwhile, most previous scholarship on the Odessans as a group has attempted to show how life in the cultural milieu of pre-Revolutionary Odessa was formative for the Odessa writers. Proof of this superficially logical hypothesis is offered in the form of certain recurring themes, motifs, and imagery that appear in the works of the Odessans: for example, depictions of sun and sea, references to summertime activities, soccer, the circus, popular song, exhibitions of physical prowess, Jewish characters and "types," nonstandard Russian idioms, and so on.[28]

While these references are now seen as unmistakably "Odessan," it is hardly creditable that the Odessan writers, by virtue of their origin, were unable to write of anything else. (In any case, such a theory could hardly explain Paustovsky's enthusiastic embrace of the same themes.) Rather, it seems reasonable to suppose that, like their migration to Moscow, the Odessans' choice of material represented a set of conscious artistic decisions: having emerged from the literary *culture* of Odessa, they went on to promote a literary *cult* of Odessa in their works. In the chapters that follow, I shall first outline the historical and poetical underpinnings of the Odessa mythology, and describe some ways in which the literary idiom developed by the Odessan writers emulates the features of that myth. I then go on to examine three unconventional "autobiographical" works by Odessan authors: Babel's childhood tales, Olesha's *No Day Without a Line,* and Kataev's *My Diamond Crown.* I also explore the sites of interaction among these three texts and a fourth, richly mythologizing text, Paustovsky's *Time of Great Expectations.* My analysis focuses on how these three very different texts participate in, experiment with, and creatively deform the genre of autobiography; how they may be viewed as drawing on or contributing to Odessan discourse; and how each conceives and projects a specifically "Odessan" authorial identity, which profoundly affects the reception of the text.

As I shall argue, the "Odessa text" was entwined with, but distinct from, the historical reality of Odessa; it was unique in that it developed through the paradoxical reconciliation of diverse ethnic, political, and cultural perspectives; and it formed a deep reservoir of motifs upon which the writers of the Odessa school drew, and to which they also contributed. Finally, it provided the ideal milieu in which these writers—modernists, but with a narrative orientation; shaped by a revolution that radically altered the perceived relationship between language and reality—could play with, and even cross, the boundaries between truth and fiction.

City Through the Looking-Glass: Literary Odessa

THE RUSSIAN CULTURAL IMAGE of Odessa is a kind of mirror image, a faithful but inverted reflection of the "abstract and intentional" Petersburg. Each of the two cities, marking a highly prized seaport, stands as an architectural monument to the martial triumph of a specific Russian monarch (Peter I and Catherine II, respectively); but Petersburg is grammatically and associatively masculine, Odessa feminine. Both cities serve as "windows on the West," but Petersburg's window opens toward the chilly north, Odessa's toward the balmy south. The very architecture of the two cities is similar, boasting colonnaded, Italianate palaces in gay hues of yellow and green (and later, in Soviet times, ringed by the same indistinguishable concrete housing complexes); yet if Petersburg was, in its heyday as capital of the Empire, a city full of lawmakers, Odessa was always popularly perceived as a city full of lawbreakers. According to a local police chief in 1912, Odessa was home to more than 30,000 "suspicious characters," mostly concentrated in the notorious Moldavanka district, on certain blocks of which "every single resident is a criminal."[1] The historian Roshanna Sylvester reports that early twentieth-century newspaper accounts "portrayed Moldavanka as a kind of 'looking-glass world' in which the values, attitudes, and identities of respectable middle-class society were systematically subverted."[2] It was this world that Isaac Babel would immortalize in his *Odessa Tales* (written 1921–24; published 1931), which made that quintessentially Odessan Jewish gangster, Benya Krik, a household name.

The "looking-glass world" evoked by Sylvester alludes, of course, to Lewis Carroll's 1872 novel *Through the Looking-Glass, and What Alice Found There,* which similarly depicts a world where all normal values are reversed. Carroll famously imagines that on the other side of the mirror, one must run as fast as possible simply in order to stand still, and quench thirst not with water but with a biscuit; similarly, in Odessa, "success in crime rather than in legitimate business led to high status and social prestige."[3] The logic of the looking-glass world thus depends upon the logic of the ordinary world: it is illogic, but only when viewed from within the framework of what Sylvester calls "respectable middle-class society." Running to stand still is nonsensical to Alice, but second nature to the Red Queen; both these perspectives, normative and subversive, must be present simultaneously in order for the meaning of the episode to be understood.

Michel Foucault uses the term "heterotopia" to describe this aspect of the mirror image, the way in which it simultaneously depends upon and subverts the "real world" space that casts the reflection:

> In the mirror, I see myself there where I am not, in an unreal, virtual space that opens up behind the surface; I am over there, there where I am not, a sort of shadow that gives my own visibility to myself, that enables me to see myself there where I am absent: such is the utopia of the mirror. But it is also a heterotopia in so far as the mirror does exist in reality, where it exerts a sort of counteraction on the position that I occupy. From the standpoint of the mirror I discover my absence from the place where I am since I see myself over there. . . . The mirror functions as a heterotopia in this respect: *it makes this place that I occupy at the moment when I look at myself in the glass at once absolutely real, connected with all the space that surrounds it, and absolutely unreal,* since in order to be perceived it has to pass through this virtual point which is over there.[4]

When the mirror merely causes me to "see myself . . . where I am not," it functions as a utopia, an obviously nonexistent and disembodied space; when, however, it shows me "my absence from the place where I am," in other words when the reality of the mirror eclipses the reality of the space where I am standing, it functions as a heterotopia, a place that is real and fictional at the same time.

Unlike a utopia, which in Foucault's formulation is either directly or inversely analogous to the real world, and is fundamentally unreal, heterotopias are real (i.e., physically existing) spaces within which multiple conflicting perspectives on and relations with "the real space of Society" are simultaneously enacted:

> In every culture, in every civilization, [there are] real places—places that do exist and that are formed in the very founding of society—which are something like counter-sites, a kind of effectively enacted utopia in which the real sites, all the other real sites that can be found within the culture, are simultaneously represented, contested, and inverted. Places of this kind are outside of all places, even though it may be possible to indicate their location in reality. Because these places are absolutely different from all the sites that they reflect and speak about, I shall call them, by way of contrast to utopias, heterotopias. . . . The heterotopia is capable of juxtaposing in a single real place several spaces, several sites that are in themselves incompatible.[5]

As the anthropologist Tanya Richardson has noted, the city of Odessa itself functions as a heterotopia in at least three of the overlapping cultures within which it is situated: Russian, Ukrainian, and Soviet. In the nineteenth century, Richardson observes, Odessa's "rapid development, Mediterranean atmosphere, ethnic diversity, and commerce were a mix that appeared novel and exotic to observers from the cultural metropole [i.e., Petersburg]." At the same time, its urban and, especially, its cosmopolitan character stood in contrast to the dominant model of Ukrainian identity, which emphasized a rural, peasant-based culture and traditional folkways. Finally, during the Soviet period, Odessa constituted itself as a site of nostalgic and playful resistance to the "homogenizing impulse" emanating from Moscow.[6]

For the Jews who made up an increasing proportion of Odessa's population as the nineteenth century progressed, the city likewise entered popular mythology as a "novel and exotic" space in which normal "values, attitudes, and identities . . . were systematically subverted." Two colorful Yiddish expressions, *"Er lebt vi got in odes"* ("He lives like God in Odessa," suggesting both that a good time is to be had in Odessa and that its residents are impious, making it possible for God to live there unmolested) and *"Tsen mayl fun odes brent dos gehenem"* ("Hell burns ten miles from Odessa") underline the popular Jewish image of Odessa as "a Russian El Dorado,"[7] in which secularized Jews enjoyed "maximum freedom from [religious] restraint, maximum access to comfort and self-indulgence."[8] Sholem Aleichem, in his only explicitly Odessa-centered work, *The Letters of Menachem-Mendl & Sheyne-Sheyndl,* references the same stereotypes of wealth, luxury, and religious permissiveness:

> This town is so rich, and its Jews are so busy getting richer, that no one thinks about Sabbaths or Jewish holidays. . . . The Odessa synagogue is something to see. It's called the Choir Synagogue and everyone wears a top hat and sits on all sides of the cantor. His name is Pini and can he sing, even if he doesn't have a beard! . . . You can pass out from just listening to him. I tell you, they could sell tickets![9]

The inversion of values suggested by Menachem's confusion of religious worship with commercial entertainment is a close cousin to the topsy-turvy logic of Babel's *Odessa Tales* or Ilf and Petrov's Ostap Bender novels.

Odessa, then, represents a "looking-glass world" in more ways than one: not only has the city enjoyed, throughout its existence, a reputation for disregarding or subverting the norms of law-abiding metropolitan society, but each of the cultures with a stake in mapping its signifying spaces has construed Odessa as a space within that culture wherein the very identity of the culture is contradicted or undermined. Russian literature in particular has extensively elaborated upon this image of Odessa as a place simultaneously real and impossible, canonical and yet subversive, generating the rich "Odessa text" which I will analyze in detail later in this chapter. But where did this paradoxical vision of Odessa as a space simultaneously contained within many cultures, yet conforming to none, come from?

As the historian Jarrod Tanny points out, while in one sense Odessa is not a city at all but a "body of lore—the legends, the folksongs, the anecdotes—that has been collected, embellished, and passed down for two centuries," this lore does have roots in a real history: "There certainly were millionaire merchants, Jewish gangsters, prodigious fiddlers who preferred the seedy taverns to the conservatory, and subterranean smugglers who operated in the catacombs at various times in Odessa's past, and perhaps they persist even today."[10] This history, in turn, is rooted in a real geography: the gangsters, smugglers, and seedy taverns throve on the bustle of Odessa's international seaport, while the city's exotic character and popularity as a resort owed just as much to its "balmy climate, pleasant beaches, and lush vegetation" (a stark contrast to the icy northern metropoles). Before delving further into the literary image of Odessa, then, it is worth dwelling a bit on the city's checkered political history.

Originally a Tatar outpost, located on the site of an old Greek colony, and captured by Russia from the Turks in 1789, Odessa was formally incorporated into the Russian Empire (a designation then less than a century old) and given its Greek-inspired name by Catherine the Great in 1794.[11] The city thus represented a kind of capstone on the imperial achievements of the preceding two decades, a monument not only to Russia's ongoing expansion but to the radical fluctuation of territorial borders in the late eighteenth century.[12] The building of a Russian city—laid out by a Dutch engineer and adorned by the then-fashionable Italian architecture[13]—on this newly Russian territory established a capsule of Russian political and cultural space, even as it commemorated the recent (and ongoing) cultural "otherness" of that space. In accordance with this "otherness," the city's first two governors, commemorated in the names of two of its major boulevards, were not Russian but French: displaced from French society by the Revolution, the Duc de Richelieu and the Comte de Langeron volunteered for service in the Imperial Russian Army in 1790, and, having (severally) distinguished themselves in the battles that established Novorossiia, were appointed to govern the region in 1803 and 1815, respectively.[14]

Having made their way to Odessa as exiles and adventurers, each of these two could be said to represent what would become central Odessan traditions of one kind or another. The Comte de Langeron, a decade before his appointment as the city's governor, suffered disgrace at the Battle of Austerlitz and was ingloriously exiled to Odessa—a fate later to be shared by various Russian *personae non gratae,* including Alexander Pushkin in

1823–24. The Duc de Richelieu—a grandson of the Duc de Richelieu who appears in Pushkin's *Queen of Spades*—served, in his turn, as a model for Byron's *Don Juan,* thus becoming a sort of literary grandfather to the heroes of the poems Pushkin would work on during his Odessa exile: *The Fountain of Bakhchisarai, Gypsies, Eugene Onegin.*[15] A statue of Richelieu, erected in 1826, today presides over Odessa's most famous architectural monument, the giant staircase immortalized by Eisenstein in *Battleship Potemkin* (1925). "Clothed inexplicably in a toga"—a symbol at the time closely associated with the French Revolution and Napoleonic Empire, and thus wholly inappropriate garb for an aristocrat displaced by those phenomena—Richelieu's statue seems an appropriately paradoxical monument to the first governor of the looking-glass city. Or perhaps it implicitly celebrates the events that drove Richelieu out of Paris and, indirectly, into the governorship of Odessa.

The formal creation of Odessa, and the early development of its harbor and infrastructure, took place under the supervision of yet another foreign adventurer, the Neapolitan-born Spaniard José de Ribas, who was instrumental in the conquest of Hadjibey and subsequently tasked with founding Catherine's new city on that site.[16] Dismissed from his post in early 1797 following the death of Catherine and the accession of her nephew Paul, de Ribas is commemorated in the name of Odessa's most famous street, Deribasovskaia (which runs parallel to Lanzheronovskaia [Langeron] and is intersected by Rishelevskaia [Richelieu]). In the 1820s, the signs directing traffic along these French- and Spanish-sounding avenues appeared in both Russian and Italian;[17] these days, they appear in both Russian and Ukrainian, but, as if to perpetuate the Odessan reputation for trickery and mischief, are "often twisted in the wrong direction."[18]

Odessa's physical location—in the outskirts of the Russian Empire, within the Jewish Pale of Settlement (another Catherinian innovation), connected by sea to western Europe and, after the completion of the Suez Canal in 1869, to the Near East—contributed significantly both to the city's prosperity and to its evolution as a nexus of disparate cultures. Its privileged status as a free port from 1817 to 1859 similarly fed both the rapid growth of the city and its cosmopolitan character: since foreign goods could enter and leave Odessa duty-free, there was a far greater fortune to be made from developing commercial ties beyond the limits of the Empire than within them, and the port teemed with ships bound to and from western Europe, the Near East, and the Caucasus. A nineteenth-century observer went so far as to argue that its free-port status "cut off Odessa from the remainder of Russia. . . . so that the territory of the Odessa port and today's municipality had closer ties with the European and Asiatic ports of the Black and Mediterranean Seas than with the rest of Russia."[19]

If Odessa's climate, geography, and administrative setup tended to strengthen its ties to foreign lands, they served equally to complicate the city's relationship with the Empire of which it was an outpost (or "portal," according to a visitor of 1912).[20] On the one hand, Odessa boasted relatively balmy temperatures, plentiful sunshine, and a waterfront that suited the needs of vacationers as well as merchant seamen. On the other, it was located at a convenient remove from the imperial capitals. Thus, in addition to its fundamental economic identity as an international port, Odessa served metropolitan Russia both as a holiday resort and as a site of exile. It was in the latter capacity that Alexander Pushkin famously formed his acquaintance with the city, where he lived for a year from 1823 to 1824;[21] and in the former that early twentieth-century writers from metropolitan Russia—most notably Alexander Kuprin, Konstantin Balmont, and Ivan Bunin—came to spend time in the city and contribute to its literary culture.[22] To these writers, Odessa represented a place whose very identity was bound up in "otherness," a place defined by its nonnormative and nonmetropolitan status.

The city's relatively free and easy atmosphere and its distance from the capital also attracted yet another set of cultural outsiders: numerous "reformers and revolutionaries," ranging from local liberal societies to the "southern wing" of the Decembrist movement, had ties to Odessa (in some cases, through exile), and literature that was censored elsewhere, such as Alexander Herzen's *The Bell,* could still be obtained there.[23] Greek, Bulgarian, Polish, Ukrainian, and Jewish (Zionist) nationalists all established bases in Odessa between the 1820s and the 1870s, as did a branch of the First International. From the 1870s on, industrial action was added to the mix, with "several dozen strikes . . . recorded from the mid-1860s until century's end."[24] It was no accident that the Potemkin mutiny and its attendant riots—which would later, thanks to Eisenstein's 1925 film, come to stand for the entire Revolution of 1905—took place in Odessa.

On the basis of its climate, bustling trade, rough-and-ready dockside culture, and reputation for legally suspect and politically unruly activities, Odessa has often been compared to Naples or Marseilles, inviting a contrast with the Western analogies usually found for St. Petersburg—Venice and Paris.[25] (Babel, who refers to Odessa in "The End of the Almshouse" as the "Russian Marseilles on the site of Hadjibey," probably bears some responsibility for this trend.)[26] The implication is that, while Odessites were not immune from the perennial drama of Russia's conflicted relationship with "the West," they framed this drama differently from their metropolitan compatriots, looking toward another, saltier West than the dainty societies on which Westward-looking Petersburgers modeled themselves. This, too, marked a difference between the culture of Odessa and that of the other cities in which the Russian intelligentsia was collected.

By 1900, Odessa was the fourth-largest city in the Russian Empire, after Moscow, Petersburg, and Warsaw.[27] The cosmopolitan atmosphere that had characterized the city from the outset persisted through the nineteenth and early twentieth centuries, though the source, flavor, and political significance of this cosmopolitanism changed continuously. Though only a scant 10 percent of Odessa dwellers in the 1897 census reported their nationality as Ukrainian, the influence of Ukrainian national sentiment would become increasingly important as the political situation in the Empire grew more volatile; meanwhile, the city's demographic composition shifted dramatically from one dominated by western Europeans (who comprised nearly three-quarters of the city's population in 1819, down to about 5 percent in 1897), to one dominated by Jews.[28]

In 1897, the year in which the Odessan writers Ilya Ilf, Valentin Kataev, and Eduard Bagritsky were born, Jews already comprised nearly 35 percent of the population (up from 14 percent in 1858) and made up the city's second-largest national group, after ethnic Russians (46 percent).[29] The Jewish population boasted, moreover, internal diversity: in addition to the Jewish gangsters of the Moldavanka immortalized by Babel in the *Odessa Tales,* Odessa was home to yeshiva Jews, secular bourgeois Jews, prodigious violin-playing Jews, and illustrious *maskilim*—figures of the Jewish Enlightenment, or Haskalah. The city was a center both of the Haskalah and of Zionism. The end of the first decade of the twentieth century saw the emergence of several Jewish educational societies and scientific research organizations; in November 1909, soon after the founding of the Jewish Literary Society in the Russian capital, St. Petersburg, a branch was opened in Odessa, headed first by the Hebrew poet Shimon Frug (1860–1916), and later by the future Israeli national poet, Chaim Nahman Bialik (1873–1934).

As the last two names suggest, Jewish literature in three languages— Hebrew, Yiddish, and Russian—flourished in Odessa even before the city boasted its first homegrown crop of Russian writers. While Russian literature took ownership of Odessa and its mythology, founding writers of modern Hebrew and Yiddish literature, including Bialik, S. Y. Abramovitsh (1836–1917), and Sholem Aleichem (1859–1916), were also associated with the city.[30] Yet to the Jews, as to the Russian exiles and holidaymakers, Odessa could be only a borrowed, not a permanent, home. Quotas for Jewish participation alongside Russians in education and public life, as well as the pogroms that burst out in 1871, 1881, and 1905, served as reminders that even though Odessa's Jews might be "for the most part assimilated, Russified, educated, and cultured," and their city the one "in which Jews lived better and more pleasantly than in any other in Russia," their existence was a contingent one, based on local tolerance rather than absolute acceptance.

According to some accounts, on the eve of the Revolution, when the Odessan writers were coming of age, Jews made up fully one-half of the city's population, displacing Russians as the largest national group.[31] While this figure may be exaggerated, it suggests that in 1916 (when, according to himself, the 21-year-old Isaac Babel "began to take [his] literary works around the editorial offices" of St. Petersburg)[32] Odessa lacked an unequivocal ethnic majority: in the words of a 1913 Italian visitor, the city was "a-national, an esperanto city."[33] Demographically speaking, pre-Revolutionary Odessa was nationless.

After the Revolution, the turmoil of the Civil War only served to increase the confusion surrounding Odessa's national identification. In the years from 1917 to 1920, Odessa changed hands nine times, controlled in turn by Bolshevik, Austro-German, French, and West Ukrainian nationalist forces—and, of course, always by the anarchic forces that thrive on such military and political confusion.[34] The city's printing presses in those same years churned out hundreds of periodicals, of which most were in the imperial language, Russian. Ukrainian-language publications came in only third, behind Yiddish ones; French, German, and Polish speakers also enjoyed substantial offerings in their native tongues.[35] The reading population was, therefore, as fragmented as the city's political status was changeable. Moreover, the very Russian spoken by the majority—the language on which the Odessan writers would draw for their works—bore traces of its multicultural environment, including Gallicisms (adults were addressed as "Madame" and "Monsieur," a practical joke was a "roulette"), Yiddishisms (*gesheft, shabesgoi, Bud'te mne zdorovy*—a calque from Yiddish *Zayt mir gezunt*), and Ukrainianisms (*Ia skuchaiu za toboi* for *Ia skuchaiu po tebe*).[36]

While all these historical, cultural, and linguistic factors marked Odessa as "other" within the Russian Empire, the special heterotopian status that would characterize the city in the writings of Russian and Jewish authors seems to have been invisible to many Western visitors, who often noted (with pleasure or disappointment) that there was nothing special about the city at all. Even Judah Waten, the Australian-raised child of Odessite parents, found no trace of the Odessa they had described to him (in by-now-familiar terms) when he made a pilgrimage there in the 1960s:

> I kept staring at the passing faces; not even a descendant of Benya Krik and his colorful Jewish bandits. This was not the Odessa of my father, the Black Sea Baghdad of the Odessan Thousand and One Nights. . . . My father's stories, the writings of Odessa were entrancing, colorful, but that was all.[37]

American tourists, far from romanticizing Odessa's uniqueness, went out of their way to extol its familiarity. In *The Innocents Abroad*, Mark Twain describes 1867 Odessa as looking "just like an American city" (a claim hard to square with the city's Italianate architecture), and exclaims:

> I have not felt so much at home for a long time as I did when I "raised the hill" and stood in Odessa for the first time. It looked just like an American city; fine, broad streets, and straight as well; low houses (two or three stories), wide, neat, and free from any quaintness of architectural ornamentation. . . . Look up the street or down the street, this way or that way, we saw only America! There was not one thing to remind us that we were in Russia.[38]

If Twain's lack of discrimination might have struck a hypothetical 1867 Odessan as deplorable, how much more so would seem the conclusion of the journalist and illustrator Sydney Adamson, writing about the city for *Harper's* in 1912: "How like the rest of the world!"[39] To be sure, what Adamson finds familiar in Odessa is not the architecture, but the arguably universal tourist experience of being swindled by porters, who matter-of-factly take advantage of the language barrier between themselves and the traveler. For the most part, though, Adamson's description of Odessa, where he spent several months, is neither of an "American" nor of a "European" city, but of one that for him epitomizes Russia. The only traces of the Russian Odessa mythology to be found in Adamson's article are references to the diversity of faces that pass in the street, and a comparison of Café Fanconi, an establishment also immortalized by Babel and Aleichem, to a French (albeit "Parisian") patisserie. In all other respects the author is agreeably impressed to find everything—from the "celebrated Russian cold table" to the opera— "purely Russian."

Odessa, in Adamson's account, might as well be Moscow: its weather is "Arctic," no one speaks English, and everyone is so swathed in furs that only their eyes peep out; Lent and Easter are both ardently observed, and the Orthodox Cathedral is "the heart of Odessa."[40] During his stay, the author is cheerfully overcharged at every turn and even arrested at one point for sketching in the marketplace. Needless to say he is released once his sketches are shown to be harmless; levities are exchanged, and no hard feelings are expected on either side. How Russian! There is an almost Gogolian aspect to the proceedings, as some sort of local official, small in person but large in authoritative accoutrements, expresses enigmatic sentiments by means of an ambiguous monosyllable:

> The prisoner bowed and a little man with sharp eyes and a grisly beard, who stood in big boots, wore a gray uniform and a big sword, ejaculated, "Ha!" The policeman explained, and once more, with too much real satisfaction for the prisoner's liking, he repeated "Ha! ha!"[41]

Adamson's Odessa experience illustrates the extent to which the Odessa mystique that is so palpable to readers of Babel and the other Odessans was not, in early twentieth-century Odessa, there for all to see. A foreign observer, even one with so much leisure and curiosity as Adamson, stood outside the Odessa tradition in Russian literature; the features of the "Odessa text" were, apparently, imperceptible to him.

THE ODESSA TEXT

Like the city itself, the Odessa text had existed for about a century by the time the Odessan writers became a part of it. Boris Briker, examining the mythology surrounding Odessa in the terms set forth by the Tartu semioticians, notes that "an image of Odessa had been formed well before Babel provided the material for his picture of Odessa and its Moldavanka district."[42] Among the elements contributing to this "Odessa text," according to Briker, are "the history of the city, newspaper reports, urban folklore, and also the structure actualized in literary works."[43] In other words, the text is part historical, part mythical, and part literary. Real events play a role in the construction of the city-text; however, the relationship between its historical and its fictional elements is not, as might be supposed, a simple matter of "theme" and "variations," where the "original" is easily distinguished from its embellished offspring. Rather, this relationship should be envisioned as a reciprocal one: early twentieth-century Odessa was not only instrumental in creating a certain kind of literature, but was, in turn, partly *created by* that literature.

In particular, the ethnic and cultural fragmentation of Odessa's real-life population had important ramifications for the structure of the "Odessa text." The proliferation of ethnic, religious, linguistic, and social concerns simultaneously organizing the life of the city meant that Odessa, in its capacity as *sign* rather than as geographic entity, resisted classification under any fixed category of national identity, instead fluctuating according to the nature of the gaze trained upon it. If Moscow and Petersburg represented, respectively, a Russian gaze directed inward toward its own traditions and a Russian gaze directed outward toward western Europe and modernity, Odessa represented a layering of many gazes, a kind of Cubist mélange of perspectives in which the terms "self" and "other" had no fixed referents but occupied a constantly shifting semiotic space. It was a place where Russian culture appeared as if seen through a kaleidoscope, formed by the interaction of multiple coexisting yet irreconcilable "lenses": the gaze of metropolitan Russia (personified by its exiles and holidaymakers) toward its margins, the gaze of the margins back toward the metropole (which grew more urgent after the Revolution, as Moscow consolidated its position as "cultural and political center of the Soviet Union," relegating other cities to the provinces),[44] the similarly reciprocal gazes between Russia and the West and among Odessa's various ethnic groups.

Pushkin, that most canonical of Russian writers, established what would become the founding literary image of Odessa in the fragments of *Onegin's Journey,* originally intended as the eighth chapter of *Eugene Onegin:*

> I lived then in dusty Odessa. . . .
> There for a long time skies are clear.
> There, hustling, an abundant trade
> sets up its sails.
> There all exhales, diffuses Europe,
> All glistens with the South, and is motleyed
> with live variety.
> The tongue of golden Italy
> Resounds along the gay street
> where walks the proud Slav,
> the Frenchman, Spaniard, Armenian,
> and Greek, and the heavy Moldavian,
> and the son of Egyptian soil,
> the retired Corsair, Moralí.[45]

Almost as significant as the content of this stanza is its doubly marginal status, as an exile's description of Odessa which is itself "exiled" from the final version of Pushkin's *poema;* standing outside the main body of the text, and describing matters not integral to its plot, this fragment seems to take on some of the heterotopian qualities of the city it immortalizes.[46] Pushkin, whose sojourn in Odessa was not exactly voluntary, nonetheless chooses to frame it enticingly here, dwelling on the sunny weather, the window on Europe, the cosmopolitan atmosphere, the constant coming and going of things and people from foreign lands, which "imbued the landscape with glitter and color."[47] The use of anaphora—"There . . . There . . ." (*Tam . . . Tam . . .*)—reinforces our sense of place, emphasizing that the qualities described are specific to the city whose literary image Pushkin is constructing. The listing of nationalities and languages creates a sense not only of ethnic and cultural diversity but of abundance, an inexhaustible supply of exotic human types to go along with the inexhaustible supply of exotic goods routinely trafficked (or smuggled) through Odessa's port.

This trope of abundance persistently characterizes poetic images of Odessa, which emphasize the profusion and diversity of colors and flavors to be found in its markets. A poem by Eduard Bagritsky, "Encounter" ("Vstrecha," 1923), captures the feeling of being surrounded by opulent produce:

> And on that day in Odessa at the market
> I lost myself in the bosoms of tomatoes,
> I couldn't find a path among the watermelons,
> Cherries led me into a blind alley,
> A wall of cottage cheese blocked me in,
> Flowing like whey over the cobblestones,
> And porous cliffs of cheese
> Threaten to crush me in a landslide.[48]

Even the sun—described as "Odessan, thick, and big" (*odesskoe, gustoe, bol'shoe solntse*)—partakes of this overstocked atmosphere. This abundance that overflows into lists (of foods, languages, or national types), not unlike shopping lists, suggests not only the bounty of Odessa's international port— the city famously sent a shipment of oranges to Catherine's disaffected son, Tsar Paul I, as an inducement to maintain the port[49]—but also the diversity of its multiethnic culture, reflected in its cuisine, of which "Ukrainian and Jewish cooking are the basis," ornamented by Greek, German, Polish, Moldavian, Armenian, and Eastern flavors, according to a book of local food lore.[50] "Delightful to all five senses," Odessan food not only provoked nostalgic reminiscences from the Odessan writers after they had severally relocated to Moscow (Ilya Ilf, in a 1926 letter: "I'll have vacation on August 10. . . . I'll leave, probably, on the 9th and arrive on the 11th. I dream of eating the following: mackerel in all its forms, tomatoes, couscous, watermelons, kefir, *brynza,* and muskmelons") but poured out of their works, in the groaning tables at wedding feasts, the ice cream at Café Fanconi, even the "chocolate jacket, cream trousers, and raspberry boots" worn by Babel's gangster hero Benya Krik.[51]

The sheer fecundity of this imagery reminds us of the city's nickname, "Odessa-Mama," and also draws our attention to the visibility—in literature as in life—of Odessa's merchant class, a layer of society that, as Julie Buckler has shown, was systematically excluded from the literary image of Petersburg.[52] (The restoration to literature, via the Odessa text, of what Buckler calls "the sociocultural middle" suggests one reason why literature about, or inspired by, Odessa enjoyed such popularity during the NEP years of the 1920s—but also one reason it began to disappear from view, almost on cue, during the first Five-Year Plan.) The abundance of goods to be traded (on markets "black" or otherwise), as well as the abundance of buyers and sellers interested in trading them, served as an apt metaphor for the cultural interchange and mingling that was a hallmark of Odessa life and of the Odessa text: Amelia Glaser has shown how the town market square, often a "vernacular space" located directly in the shadow of a sacred one (the town church), is used in literature to embody "the everyday encounters between groups that differ in culture, religion, language, ideology, and profession."[53]

In the one brief stanza quoted above, then, Pushkin manages to capture practically all the salient features of what would become the "Odessa text" of Russian literature: sun, sea, trade, color, glitter, variety, and plenty. By institutionalizing the image of Odessa as a kind of carnivalesque alternative to Peter's northern "window to Europe," the poet seems to prepare the way for the Odessan writers' entrée into the canon of Russian literature a century later. But—with Pushkin there is always a "but"—he goes on, in the very next stanza, to dismantle his own illusion, noting that "our friend Tumanski" (a poet and associate of the southern wing of Decembrist would-be revolutionaries)[54] has already described the delights of Odessa; "but he with partial eyes/gazed on it at the time." The truth is that Odessa, like any young provincial city, is not only dusty but muddy; the trees that will someday provide ample shade, and help with the dust problem, are still small; the paving of the streets is not yet finished; there are even problems with the water supply.[55]

While the latter are typical problems of a still-young municipality (one that has yet to reach its golden age), Pushkin manages at the same time to convey a sense of nostalgia for a *bygone*, unironically delightful vision of Odessa represented by the "partial" Tumansky, with his "enchanting pen." Tumansky, it seems,

> like a regular poet,
> went off to roam with his lorgnette
> alone above the sea,

leaving Pushkin, an irregular poet with a disenchanting pen, to notice the deficiencies of paving and plumbing. (Fortunately, these will be compensated for in some degree by Odessa's deservedly famous opera theater and the "beautiful and gleaming" merchants' wives who frequent it.)[56] Here, as elsewhere in *Eugene Onegin*, Pushkin's first-person lyric persona forces himself on our attention, apparently losing sight of his protagonist altogether as he indulges in reminiscences of his 1824 exile. With its combination of nostalgia, playfulness, and autobiographical fabulation, this text presages the twentieth-century Odessan text in form as well as in content.

The features of the Odessa text as set out by Pushkin remained substantially unchanged by the time Konstantin Paustovsky (1892–1968), who adopted Odessa as a kind of spiritual hometown after living there in the turbulent early years of the post-Revolutionary period, offered his own lyrical description in *The Black Sea* (*Chernoe more*, 1935):

Odessa is the Levant. It is the Black Sea, the warm winds from the Bosphorus, the former Greek smugglers and hagglers of Piraeus, Italian Garibaldians, captains and port laborers. The wealth of all countries, the influence of France, the ghetto in Moldavanka, bandits who valued wit above everything, gray-whiskered merchants from Peresyp, the Italian opera, memories of Pushkin, acacias, yellow stone, flowers, love of jokes, and extreme curiosity about every little detail. All this is Odessa. [57]

Again we sense a kind of surplus that overflows into lists, as well as a number of individual list items that seem familiar: the warm breezes, the breath of Europe, the intermingling of cultures and classes, the opera, the jokes. Paustovsky, who frequently acts as a kind of self-appointed evangelist for Isaac Babel,[58] makes use of his list to build a textual bridge between his protégé and Russia's most canonical poet, expanding Pushkin's imagery of "live variety" to include some additional figures: Pushkin himself (fittingly, in the form of a "memoir") and the Jewish milieu that fostered Babel. Devotees of the latter writer will not miss the homage to the *Odessa Tales* embedded in Paustovsky's inventory: the Moldavanka, an unlikely site of nostalgia for Paustovsky in real life, represents the world of Benya Krik, and the "gangsters" for whom he evinces such affection are in all likelihood Babel's fictional ones, rather than their real-life models. The characterization of the Moldavanka as a "ghetto," which it technically was not, is Babel's too (although it could equally reflect an honest misconception on Paustovsky's part). The references to "the influence of France" and to Italian opera (the subject of Babel's 1937 story "Di Grasso," as well as of Pushkin's stanzas) also read as Babel signifiers, making the implicit Babel a shadowy counterpart to the explicit Pushkin in Paustovsky's Odessa canon.

Indeed, Paustovsky here echoes in part the essay of Babel's, mentioned in the introduction to this study, that was published in 1916 under the simple title "Odessa." In this short but often-quoted sketch, Babel undertakes to explain just what it is that makes Odessa so different from other Russian cities—St. Petersburg (then Petrograd) in particular. After making fun of the idiosyncrasies of Odessan Russian and extolling the city's "atmosphere of lightness and clarity," which he credits to the preponderance of Jews in Odessa's population, Babel goes on to describe "the typical Odessite" as

exactly the opposite of the typical Petrogradian. Nowadays it is a cliché how well Odessites do for themselves in Petrograd. They make money. And being dark-haired, they get limpid blondes to fall in love with them. In addition, Odessites have a tendency to settle on the Kamennoostrovsky Prospekt. You will say this smells of a joke. No, sir![59]

Whether the joke in question is to be about the stereotypical Odessites (many such jokes exist), or told by them—or both—is the reader's guess. The choice of idiom, "smells of a joke," recalls Babel's attention to the smells of his hometown in the 1915 story "Childhood. At Grandmother's" ("Detstvo. U babushki"), where he compares his treasured memories of the city to "the scent of our mother," and prefigures his description of Bagritsky in the foreword to a 1923 anthology of works by seven Odessan writers: "He smells like mackerel, freshly fried by my mother in sunflower oil. He smells like fish soup prepared on the aromatic coastal sand by fishermen from the Malofontanskaya neighborhood at noon on an unbearable July day." Like Odessan cookery, "delightful to all five senses," the Odessan spirit of humor and lightheartedness can be sniffed out in the environs of the colonized Kamennoostrovsky Prospekt: "Dark-haired Odessans simply bring with them a little bit of sun and lightness."[60]

It is for this reason that Russian readers should, according to the author, look to Odessa for the advent of the "Literary Messiah, so long and fruitlessly awaited," who will be the first to introduce into Russian literature "a clear description of the sun."[61] Commentators have often skipped straight from Babel's prophecy of an Odessan "literary Messiah" to the rather obvious point that Babel himself (some even add, "ironically") turned out to be that "Messiah." Indeed, it is hardly to be supposed that Babel had anyone else in mind for the job; the terms in which he couches his "prophecy" very carefully lay the groundwork for his own imminent "invasion" of Russian literature, where he proposes to create a uniquely Odessan niche for himself, redolent (like the Kamennoostrovsky Prospekt) of Jewish humor and mackerel. As Barry Scherr observes, Babel does not seem intent either upon recapturing the milieu of his childhood (which was spent not in the "overcrowded, suffering Jewish ghetto" mentioned in this essay, but rather in "some of the better parts of town"), or upon introducing the setting and mood of the *Odessa Tales* (which differ rather sharply from the Odessa portrayed here).[62] Rather, Babel's project in this essay is to outline an emphatic argument for Odessa's Russianness, for its importance as a "significant and enchanting city of the Russian Empire"—the only city in that Empire, he contends, whose sunshine and lighthearted atmosphere can hold their own against the creeping fogs and ghosts of literary Petersburg.

Babel is clearly aware here that, in making this "postcolonial" move— using "exotic" metropolitan stereotypes about his marginal birthplace to insert himself into a position of power within the metropolitan culture—he is following in the footsteps of Gogol, who had done the same thing with Ukrainian folkways a hundred years earlier. As Emma Lieber notes, "in 'Odessa,' Babel both sanctions later critical comparisons between himself and his Ukrainian predecessor and also guides their focus." (Lieber gives a catalogue of later critics who have drawn comparisons between Gogol and Babel; Shklovsky, in "South-West," would invoke Gogol as a literary ancestor to the entire group of Southwestern writers.) Tracing the trajectory of Gogol's career from *Taras Bulba* to the Petersburg tales—and stressing his illustrious predecessor's "almost mystical progression from utopia to decay,"[63] from southern sun to northern fog and sleet—Babel uses the "Odessa" essay to position himself so that Gogol stands in his shadow, rather than the other way around. Not being from Odessa, Gogol could not hang on to his artistic vision of "the life-giving, bright sun" in the face of Petersburg's ghosts; as a southern emissary to Russian literature, he achieves at best the status of a minor prophet. The role of "literary Messiah" remains Babel's for the taking; all he has to do is convince his readers that such a Messiah is actually needed.[64]

To make his case for Odessa as a source of literary salvation, Babel takes the features of the existing "Odessa text"—the sun, the sea, the dust; the "live variety" of languages and nationalities, composed of sailors, traders, holidaymakers, Italian singers, Jewish fiddlers, and Russian poets, with a seamy admixture of smugglers, gangsters, and exiled Russian malcontents—and turns them into a literary program, taking care to leave us in no doubt that it is a program for *Russian* literature. His birthplace—"Russian Odessa" in "the Russian south"—is named as "perhaps (*qui sait?*) the only city in Russia where our national Maupassant, of whom we stand in such need, may be born." The unnecessary little French tag accompanying this invocation (one of several that pepper this text: *"pur sang," "quand même et malgré tout," "parole d'honneur!"*) leaves us in little doubt about who this "national Maupassant" is supposed to be.[65] Odessa, a city surrounded by Ukrainian steppe and demographically dominated by Jews (as Babel readily acknowledges), is firmly proclaimed to be a new epicenter of *Russian* "national" culture—which Babel paradoxically hopes to join by posing as a Frenchman. The ethnic schizophrenia of this position seems quintessentially Odessan.

Indeed, this unification of seemingly irreconcilable perspectives is a crucial element of Babel's art. Many critics have remarked upon the way his narrative voice—even in seemingly disparate works—collapses opposites; a famous example is the androgynous imagery in "My First Goose," where a passage describing the macho divisional commander (*nachdiv*) Savitsky extols "the beauty of his gigantic body" with its "long legs . . . like girls clad to the shoulders in shining jackboots."[66] Within the "Odessa" essay, as Scherr notes, "Babel' seems unable to refrain from mixing the positive and the negative," moving in the space of a single thought from "the muscled bronze figures of youths playing sports" to "pimply and emaciated dreamers," and "from the . . . suffering Jewish ghetto to the sweet spring evenings with their pungent scent of acacias."[67] Even the peculiarities of the

Odessa idiom Babel makes fun of in his first paragraph seem to reflect this "double vision": according to Babel, Odessites talk of "two big differences" (*dve bol'shie raznitsy;* in standard Russian, *raznitsa* is never pluralized) instead of "a big difference" (*bol'shaya raznitsa*), as if they saw the concept of "difference" as inherently double (which, of course, it is; as an Odessan might argue, it takes two to differ).[68] Scherr sees this two-edgedness, this collapsing of mutually irreconcilable perspectives (positive/negative, masculine/feminine), as the main—perhaps the only—way in which "Odessa" prefigures Babel's later Odessa-based texts. However, I shall argue that this kind of verbal paradox is just one of several recognizable characteristics of Odessan modernism, and that these characteristics can be found not only in Babel's works, but in those of other Odessan writers as well.

ODESSAN MODERNISM

The "double vision" (or multiple vision) of an idiom that sees "two big differences" where standard Russian allows only one is a good example of the Odessan tendency to evoke simultaneously opposite sides of, or opposite sensations elicited by, the same phenomenon. The obverse tendency—to collapse distinctions between more or less opposite phenomena—is equally characteristic: Shklovsky writes of Babel that his "principal device is to speak in the same tone of voice of the stars above and of gonorrhea."[69] A comparable impulse can be seen in Olesha's *Envy* (1927), for example in the androgynous imagery used to describe Andrei Babichev (who has "the groin of a progenitor" and breasts that bounce when he walks down stairs) or in the juxtaposition of high discourse (Ivan Babichev's philosophical disquisitions) with low venues (dive bars). In his monograph on Olesha, Victor Peppard connects this device to the topsy-turvy logic of Bakhtinian carnival.[70] Indeed, since Odessa was—to metropolitan Russia—a place outside the everyday, a place of exile or holiday where quotidian laws did not apply, it makes sense to consider the paradoxical conflations of Odessan literature as a form of carnival, the aesthetic inversion or subversion of conventional dichotomies and hierarchies. A favorite target of such subversion was the division between truth and fiction—a division Babel, Olesha, Kataev, Shklovsky, and Paustovsky all sought to destabilize in a variety of ways.

The Odessa Rogue

Related to this subversion, or submersion, of conventional oppositions is a second indispensable feature of Odessan modernism: the figure of the

Odessa rogue. This character is an often, but not always, Jewish trickster whose success in navigating the criminal underworld (or, sometimes, another challenging historical milieu) serves as an inspiration for literature itself. Briker and Sylvester both note that the criminal enterprises of Odessa's "looking-glass world" expressed themselves in writing: "A typical raid in Odessa would begin with a letter of extortion received by the owner of a business, [in which] the extortionist would demand that the owner amass a prescribed sum of money and deliver it to a designated place." The language of such documents, laced with "the same clichés found in business letters," produced "a pure parody of business correspondence."[71] (One might think in this connection of Babel's story "Answer to Inquiry" ["Spravka," undated], which similarly borrows language from the business letter but converts it into literature.)[72] In other words, the real-life Odessa rogue was a successful author as well as a powerful protagonist, in full command of his surroundings. He was also an incorrigible subverter of convention: a popular *blatnaia pesnia*, or criminal song, associated with Odessa declared, "With us in Odessa, joking is serious!" (*U nas v Odesse—shuti vser'ez!*)—and the inverse of that sentiment could be asserted with equal truth.[73]

The Odessa rogue is a version of the trickster figure described by Lewis Hyde: a cunning thief who "invents the art of lying," and with it, art itself—that is, the use of linguistic signs to manipulate, rather than reflect, reality. Hyde argues that "theft is the beginning of meaning"—Odessa rogues are all, in one way or another, thieves—and that therefore "a prohibition on theft is an attempt to constrain meaning, to stop its multiplication, to preserve an 'essence,' the 'natural,' the 'real.'" By taking things from their proper places and putting them in other places, just as the real-life Odessa gangsters took clichés from business correspondence and inserted them into extortion letters, or as Babel would take events from literary works or from his own imagination and insert them into his autobiography, we alter their meanings and confound efforts to maintain a firm distinction between "truth" and "fiction"—or between "fiction" and "lie." According to Hyde, "both lying and thieving multiply meanings against the grain, as it were"; both are subversive, but also (or rather, *and therefore*) creative acts.[74] As Hyde's title (*Trickster Makes This World*) suggests, roguery is an important model for artistic creation that works "against the grain."

Perhaps the most telling description of the Odessa rogue is one offered by a writer who was not from Odessa at all, but who deliberately cultivated an "Odessan" authorial persona in his "criminal," dissident writings: Andrei Sinyavsky (aka "Abram Tertz," 1925–1997). As Catharine Theimer Nepomnyashchy relates in her definitive study of Sinyavsky/Tertz, the author borrowed his pseudonym "from Abrashka Tertz, a legendary Jewish outlaw whose exploits were celebrated in a thieves' song popular in Odessa in the

1920s."[75] The choice of this pseudonym by a writer who was himself neither Jewish, nor from Odessa—and whose identity as a criminal was due solely to his activities as a writer—reveals the importance of the Odessa rogue as a model both for the creation of fiction (along the lines that Hyde suggests) and, more specifically, for what Mark Lipovetsky calls "the practices of the 'shadow' economy and sociality" under socialism: practices which may have begun as politically innocent forms of economic chicanery under the NEP, but which evolved to include "different strategies of the intelligentsia's self-identification in the late Soviet period," from the everyday manipulation of personal identity in response to the demands of the state, to the dissident creativity of an "Abram Tertz" or a "Nikolai Arzhak."[76]

Sinyavsky conceived of his literary production under the Tertz pseudonym as a form of literary roguery—running in parallel to but on the opposite side of the law from his official literary career much as the criminal "looking-glass world" of early twentieth-century Odessa mirrored the world of regular business, and affording, through the manipulation of boundaries between "self" and "other," "reality" and "fiction," a degree of authorial power and freedom that could not be accessed within the sphere of officially sanctioned Soviet literature. In *Goodnight* (*Spokoinoi nochi*, 1984), Sinyavsky describes his borrowed alter ego as follows:

> I see him as if it were now, a robber, gambler, son of a bitch. . . . Intense, irrefutable. He'd slit your throat at the drop of a hat. He'll steal. He'll croak, but he won't betray you. A businesslike man. Capable of writing with a pen (on paper)—*with a pen,* which in thieves' language is a *knife,* dear children. In a word—a *knife.*[77]

Writing and knifing are as one activity for the Odessa criminal: one is irresistibly reminded of Babel's famous aphorism from the story "Guy de Maupassant" (1932), "No steel can enter the human heart as chillingly as a period in the right place."[78] The equation between verbal art and physical violence is not accidental; again and again we will see that the two are intertwined, even perhaps interchangeable, in Odessan modernism. When Babel spoke of giving up "the right to write badly" in his speech at the 1934 All-Union Congress of Soviet Writers, his listeners understood him to be referring to writing that was aesthetically "bad," unacceptable under the guidelines for literary art adopted by the Writers' Union at that same meeting. But he was also referring (those guidelines having become, effectively, the law of the land—the very law that "Abram Tertz" would wantonly violate) to writing that was "bad" legally: a crime equivalent to the slitting of throats with a pen.

A few sentences later in *Goodnight,* Sinyavsky characterizes Tertz as "a clown, a jester, *a rogue in the bazaar of writing,*"[79] making clear the connections among the three key aspects of the rogue persona: literature, wit (of the subversive, carnivalesque, court-jester variety), and crime. We can recognize these characteristics not only in the heroes of the *blatnye pesni* from which Sinyavsky borrowed his pseudonym, but in the literary rogues who populate the narratives of the Odessan authors, some Jewish, some not: Babel's Benya Krik, Ilf and Petrov's Ostap Bender, Olesha's Ivan Babichev (and Ivan's sidekick, Kavalerov).[80] All are loquacious, protean, masters of genre, and—importantly—autobiographical liars, a point to which I shall return shortly.

To the extent that the figure of the Moldavanka gangster overturns standard literary conventions surrounding the figure of the "small, bent, weak, and pathetic" Jew, he belongs not only to the category of Odessan rogues but also to the category of "New Jewish Men," who featured prominently in the works of Odessan writers as well as those of other Soviet writers of the 1920s.[81] Babel's El'ia Isaakovich, Benya Krik, and the eccentric forebears ascribed to the narrator of the "childhood" tales, can be placed in this category, as can Bagritsky's Kogan in *The Lay of Opanas* (*Duma pro Opanasa*, 1926), who coolly faces down and shoots the poem's eponymous antihero, or Kataev's David Margulies in *Time, Forward!* (*Vremia, vpered!*, 1932), who successfully oversees a record-breaking bout of concrete production (and ushers in the era of the production novel). Thanks in large part to Babel's Odessa tales, such radical images of Jewish brawn and potency ("You can spend the night with a Russian woman, and the Russian woman will be satisfied with you"),[82] and in particular of Jewish gangsters, have become closely identified in the Russian imagination with Odessa. In fact, however, Jewish gangsters and strongmen were a relatively common phenomenon in the early twentieth century (they were found in New York, Chicago, and Los Angeles in addition to eastern Europe);[83] moreover, contemporary Yiddish literature enjoyed, according to David Roskies, a "longstanding romance with the Jewish gangster" who, in the guise of a stock character known as the *ba'al guf* (after the hero of Bialik's 1899 Hebrew novel *Arye Ba'al-guf*), "enjoyed something of a vogue between 1910 and the 1930s, both in fiction and on the stage."[84]

It was *Russian* literature that lacked such characters, and in providing them, the Odessans wove together three previously separate strands of the "Odessa text": the "Jewish question," particularly urgent at the turn of the twentieth century; a certain tincture of the carnivalesque; and a related preoccupation with physical prowess, as exemplified by the clientele of Kuprin's "Gambrinus":

All these people—sailors of various nations, fishermen, stokers, merry ship's boys, harbor thieves, machinists, workers, boatmen, dockers, divers, smugglers—they were all young, healthy, and steeped in the strong [*krepkim*]

odor of sea and fish; they understood hard work, loved the allure and terror of daily risk, and valued above all strength [*silu*], prowess, and the sting of
strong [*krepkogo*] language; when on dry land they gave themselves up with
savage relish to debauchery, drunkenness and fighting.[85]

This sentence, in which "strength" (of odor, of body, and of language) is repeatedly evoked alongside verbs of enjoyment (*liubili, tsenili, predavalis' s
dikim naslazhdeniem*), lays out the vocabulary subsequently used by Babel
and Olesha to describe the world from which their narrators are debarred.

It is interesting to note that while Babel stocks his stories with Jewish
characters who impress the reader with, to use Gorky's phrase, "the amazing tension of [their] will to live," he reserves for his first-person narrators
(*Red Cavalry*'s Lyutov; the narrator of the "autobiographical" tales) a Jewish self-consciousness based on the more conventional image of the "small,
bent, weak, and pathetic" Jew.[86] Olesha's first-person narrators (Kavalerov;
the seemingly autobiographical narrators of "The Chain" and "The Cherry
Pit") suffer from a similarly frail self-image, though they are not Jewish. Indeed, Babel's and Olesha's first-person narrators have in common a sense of
alienation from the raw, sexy, and brutal physicality described by Kuprin and
embodied by characters such as Benya Krik and Andrei Babichev. It is as
if both the myth of Jewish frailty and the images of physical and sexual potency to which it was opposed have been cut loose from their ethnic moor-
ings; the images are the same, but the division is between "self" (the narrator) and "other," rather than between Jew and Russian.[87] In a heterotopia, a
place "outside of all places," everyone is an outsider; to be self-conscious is
to be conscious of one's own "outsiderness."

Exilic Anxiety and Nostalgic Longing

The anxiety, as well as the secret joys, of "outsiderness"—a historical reality
for the Jews, but a literary pose for Babel, Olesha, and the other Odessan
writers who settled in Moscow—underlie a third characteristic of Odessan
modernism, albeit one that is shared by modernist literature more generally.
Indeed, the coincidence of the Odessan moment in Russian literature with
the epoch of modernism was probably not random: it is worthy of note that
despite its frequent visits from (and romanticization at the hands of) illustrious Russian writers, and despite its status as a center of both Yiddish and
Hebrew literature in the nineteenth century, Odessa did not make its major
homegrown contribution to Russian literature until the Revolutionary generation. Even then, it was not until the Odessans had left Odessa for metropolitan Russia that they wrote most of the works, from Babel's "Odessa"
(1916) to Kataev's *My Diamond Crown* (*Almaznyi moi venets*, 1977), for

which they are justly celebrated, and with which they mutually assured their collective fame. That most of these works were, moreover, written during the two decades following the Revolution—decades in which the Odessa they had known underwent tremendous upheaval and, arguably, ceased to exist—means that Odessa was both spatially and temporally absent for the Odessa writers at the moment when they became Odessa writers. It is not too far-fetched to speculate that they wrote as they did partly to make it present.[88]

A peculiar paradox (one, as must by now be evident, among many) of the Odessa myth was that Odessa was always already "over," perceived as being in a decline from its golden age when the gangsters were *really* gangsters, the exotic people and commodities *really* exotic, the sunshine *really* sunny (Alexander Deribas, in 1913: "I have not forgotten the old Odessan sun. It was brighter and its smile was more affectionate than it is today. It used to illuminate Odessa without restraint").[89] One can sense a nostalgia even, as I suggested above, in Pushkin's early canonizing stanzas: Pushkin, coming after the poets who could ignore inconvenience and selectively "glor[y] the gardens of Odessa," but before the construction of such impressive monuments as the Primorsky (now ".Potemkin") Staircase (1837–41) and the Viennese-designed Opera and Ballet Theater (1884–87), could make a case for having missed an Odessan golden age, which other nineteenth-century writers reported as having taken place between 1815 and 1820. Jarrod Tanny documents how subsequent accounts mourned the passing of Odessa's prime, variously identified as the 1840s, 1870s, 1900s, and 1920s, and concludes: "An analysis of the Odessa myth from the early nineteenth century to the present demonstrates that Odessa's golden age has been mourned for its apparent passing from the city's very inception."[90] Two centuries later, the tradition persists: on a research trip to Odessa in 2007, I was told in my turn—by a very serious young scholar, aged twenty-four—"You've come too late; Odessa isn't what it used to be." Further inquiry revealed that the lost golden age he had in mind was, improbably, the 1980s—the first years of his life, and the last in the life of the Soviet Union.

The loss of, or sense of disjuncture from, one's personal past is a widespread theme in early Soviet (as now, in post-Soviet) literature. For writers whose youth was divided from their adulthood by the irreversible turnstile of the Revolution, the price to be paid was, in Carol Avins's phrase, "the loss of one's personal past, and particularly of home, the place where one most fully belong[ed]."[91] The return to a personal home grounded in a personal past—to one's proper and private spatiotemporal coordinates—is an ancient literary dream, embodied in Homer's *Odyssey* and rehearsed in innumerable works over the subsequent centuries. However, as Svetlana Boym points out, in a rapidly changing world "a return home does not involve only a journey in space, but also an adventure in time": return is sometimes chronologically impossible.[92] Petersburgers of the Revolutionary generation repeatedly found their hometown literally erased from the map, replaced first by "Petrograd," then by "Leningrad." They also suffered the loss (to Moscow) of their city's former position as imperial capital, and a corresponding relegation to provincial status. Odessa, arguably, represented an even more troublesome case, since the defining feature of its semiotics was a radical ethnic and cultural undecidability: though *home* to about half a million people, it was *homeland* to none—a notion reinforced by Odessa's image in Russian culture as a perpetual destination of holidaymakers and exiles. The whole identity of Odessa was bound up in contradictory multiplicity: it was a shifting sign, not the kind you could navigate toward with a nostalgic compass.

Moreover, many of the Odessan writers, including the three whose works form my principal object of study in the succeeding chapters, spent their early careers in agitprop journalism. That gave them a professional interest in the progress of the Civil and Polish-Soviet Wars—wars that, as Avins suggests, imbued the territorial with the ideological.[93] The advancing and retreating fronts of the conflict acquired the significance of advancing and retreating time: the Polish effort to restore its 1772 borders and prestige versus the Soviet effort to catalyze a new European order, the White effort to restore a semblance of pre-Bolshevik Russia versus the Red effort to buttress its futuristic vision of communist utopia. These fronts passed several times through Odessa.

The search for a fixed point of reference becomes all the more urgent amid uncertain surroundings and changeable winds. As yet unaware that his life story will be defined by a twenty-year absence from home, Homer's Odysseus (a quintessential trickster and a master craftsman) carves his marriage bed from a mighty and firmly rooted tree trunk; upon his return, after numerous detours and delays, this immovable object of his own making will become the key not only to his homecoming but to his true identity. In Homer, this kind of activity, converting a "raw" natural object to a "cooked" human artifact, tends to stand for the creation of poetic meaning (which lasts) from mortal phenomena (which decay).[94] *Being*, in itself senseless and ephemeral, acquires both significance and permanence through the act of *making*; the tree-bed becomes synonymous with Odysseus's identity, standing for him throughout his absence and providing the key whereby he is recognized on his return.[95] That the final proof of continuity between Odysseus the bridegroom and Odysseus the returning wanderer is furnished by an artifact, rather than a sentiment, shows us that making, not memory, is the engine by which identity is established; or as Boym puts it, "The literal is less truthful than the literary."[96] In the same spirit, the articulation of a coherent Odessan identity based on a common Odessan "home" must be seen as a creative, rather than a recuperative, act.

Self-Invention and Odessan Modernism

Odysseus is, in addition to being the quintessential literary representative of homesickness, the first great autobiographical liar in European literature: famously, upon his long-awaited return to Ithaka,

> he poses as a Cretan and tells three notoriously elaborate autobiographical stories, all of which contain elements from what we think of as his real life. It's at this point that you start to wonder what words like "real" and "true" mean in a work that is itself a fiction.[97]

Earlier in the epic, Odysseus has—in a kind of reversal of the move made by *Onegin's* narrator, who incorrigibly inserts himself into a story ostensibly about the titular character—wrested control of his own story from the "official" narrator, recounting the events of the past ten years in his own words. It is a move that reveals the peculiarly bifurcated relationship of autobiographical narrative to what we perceive as "truth": on the one hand, in accordance with the autobiographical pact, we understand that the first-person narrator is the most qualified witness to the events of his own life. On the other, we understand that the first-person narrator is intrinsically unreliable. When Alkinoös, king of Phaiakia, responds to Odysseus's tale with the words

> "Odysseus, we as we look upon you do not imagine
> that you are a deceptive or thievish man, the sort that the black earth
> breeds in great numbers, people who wander widely, making up
> lying stories,"[98]

it is hard to tell whether he is sarcastic or serious: is he courteously abiding by the autobiographical pact, or commenting dryly on its obvious violation?

Odysseus, one of only three characters in Greek literature to be described as "polytropic" (*polutropos*, "turning many ways"), is an archetypal trickster: he uses his autobiographical lies as disguises, expertly manipulating his identity in order to shape the developing narrative of his life.[99] In this he is again a forerunner and kindred spirit of the Odessa writers, whose preoccupation with identity, as well as their keen interest in literary roguery, is reflected in the fourth major characteristic of Odessan modernism, one that is both foreshadowed in Babel's "Odessa" and hinted at by Shklovsky in "South-West": a blurring of the line (to the extent that such a line exists) between "literature" and "memoir." As I noted in the introduction to this study, the tendency of the Odessa writers to favor narrative modes that their audience took to be autobiographical, in the strictest sense, has been one of the most significant factors in their reception.

The most important principle governing autobiography is its devotion to the evolution of a central figure understood as the "self" both of the author and of the narrator; its second most important principle is the relationship of the narrative to historical "truth," of which the identity among author, narrator, and protagonist is understood as a symbol. These two rules are particularly significant in the context of Russian and early Soviet literature. If autobiographical forms came to be viewed during the Thaw as a form of testimony, especially against the atrocities committed by the Stalinist regime, in the early Soviet period they served as a literary sanctuary for the "private" voice, at a time when literary language was increasingly being reserved and refurbished for "public" uses. In both periods, the stakes for self-narrative were high, and so, correspondingly, was the expectation of truthfulness (even at a moment when the daily reality of coerced confessions and insincere professions of political faith created a dark parody of autobiography that might call to mind the "parody of business correspondence" engaged in by the Odessa gangsters).[100]

At the same time, the idea that literature could, and should, act upon and refurbish reality was current in Soviet Russia even before the formal institution of Socialist Realism in 1934. Autobiographical discourse, by offering the author control over a narrative "contractually" rooted in reality, afforded an opportunity to rewrite the past, much as Socialist Realism would seek to rewrite the present and future.[101] In the chapters that follow, I will examine some of the ways in which the Odessa writers roguishly manipulate the boundaries of autobiographical discourse, subverting the logic of Socialist Realism for their own purposes; and the techniques by which they create the signs of personal authenticity, as a substitute for "objective," publicly recognized truth. Because their autobiographical acts bordered upon and implicated one another, the Odessans furnish particularly interesting territory for such an investigation: in inventing themselves, they were also inventing a narrative of each other, of Odessa, and of Soviet literature that would compete for authority with the "scientific" version advanced by historians.

Stories That Come True

This circle of themes (carnivalesque inversion and the collapsing of opposites, creative rogues, exile and nostalgia, autobiographical fabulation and self-invention) leads us back to what, for me, is the most interesting characteristic of my Odessan writers' works: their shared interest in stories that come true, and conversely in truths that become stories. As I suggested in my introduction, Shklovsky's critical narrative of the Southwestern school can be read as an impression taken from life (a "truth"), which became a story, which in its turn "came true" in both expected and unexpected ways. The haste and vehemence with which more-Party-minded writers rushed to refute Shklovsky's propositions may be compared to the similar rebuttals directed at Babel's *Red Cavalry* by Cavalry Commander Budyonny, at Kataev's *My Diamond Crown* by contemporaries on both sides of the Iron Curtain, and at Babel's and Olesha's autobiographical narratives by Kataev himself.[102]

In all these cases, stories seen as having pretensions to "truth" are tested and found wanting—all the while giving rise to very nonfictional consequences. Conversely, stories that declare themselves as fictional—a short story by Kuprin, a poem by Bagritsky, the tall tales of an invented great-uncle—are suddenly revealed to be truer than the "autobiographical" narratives surrounding them, possessing a solid historicity borne out by material evidence (a grave site, a stone wall, an eyewitness). The fluidity of the boundaries between "truth" and "fiction," and the Odessan writers' roguish play with these boundaries, will be a central theme of the literary analyses that follow. Babel in particular is an autobiographical liar on a par with Odysseus, and the next two chapters examine his development of this very Odessan literary technique.

Isaac Babel: Stories That Lie Like Truth

I pull in resolution, and begin
To doubt th'equivocation of the fiend
That lies like truth.
—Macbeth

I was a deceitful [*lzhivyi*] boy. This was the result of reading. My imagination was always inflamed. I read during lessons, in the recesses, on my way home, at night under the table. . . . Who would have wanted to consort with such a fellow?[1]

With these words, Isaac Babel begins his short story "In the Basement" ("V podvale," 1931), one of a cycle of childhood stories ostensibly narrated by, and starring, the young Isaac Babel himself. As indicated in notes Babel appended to the stories as they were published, this cycle includes four stories: "The Story of My Dovecote" ("Istoriia moei golubiatni," 1925), whose title Babel apparently intended to use as the name of the whole cycle; "First Love" ("Pervaia liubov'," 1925); "In the Basement" ("V podvale," 1931); and "Awakening" ("Probuzhdenie," 1931). In my consideration of this "childhood" cycle, which occupies the bulk of the next two chapters, I add a fifth story, "Childhood. At Grandmother's" ("Detstvo. U babushki," dated 1915, and unpublished at the time of Babel's death). As I will argue, placing this early story at the beginning of the cycle creates a pleasing formal symmetry and also provides the reader with indispensable clues about how to read the cycle as a whole.

In the story quoted at the head of this chapter, the narrator almost immediately answers his own question—"who would have wanted to consort with such a fellow?"—by describing the instant popularity he has enjoyed among his classmates upon revealing his talent as a spinner of yarns. His teachers, too, are beguiled by the young narrator's gift for storytelling, awarding him quasi-respectable grades, instead of the *dvoiki* (equivalent to Ds) his neglected schoolwork really merits. It would seem, then, that in fact quite a lot of people "would want to consort with such a fellow." But who on earth would actually swallow his "deceitful" stories?

Surprisingly, the answer here too is "quite a lot of people." So cunningly does Babel blur the line between truth and fiction in his childhood stories that his readers are apt to overlook the clues provided by the stories' form and the narrator's many hints, and invest heavily in his counterfeit coin, all the more so since reliable autobiographical, or even biographical, information about Babel has been hard to come by. Even so eminent a critic as Lionel Trilling proved susceptible to Babel's blarney, apparently mistaking a scene from the Babel story "First Love" for historical fact:

> But Babel had seen his father on his knees before a Cossack captain on a horse, who said, "At your service," and touched his fur cap with his yellow-gloved hand and politely paid no heed to the mob looting the Babel store. Such an experience, or even a far milder analogue of it, is determinative in the life of a boy.[2]

As the last sentence suggests, Trilling assigns this event a great deal of significance in Babel's life, going so far as to conjecture that Babel's decision to ride with a Cossack regiment in the Civil War—the experience that would later provide material for his best-known work, *Red Cavalry* (*Konarmiia*, 1923–26)—was prompted by the memory of this early, harrowing encounter with a Cossack officer. The only problem with this perceptive analysis is that the encounter in question is fictional.

Such a transferal of story material from the realm of fiction to that of history, apparently effected unilaterally by the reader, has interesting generic implications. Usually, the reader of a fictional text implicitly enters into the "fictional pact," whereby the suspension of disbelief allows her to respond to the events of the story *as if* they were true, without admitting them to the set of things that are *actually true,* that is to say, mistaking them for real life.[3] When, however, the fictional pact breaks down, and with it the boundary between the fictional content and "real life," the story is no longer a fiction. Instead, it becomes a lie: a deliberate invention masquerading as the truth.

Conventionally, of course, fiction (the fabrication that does not masquerade as truth) and the lie (the fabrication that does) represent mutually exclusive categories of discourse. The problem in distinguishing between them lies in the inconvenient fact that the distinction is one of intent, a notoriously slippery quantity, especially when the object of examination is a work of literature by an author no longer living. In literature, the intent underlying a given fabrication cannot be fully known, and efforts to discern it can only lead the investigator into the territory of the intentional fallacy. However, all is not lost: the formal qualities of the story itself telegraph a kind of intent—not that of the author, perhaps, but that encoded in the work of art—and can be examined for concrete clues, to decipher which only an attentive reading is required. Some scholars of literature have specifically explored the relationship between fiction and lies: Michael Riffaterre draws a firm line between the two with the assertion that "fiction is a genre whereas lies are not."[4] While the first part of that claim is problematic—surely so general a category as "fiction" cannot accurately be termed a "genre"—the gist of Riffaterre's assertion, that fiction represents a legitimate artistic enterprise to which mere lies do not aspire, provides a useful starting point from which to consider the Babel dilemma. For Riffaterre, the distinction between a fiction and a lie resides in the "intention," not of the author, but of the text itself: fiction "specifically, but not always explicitly, excludes the intention to deceive." The "intentions" of the fictional text are formally encoded in the fictional narrative, which "points" to its own fictionality by means of intratextual "signs whose function is to remind readers that the tale they are being told is imaginary."[5]

One might surmise that Babel had omitted to include a sufficient quantity of such "signs" in his childhood tales, since Trilling along with numerous other respected critics was lulled into accepting their content as authentic.[6] However, the stories I will examine in this chapter and the next are alive with fictionality markers, both on the formal and on the thematic level. For example, there is something disjointed about reality as it is presented by Babel's narrator; the vision he presents of his world is fragmented, sometimes verging on the absurd; realism is disrupted by violently inapposite, freighted metaphors and irruptions of a frenetic illogic. Even in its calmer moments, the language of the stories does not play a strictly mimetic role; a careful reading of all five stories reveals a painstakingly constructed vocabulary of symbols, which functions at least partly as an artistic commentary on the relationships among reality, perception, and imagination.

Particularly noteworthy among these Riffaterrian "signs" is a preoccupation, throughout Babel's childhood tales, with stories as such. The events recounted in "Childhood. At Grandmother's," for example, include the narrator's perusal of Turgenev's novella *First Love* (*Pervaia liubov'*, 1860), a work that, in turn, is itself explicitly concerned with stories and the art of telling them. The Turgenev work reappears later, like an authorial wink, in the title of Babel's third childhood tale, also called "First Love." A different kind of storytelling, less literary but with formal characteristics of its own, is represented by the postprandial reminiscences of the narrator's grandmother. And in "The Story of My Dovecote," a narrative studded with "creative" (read: misleading) utterances ranging from euphemisms to encomia is crowned by the "lying stories" of the narrator's great-uncle Shoyl, a consummate narrative rogue and autobiographical liar who seems to serve as a model for the narrator (and author?) himself. Shoyl is only one among many characters whose statements are measured for truth-value by the narrator: all the Babel men are characterized as discursively unreliable (whether from deliberate fraudulence or from one or another dementia), as I will discuss later. The narrator himself is by no means exempt from this unreliability; a "deceitful little boy" (2:179/49), he is "tormented" by "unbridled fantasies" (2:154/42). "By day," he reports, "I told tall stories to the neighbors' urchins[;] by night I transferred them to paper" (2:172/61).[7]

Each of these allusions seems designed to remind us that the telling of stories is an enterprise quite distinct from the living of stories; that good material does not automatically make a good story, and conversely that a good story—which, we may assume, Babel wants his own to be—may not always be a true one. Moreover, as I shall show later in this chapter, a closer examination of the way these various extrinsic stories are treated in Babel's narratives reveals that, as symbols, they undermine themselves in interesting ways, adding layers of complexity to their Riffaterrian significance.

THE PROBLEM OF GENRE

Given that it is the nature of fiction not to be true, it should hardly come as a surprise that some of Babel's fiction is made up; if anything, we ought to be surprised that some of it is not. And yet for all the fiction-signifying apparatus described above, the relationship of Babel's stories to extratextual "reality" has remained a vexed issue—not only for early Western scholars of Babel (who wrote on him without the benefit even of the limited reliable information we now possess about his life), but for their better-informed and more skeptical successors. The prospect of falling into an error like Trilling's has driven illustrious readers of Babel, from his daughter Nathalie to the writer Cynthia Ozick, to call plaintively for an authoritative biography of Babel—a demand that has proved difficult to meet, since Babel, in his daughter's words, "loved to confuse and mystify people," and the Stalinist government that purged him was hardly more candid.[8] Patricia Blake, a would-be biographer of Babel who has invested many years in researching his life, reports feeling "despair that a biography of this great writer can ever be rendered in the amplitude it deserves," since "much of Babel's life story continues to elude me."[9] It is precisely this elusiveness that compels readers to attempt to fill in the blanks of Babel's life from his stories—or their own; recent novels by Robert Rosenstone and Travis Holland, as well as an idiosyncratic, colloquial study by Jerome Charyn, pursue through flights of imagination the prey that has eluded capture in documents and archives.[10]

Meanwhile, the relationship between Babel's fiction and his life has remained a point of contention among critics. As Elif Batuman puts it, "a straightforward relationship to factual truth never was one of Babel's top priorities."[11] Jerome Charyn writes of Babel, plausibly, that

> he suffered from mytholepsy, the maddening need to narratize oneself. It would plague him continually, so that it was impossible to tell where the myth of Babel ended and where Babel began. Like many Odessans, he loved to tell a tall tale.[12]

"Impossible" to answer though it may be, scholars and lay readers alike have returned repeatedly to the question of "where the myth of Babel ended and where Babel began." Aware that Lionel Trilling is not alone in having been taken in by Babel's Cretan tales, critics writing on Babel since his posthumous rehabilitation in 1956 (as various corrections to the record have been made) have been careful to distance themselves from the mistakes of their misinformed predecessors and, where possible, to bolster their own propositions about the author's life and character with testimony from Babel's acquaintances, colleagues, and family. Here is Cynthia Ozick on Lionel Trilling:

> For one thing, Trilling mistakenly believed that Babel . . . was actually a member of the regiment. . . . Worse, in the absence of other sources, Trilling fell into a crucial—and surprisingly naïve—second error: he supposed that the "autobiographical" tales were, in fact, autobiographical. . . . One may suspect that Trilling's cultural imagination (and perhaps his psyche as well) was circumscribed by a kind of either/or: either worldly sophistication or the ghetto; and that, in linking Jewish learning solely to the ghetto, he could not conceive of its association with a broad and complex civilization. . . . Trilling's Freudian notion of the humiliated ghetto child could not have been more off the mark.[13]

Evidently the temptation to infer a psychological diagnosis from a literary text is not unique to Trilling! But whether or not Ozick's psychoanalysis of Trilling is correct, the portrait she herself offers of Babel is scarcely better supported than his:

> For Babel, lamp oil and fearlessness were not antithetical. He was a man with the bit of recklessness between his teeth. One might almost ask how a writer so given to disguises and role-playing could *not* have put on a Cossack uniform.[14]

Like Trilling's, Ozick's characterization of Babel is as indebted to the fictions Babel wove about himself as to any verifiable facts. The bit about "disguises and role-playing," however, connects to the Odessan "trickster" persona that Charyn references, and that Babel certainly cultivated in his works. As Ozick puts it elsewhere: "Amusing and mercurial, Babel 'loved to play tricks on people,' according to Lev Nikulin, who was at school with Babel." This theme is echoed by Nathalie Babel, who, on a quest to exhume an authentic memory of her father (whom she had seen in person only briefly, when little more than an infant), insists firmly on the mischievous bent that renders his own testimony unreliable.[15]

Some critics' mistrust of Babel extends so far as to question *any* direct relationship between his fiction and his real life. Frank O'Connor writes of *Red Cavalry:*

> What I am saying is that when a Jew with an uproarious imagination describes scenes of violence one should ask oneself whether he is describing what he saw or what he thought he should have seen. Some of the things Babel describes I am quite certain he never saw.[16]

O'Connor's skepticism is reminiscent of the indignant "Open Letter to Maksim Gorky" published, over the signature of First Cavalry Commander Semyon Budyonny, in the *Red Gazette (Krasnaia gazeta)* in 1928. (The text of the letter is almost identical to a critique penned by a Budyonny subordinate, S. Orlovsky, entitled "In the Backyards of *Red Cavalry*.")[17] Budyonny, fiercely defending the honor of the First Cavalry against the defamation of *Red Cavalry*, protested:

> Babel . . . invents things that never happened, slings dirt at our best Communist commanders, lets his imagination run wild, simply lies. . . . I happen to know for certain that while Babel saw women's breasts and bare legs around the army's field kitchens, Pani Eliza's servants' quarters, in the middle of the forest, awake and asleep, in various combinations, there were a few other things the First Cavalry was doing that Babel did not see.
>
> And that's quite natural and understandable. How could Babel possibly have seen from the deep rear the spots where the fate of the workers and peasants was being decided? He just couldn't have.[18]

One may chuckle, as Babel did in a letter dated the same day, over the professional soldier's inability to distinguish between art and libel, and simply accept Budyonny's and O'Connor's explanations for the "wild" stories of *Red Cavalry*. Yet, unless we are to assume that Babel's playful desire "to confuse and mystify" his readers extended even to himself, Babel's 1920 diary offers reasonably clear evidence that he *did* see scenes of violence like the ones he describes. Thus, O'Connorian skepticism seems no better a strategy for reading Babel than Trillingesque credulity. Babel has violated both the fictional and the autobiographical pacts. What we are confronted with is a problem of genre.

Given the unlikelihood that research will ever yield definitive answers to all the questions surrounding Babel's life, the question "what *really* happened?" seems something of a red herring. A more salient question might be: why are Babel's readers so preoccupied—even to the point of readable anxiety—with getting at the truth? Part of the answer lies in the very impenetrability of the veil that hangs over parts of Babel's life, which for many years was made even more opaque by the Soviet cover-up of the facts surrounding his execution. But part of the answer lies, too, in the nature of Babel's fiction. As Gregory Freidin observes, "its apparent autobiographical character" is one of the "essential attributes of Babel's art." What, then, is Babel doing, in his "autobiographical" stories, that prompts his readers to invest so much in the factuality, or otherwise, of his narrative? To solve these puzzles, we must reopen the question of the stories' genre, looking this time at the way they define *themselves* generically.

The practice of embedding autobiographical material in a fictional narrative is not in itself a radical step; many celebrated works in the Russian canon (for example, Tolstoy's *Childhood, Boyhood, Youth* or Dostoevsky's *Notes from the House of the Dead*) offer first-person narratives drawn largely from the lived experience of the author, with a thin veneer of fictionalization. Typically, such "hybrid" narratives do not present the reader with severe epistemological or generic difficulties; they simply invite her to participate in the ordinary readerly activity of "pretending" that the story is true, with the additional gratification of knowing that parts of it actually are. What, then, makes Babel's "hybrid" text so much more troubling than those of other celebrated writers of fiction who took their material from life?

Simple though it may seem, the answer lies in the way Babel constructs the hybrid. By fashioning a narrator from the details of his own birth certificate, Babel roots his narrative in "a single subject whose identity is defined by the uncontested readability of his proper name";[19] in other words, he invokes the defining condition of autobiography, and along with it, Lejeune's "autobiographical pact."[20] Babel enters into the pact disingenuously, since the facts of his biography and those of his "autobiography" are at variance with each other; but he does enter into it. In so doing, he creates a cycle of stories that, in Alice Stone Nakhimovsky's phrase, "*pretends* to be autobiographical."[21] Babel himself went further: describing the stories of his childhood cycle in a letter to his mother, he wrote, "All the stories are from the childhood years, *with lies added,* of course."[22] Unlike the author of an "autofiction," a term coined by Serge Doubrovsky in explicit resistance to Lejeune's strict legalistic definition of "autobiography," Babel does not merely "create a fictional framework through which to narrate biographically verifiable events."[23] Rather, he uses his own life as a frame through which to narrate compelling fictional events—events which are all the more vividly realized in the reader's imagination as a result of their *illusion* of verifiability—all the while "mystifying" and obfuscating the real events of his life so that the fictional events are bound to supersede them.

Babel's childhood stories, then, demand to be read as autobiography proper, even as they cheekily call attention to their own "deceitfulness." But what does it mean to read a text as an autobiography? Like fiction and lies, fiction and autobiography are hard to tell apart; the boundaries of both are porous, and though autobiography is conventionally viewed as a genre, it is notoriously difficult to define in generic terms, not least because of the implicit contradictions inherent in its very name. Over the course of the twentieth century, theorists of autobiography shifted their attention from the genre's central element—*bios,* "life," or the content of the narrative—to its prefix, *autos,* or the "self" projected by the narrative: what Wayne Booth would call the "implied author," who in autobiography serves as the protagonist and narrator as well. A further shift in emphasis, beginning with Roy Pascal's seminal book *Design and Truth in Autobiography* (1960), brought into focus autobiography's third component, *graphê*—the art of writing itself. To the problem of subjectivity that had led the "second wave" of autobiography theorists to question the straightforwardness of self-narrative, another complication was now added: the conscious use of art in shaping autobiographical narrative. Much of this "third wave" interrogation of autobiography has centered on how to negotiate the apparent opposition between the two elements, "truth" and "design," considered essential to its composition.[24]

This internal contradiction has complicated efforts to define autobiography as a genre. As Paul de Man complains:

> Empirically as well as theoretically, autobiography lends itself poorly to generic definition; each specific instance seems to be an exception to the norm; the works themselves always seem to shade off into neighboring or even incompatible genres and, perhaps most revealing of all, generic discussions, which can have such powerful heuristic value in the case of tragedy or of the novel, remain distressingly sterile when autobiography is at stake.[25]

Other genres do not have to face these threats to their identity. Readers of *Eugene Onegin* who argue about whether "novel in verse" is an oxymoron or a legitimate subgenre can indeed have "heuristically valuable," if ultimately irresolvable, generic discussions.[26] By contrast, those who squabble over the status of, say, Wordsworth's *Prelude* can neither admit it to nor debar it from the category of "autobiography" on the basis of its poetic structure, but only by deciding what to make of its frequent departure from what is known about Wordsworth's "real" life.[27] Generically speaking, what distinguishes Wordsworth's *Prelude* from Dante's *Inferno*—a text that would be invoked as an autobiographical model by at least one Odessan writer, Yury Olesha[28]—is not its form: both are long poems, though of course their prosodic specifications differ. Nor is it the position of the narrator within the text: each poem is narrated by an "I" who claims identity with its physical author, and asserts that the experiences recounted are his own. Rather, it is the *credibility* of what is narrated that sets the two apart. The distinction is quite purely *fabula*-driven: Dante's round-trip to the Underworld marks his poem as epic, whereas Wordsworth's more mundane adventures mark his (at least in some quarters) as autobiography.

Without historical or formal distinctions on which to base a definition of autobiography, critics have been forced to revive the "dead" author and grapple with the dismayingly pre-Formalist problem of describing autobiography in terms of its relationship to "truth" or "reality," and differentiating it from "fiction." Western autobiography theory and Soviet autobiography theory have approached the problem from slightly different perspectives: while Western theorists since Roy Pascal have sought to elucidate the role and purview of "design" in organizing the narrated experience, Soviet theorists have focused—logically, given the political context—on the testimonial aspects of autobiographical writing, which has been viewed as a genre of "documentary prose" (*dokumental'naia proza*).[29] The comparison is intriguing because it implies that the two theoretical currents differ in their conception, not only of autobiography's ethical function, but also of the relationship between autobiographer and reader.

The reader, in Western theory, is generally conceived of as a lone individual, his relationship with the text an intensely personal one. By contrast, Bakhtin, in an essay dated 1937–38,[30] traces the earliest known forms of autobiography to two ancient Greek genres, the first of which he calls "Platonic" autobiography, "since it found its earliest and most precise expression in such works of Plato as the *Apology* of Socrates" (a curious example, since although Socrates serves both as narrator and as subject matter, he cannot strictly speaking be called the author of the *Apology*). According to Bakhtin, "Platonic" autobiography takes as its theme "the life course of one seeking true knowledge," whereas "rhetorical autobiography" is based on the funeral encomium and exemplified by the *Antidosis* of Isocrates. What both these forms have in common is an orientation toward "the public square"; they are designed to be received by a large number of people collectively, in public, rather than perused alone in the privacy of one's study, or heard (like, ostensibly, Augustine's *Confessions*) only by God. Their significance is more historical than personal.

Bakhtin's choice of such publicly oriented texts as the forerunners of modern autobiography is not accidental; it is of a piece with other twentieth-century Russian conceptions of autobiography, which tended to focus on the stamp of authenticity provided by firsthand, first-person accounts, rather than on their troublesome subjectivity. Mandelstam argues in "End of the Novel" that autobiography, as a genre European writers ("plucked out of their own biographies" by the modern condition) could use to locate themselves within history, must necessarily supersede the nineteenth-century novel, with its "interest in an individual human fate."[31] In other words, autobiography is to be seen as less subjective, and more world-historical, than the great novels of the imperial age. For Soviet purposes, such a conception of autobiography implies that it is also more *useful* than the nineteenth-century novel (an essentially bourgeois genre), a criterion that is all but ignored in Western criticism but persists in the Russian discussion of autobiography throughout the Soviet period.

The uses of autobiography were various, sometimes nefarious. The Stalinist Terror made extensive use of autobiography, in the form of the secret police file, which conventionally culminated in a confession by the subject of the file in his or her "own words." As Cristina Vatulescu has shown, however, these "autobiographical" narratives were shaped by a systematic interrogation process in order to produce texts that conformed to the rules of a predetermined genre:

> From the start, two portraits of the self—the secret police's vague criminal scenario and the victim's own perception of his life—were pitted against each other. The balance of power was totally disproportionate, and the individual had value only inasmuch as he could fill in the details of the secret police case against him.[32]

The personal confession was a crucial part of the Stalinist police file precisely because of the authenticating power of the autobiographical voice: by producing self-narratives that harmonized with the official scenarios for "the transformation of a socialist citizen into an enemy," the prisoners validated both their own arrests and the state's "histrionic rhetoric of unmasking, projecting, and reforging enemies."[33] Just a few years after writing the childhood cycle, Babel would become a coauthor in this genre as well.

If, inside the prison, autobiographical voices served to validate official discourse, on the outside—and especially after the Thaw—their task was to expose and dismantle that discourse, bringing "a new measure of historical truth in the form of *belles lettres*" to the recent past. Mandelstam's argument is echoed in the post-Thaw period by Kuznetsov, who argues that the aim of autobiography is to "inform us of the most complex problems of the age" and "allow [writers] to create their new picture of the world."[34] This argument, formulated against the backdrop of an official discourse that was widely, if tacitly, perceived as inauthentic, ascribes to autobiography, by virtue of its first-person perspective, an authenticity that was lacking in official historical accounts. In the West, meanwhile, exactly the opposite was true: the personal and subjective nature of autobiographical narration attracted critical suspicion and led to the foregrounding of the "literary" properties of autobiography.

While both Russian and Western traditions of scholarship have insisted on the "literariness" of the autobiographical text, and have recognized its dual nature as a text that is both "found" and "created" (or at least aesthetically organized),[35] Western scholars have been more willing—at least in recent decades—to part altogether with the notion of historical authenticity or verifiability as the defining characteristic of autobiography. The vacuum left by dispensing with truthfulness as an absolute requirement creates freedom, but also dissent. The apparent impossibility of formulating what Timothy Dow Adams calls "an airtight definition of autobiography" has impelled critics with a stake in the problem to position themselves along the axis defined by two extreme responses to it: on the one hand, that there is, finally, no such thing as autobiography; on the other, that all texts are more or less autobiographical.[36]

It is difficult to discredit either of these two positions, which in the final analysis amount to almost the same thing; that is, they affirm the erosion of boundaries between "autobiographies" and openly fictional texts. Post-Structuralist critiques of both the concept of the self and the referentiality of language—the two main ingredients of autobiography—have complicated the task of salvaging some firm ground on which an understanding of autobiography as a meaningful generic category may be built. As the notion that an author's "I" refers to a real person, or his words to concrete things, becomes increasingly quaint, so does the distinction between autobiography and fiction. Moreover, the fallibility—or essential narrativity—of memory makes it still harder to claim any articulable relationship between "autobiography" and "truth," since what the autobiographer does consciously (i.e., organize plot around one or more aesthetic principles), the memory does without our conscious sanction. Assuming a "fallen" state of language, memory, and selfhood, it seems impossible to draw any meaningful distinctions between "autobiography" and the fictional genres on which it borders.

THE READER IN AUTOBIOGRAPHY

For all the reservations outlined above, terms like "identity" and "autobiography," which designate the articulation of the self, retain their meaning based on an intuitive consensus that there is a "there there"—a recognizable something to which they refer. As Barrett John Mandel writes, "autobiographies and novels are finally totally distinct—and this simple fact *every reader knows.*"[37] Much as language continues to function tolerably well despite the deconstruction of stable signification, autobiography continues to command a qualitatively different kind of reading from fiction, despite repeated demonstrations (dismissed by Mandel as "academic sleight-of-hand") that the two cannot be reliably separated. In an effort to preserve and codify its distinctive character as a "truth-based" genre, influential theoreticians such as Philippe Lejeune and Elizabeth Bruss have devised systems of rules governing the practice of autobiography.[38] However, since "truth" is precisely the term on whose meaning thinkers are least likely ever to agree, and since moreover "for the autobiographer, part of the game includes trying to keep the reader off balance"[39] by selectively violating the rules distilled by critics, the most successful theories are those which focus not on the relationship between "truth" and "design," but on the relationship between writer and reader.

A reception-based approach to autobiography has the benefit of allowing us to consider autobiography as a communicative, rather than an ontological, issue, which in turn invites us to take into account the indispensable substrata of successful communication: consensus and intuition. Seen in this light, Lejeune's 1975 theory of the "autobiographical pact," a quasi-legal understanding between author and reader sustained by a combination of names (the nominal identity among author, narrator, and protagonist) and extra-literary information such as the Library of Congress classification, takes on new authority. While it does not (indeed, cannot) preclude intentional or unintentional mendacity, the "pact" does create a writer-reader relationship based on the *notion,* however unattainable, of a veracious narrative.

To be sure, it is technically impossible for the author actually to abide by this contract, for the reasons explored above; however—and this is the important point—it is not the author's good faith, but rather her *signature,* that determines the genre of the work. The extraliterary cues mentioned by Lejeune, such as the library classification and title page, are of minor importance: what signifies is the identity of author and narrator. In this way, we can reconcile (however improbable it might seem) Lejeune's "autobiographical pact" with Paul de Man's description of the autobiographical text as one whose inevitable "deviations from reality," however numerous, "remain rooted in a single subject whose identity is defined by the uncontested readability of his proper name"; or in other words, as a document whose content is authenticated by the author's "signature," in the form of a narrator who bears the same name.

In this study, I take a basically Lejeunian approach to the texts under discussion. That is, I foreground the relationship between the author and the reader, as it is conditioned by the apparent equivalence between the narrator of each work and its flesh-and-blood author, without dwelling overmuch on technicalities such as the Library of Congress classification, which I view as extraneous to the reader's experience of the text. When the author (inevitably) breaks the "autobiographical pact," it is not, in my view, the case that he is no longer writing autobiography. Rather, the manner in which he breaks the contract will determine both what kind of autobiography we think we are reading, and the extent to which we deem it interesting or "literary." Such breaches of contract should be seen as creative play with the rules governing autobiography, which, like the rules governing other genres, can be traduced or undermined in productive ways. It is precisely the impossible tension between artifice and authenticity that brings autobiography to life, and that provides authors with myriad ways to play with the boundaries between truth and fiction.

This brings us back to Trilling's Dilemma: what good is the pact when Babel blithely goes on to fabricate the details of the story? And if, in light of his choices with regard to narrator and theme, Babel's fabrications violate the terms of the autobiographical pact, should we consider them fictions— or lies? As it turns out, by citing events from a Babel story as "true," Trilling brought into focus the very problem that the stories themselves insistently raise: the nature of "story" itself, refracted through the relationship between the work of fiction and the work of deception—between the short story and the tall tale.

"AUTOBIOGRAPHY" AS TEMPLATE FOR A READING STRATEGY

As a preliminary to reading Babel's "autobiographical" stories, it is instructive to take a look at his brief "Autobiography" ("Avtobiografiia"), dated 1924.[40] Though it purports to be tersely factual, this four-paragraph sketch exemplifies, in miniature, some of the truth-altering techniques Babel would put to use in the childhood tales—including the incorporation of fictional elements. In her discussion of "Autobiography," Nathalie Babel largely discounts its value as a biographical document, observing that "autobiographical facts are largely distorted" in Babel's summary of them, and enumerating three ways in which this is done. According to his daughter, Babel "does not differentiate between trivial and important details," and some of the "facts" he presents in "Autobiography" are "pure fabrication"; moreover, in this lightning summary of his first thirty years, the author "telescopes seven years of his life: 1917–1924."[41] These "imaginative distortions" may be taken as a condensed guide to Babel's autobiographical method in general:

(1) *Babel devotes excessive attention to details that are relatively trivial.* In "Autobiography," such details include a demographic breakdown of

Babel's classmates in elementary school, and a catalogue of their activities at recess. Beyond "Autobiography," an obvious example of Babel's tendency to foreground activity that takes place in the margins of his "main" plot glares at us from the title of "The Story of My Dovecote": for the first half of the story, the action is dominated by the young protagonist's struggle to gain a place at secondary school; by the end of the story, our attention has again been drawn away from the dovecote by the violent trauma of a pogrom.

(2) *Babel lies.* Among the outright fabrications in "Autobiography" we may include Babel's romanticized account of the hardships he endured during his first years in St. Petersburg, and in particular the claim that—an impecunious and illicit resident—he was driven to lodge "in the cellar of a harrowed (*rasterzannyi;* Nathalie Babel has "bedraggled," McDuff, "tormented"), drunken waiter." This, according to Ozick, "was pure fabrication: in actuality Babel was taken in by a highly respectable engineer and his wife, with whom he was in correspondence." She surmises that the purpose of the fabrication was "romantic imposture. . . . A drunken waiter would have been adventure enough—but ah, that Dostoyevskian 'tormented!'"[42] Nathalie Babel elaborates, "His father still sent him money. Moreover, although Jewish students were allowed to remain in Petersburg only for a limited period of time, this period could be extended."[43]

Similarly, in the childhood tales, Babel freely mixes material taken from life with the products of pure invention; Nathalie Babel is quick to point out, for example, that Babel's parents did not (as in "First Love") have red hair, nor was his mother's name Rachel.[44] As we shall see, by falsifying such details in his "autobiographical" stories, Babel creates a fictive falsehood that reflects the thematic emphasis in the stories on lying and on the various ways in which reality may be distorted.

(3) *Babel miniaturizes (or "telescopes") the events that are most important.* The short shrift Babel gives to the years 1917–1924 in "Autobiography" is the logical corollary to the "long shrift" lavished upon minutiae from his school days. Together, these two techniques, (1) and (3), constitute a form of prevarication, not perhaps as brazen as his outright lies, but illuminating a key aspect of Babel's literary consciousness: his concern with perception and perspective. (Yury Olesha, as we will see in chapter 4, shares these interests, although he brings different techniques to bear on them.) The discursive deformation of perspective, exemplified by the twin techniques of magnification and diminution, is one of the ways in which the narrator of the childhood tales will make us feel the correlation between language (as the medium via which we receive narrated "reality") and experience (as the medium via which we receive extratextual reality).

In addition to "miniaturizing" significant events, Babel often leaves things out altogether: as Jerome Charyn dryly observes,

"I was born in 1894 in Odessa in the Moldavanka district," Babel begins, neglecting to remind us that his family moved to Nikolaev, a little seaport eighty miles from Odessa, when he was still an infant, and that he didn't grow up in the Moldavanka, among gangsters and horse carters who could split a man's skull with their hands.[45]

Sometimes Babel's omissions have the effect of creating a kind of ersatz censorship, which actually draws the reader's attention to the missing information. The institution of state censorship—with which both Russian and Soviet literature traditionally had to contend—provided a model according to which the most salient material is that which is *not* stated. Babel, like his forerunners in Russian literature, was versed in the art of strategic omission and, as we shall see, sometimes turned it to account as a way of paradoxically highlighting certain details. Like Babel's other literary tricks, this stratagem demands close attention from the reader in order to work.

"Autobiography" and "Aesthetic Coherence"

Jane Gary Harris postulates that "the aesthetic coherence of a given autobiographical statement resides in the articulation of the tension created by this dialogue (between "experience" and "interpretation")—often expressed in the laying bare of the mediating act."[46] To the extent that a given text relies for its effect on making this tension palpable, it follows that the mediating act must, to some extent, be laid bare. In "Autobiography," the tension arising from the "dialogue"—really, a mediated disparity—between "experience" and (re-)"interpretation" is manifest. The "mediating act," however, is not "laid bare" intratextually, according to the rules laid down by Shklovsky and his fellow Formalists. Rather, the reader can become aware of the mediation only upon acquiring *extratextual* knowledge of Babel's life, from reliable outside sources. In other words, the "aesthetic coherence" of "Autobiography" as a literary text depends on the reader's knowledge of "what really happened"; in order to appreciate the aesthetic qualities of the text, the reader must—paradoxically—indulge the antiaesthetic drive to "get at the truth."

Presuming that the primary function of "Autobiography" is not a literary one,[47] it is, perhaps, of little consequence whether its "aesthetic coherence"—that is, its calculated mendacity—is available to the reader. However, it is not the relatively obscure "Autobiography" but Babel's stories themselves that "have often misled those critics who like to seek the man in his works."[48] This constitutes a much more serious problem, for if we cannot apprehend the "aesthetic coherence" of Babel's fiction without recourse to a comprehensive biography of him, we cannot hope ever to appreciate it fully. I submit that such a situation is unacceptable; we must attempt to uncover the clues the author has left for us in the texts themselves—the ways in which the "mediating act" is laid bare intratextually. With this in mind, I devote the remainder of this chapter to close readings of the first two childhood tales, "Childhood. At Grandmother's" and "The Story of My Dovecote."

"CHILDHOOD": SEEDS OF AN
AUTOBIOGRAPHICAL METHOD

"Childhood. At Grandmother's," the first of the childhood tales, is dated "Saratov, 12.11.15"—placing it among Babel's earliest works—and was not published until 1965, long after the author's death.[49] It thus falls well outside the most illustrious and productive period of Babel's literary career (roughly, 1921–27), and—being moreover available to us only in a slightly imperfect manuscript—has enjoyed a relatively obscure existence as a result. Until recently, editors as well as critics have tended to sever it from the "autobiographical" cycle headlined by "The Story of My Dovecote." However, it seems clear that the cycle without "Childhood. At Grandmother's" is incomplete, for three reasons. First, a familiarity with "Childhood. At Grandmother's" adds a great deal to the reader's appreciation of "Awakening," the final story of the cycle, which mirrors "Childhood. At Grandmother's" both structurally and thematically. Second, "Childhood. At Grandmother's" provides the reader with information without which certain discursive aspects of the other stories are inaccessible. Third, it is in "Childhood. At Grandmother's" that the fundamental thematic concerns of the cycle are established, and the symbolic language that gives them expression is introduced.

The first of these recurrent motifs to make an appearance is the characterization of the narrator as a "dreamer" (*mechtatel'*). The narrator describes the walk home to see his grandmother, with whom he will spend the remainder of his Saturday, as an opportunity to let his imagination roam. Variations on the word *mechta*, the Russian for "daydream," occur three times in the first paragraph of the story, leaving us in no doubt about the defining feature of its protagonist's personality. The world of daydreams (*mechty*) is juxtaposed early on with the world of sleep-dreams (*sny*), which the narrator enters when he crosses the threshold of his grandmother's room. In later stories, we see the dichotomy between *mechty* and *sny* developed further, as our hero is subject to both; here, we see the beginnings of a connection between the narrator's daydreams and his heightened, if imaginative, cognizance of the world around him.

Sleep-dreams, by contrast, seem here and elsewhere to be associated with a protective insensibility to the outside world. In "Childhood. At Grandmother's," sleep is repeatedly linked to blindness, and thus to a form of escape. The incorrigible sleeper of "Childhood. At Grandmother's" is, however, not the narrator but his grandmother's dog, Mimka, a "terrible sleepyhead, but a wonderful dog" who is frequently to be found sleeping "peacefully" (1:38/22). Mimka's peaceful slumber stands in contrast to the watchful, wakeful presence of the narrator's grandmother, whose constant surveillance monitors the narrator's actions, restricting him to a prescribed set of activities—lessons, reading, homework—that are designed to liberate him (eventually), but instead intensify the claustrophobic atmosphere that continues to build to the end of the tale: "I can't breathe, there is nothing to breathe, I must run outside to fresh air, to freedom, but I have no strength to raise my drooping head" (1:41/26). The tension between freedom (or "fresh air") and confinement or constraint will become crucial to the childhood tales: dreams (*mechty* when the narrator is alone, preferably outdoors, and able to exercise some subjective autonomy; *sny* when he is under familial lock and key) become, in the childhood cycle, the narrator's standard form of escape, implicitly the springboard for his activities as a writer. As Patricia Carden puts it, "The escape from reality into the world of the imagination is one of the poles of freedom. . . . The pattern is one of tension and release."[50] The seeds of this idea are sown in "Childhood. At Grandmother's."

Sleep, at the end of "Childhood. At Grandmother's," serves as a refuge both from the outside world mistrusted by the grandmother and from the claustrophobic atmosphere she creates in response. It provides relief from being looked at, but also from vision itself: the fragment that remains of the story's unfinished ending concludes, "More than that I do not see, for I sleep very soundly, sleep a youthful sleep behind seven seals in Grandmother's hot room" (1:42/27). The reader is thus alerted early on to the importance of vision to Babel's narrative language, manifested in the proliferation of verbs of looking and seeing (*videt'*, *osmatrivat'*, *zagliadyvat'*), in the attention to color and perspective, and (in this story) in the constant references to Grandmother's relentlessly watching eyes. The narrator gives especial emphasis to their improbable color: yellow—introducing a color association that will come to fruition in "The Story of My Dovecote."[51]

Grandmother's synecdoche, her yellow, piercing eyes, is juxtaposed with that of the Russian violin teacher, Sorokin: large, red hands. Sorokin, whose brief is to subject the young "Babel" to the tiresome paternal imposition of music lessons—theoretically, his potential ticket out of the constrictions of Jewish life in Russia, among them the child-stifling atmosphere to which the narrative itself is devoted, and of which Sorokin himself forms a part—simultaneously represents both the physical, outdoor world that

"Babel" so longs to master, and the oppressive cultural training that bars him from it.[52] "A splendid fellow" with "black hair in a crew cut," "big red [*krasnye*] hands and beautiful [*krasivye*] full lips" (1:39, my translation), Sorokin serves as an early exemplar of that specifically Russian heartiness (connoted by *krasnota*—redness—and fraught, in Babel, with aesthetic appeal, or *krasota*), that is at once indispensable in order to belong to the physical realm, and inaccessible to the self-conscious Jews of "Babel's" domestic sphere. "Childhood. At Grandmother's" thus lays out the beginning of a symbolic pattern that will be further elaborated in later stories: a cluster of associations among, at one pole, the color red, hands, the realm of practical action (i.e., a participatory relationship to the world), and the physical confidence and freedom of movement associated with Russians; and at the other, the color yellow, eyes, the realm of watching and looking (a spectatorial relationship to the world), and the intellectually intense, physically restrictive and claustrophobic environment the narrator associates with his Jewish upbringing.

Family, in the childhood cycle, occupies a highly ambiguous position: it is the source, on the one hand, of the narrator's literary pedigree, and, on the other, of the "otherness" that torments him. Indeed, the narrator's inner turmoil is cast, in large part, as his legacy from the men of the "Babel" family—who are conspicuously absent from this introductory story. Their physical absence is underlined by the fact that the three most important male Babel figures are mentioned in the story, thus making their presence felt indirectly.[53] The first of these absent presences is Babel's father: the narrator mentions him in passing, saying, "Of everything living, Grandmother loved only her son (Babel's father), her grandson (Babel), her dog Mimka, and flowers" (1:38, my translation). Babel's father is mentioned again, in a similar context, three pages later. His grandfather garners more attention, as the subject of one of Grandmother's stories; he is represented as a colorful figure, but with a particular combination of weaknesses which, as we read on in the childhood cycle, will come to be understood as the perennial male-Babel hamartia: an overindulgence in "stories" and an excessive credulity vis-à-vis his fellow man. These are pointed out by Grandmother in the preface to her narrative:

> "Your grandfather," she began, "knew many stories, but he didn't believe in anything, he only believed in people . . ." And Grandmother tells me about my grandfather, a tall, sarcastic, passionate and despotic man. He played the violin, wrote essays by night and knew all the languages. An unquenchable thirst for knowledge and life possessed him. (1:41, my translation)

The fact that Babel's grandfather is evidently dead by the time his grandmother tells these stories indicates that "Childhood. At Grandmother's,"

though written earlier, is actually set at a later date than the subsequent stories in the cycle (with the possible exception of "Awakening"), for in "In
the Basement" we will "meet" Grandfather Levi-Itskhok in person. Grandmother's description of him here is rather positive by comparison with the
portrait in "In the Basement," which insists more sharply on the grotesque
aspects of the apparently congenital male-Babelian mania Grandmother
only hints at here.

The moral Grandmother draws from the story of Grandfather Levi-
Itskhok is a telling one: "'Study,' she says with force, 'study, you will attain
everything—wealth and fame. You must know everything. . . . Don't have
faith in human beings'" (1:41/26). The last sentence (literally, "Don't believe
in people") represents an injunction to her grandson not to follow in his
grandfather's footsteps: that is, explicitly, not to "believe in people," and, implicitly, not to waste his time with stories ("Your grandfather . . . knew many
stories"), but to rely only on "knowledge"—the products of study, not of
imagination. She is wasting her breath on the boy, as the reader can by this
time already guess; but her advice resonates beyond the text, as an ironic
admonition to us not to trust *this* story, not to place our faith in its narrator.

Stories, in general, figure prominently in "Childhood. At Grandmother's" as they do throughout the childhood cycle, providing a metaliterary running commentary on the author's project, as well as an index of the
narrator's concern with his own development as a storyteller. The most significant event in "Childhood. At Grandmother's," in terms of its emotional
impact on the narrator, is his perusal of Turgenev's *First Love,* which, in the
narrator's reading, provides an Ur-text for the charged interrelationship of
love and violence that will come to shape the world of the childhood tales
(and, indeed, of much of Babel's work):

> I liked everything in it . . . but trembled at the scene where Vladimir's father
> strikes Zinaida on the cheek with his horsewhip. I heard the whistle of the
> whip, the supple leather dug into me keenly, painfully, instantaneously. I was
> seized by an inexplicable excitement. (24)

In fact (or rather, in fiction—that is, in Turgenev's original) Vladimir's father
lashes Zinaida not on the cheek, but on the arm. This minor discrepancy
constitutes our first evidence of the narrator's unreliability that is verifiable *without recourse to actual biographical knowledge of Babel,* and almost
without recourse to extratextual reality; although we are referred to a source
outside the childhood cycle, the source is at least a *text,* and not just any
text, but the eponym of one of the childhood tales themselves. By electing
to "plant" evidence in an intertext, moreover, Babel calls our attention even
more sharply to the theme of fiction and fictionality.

A different brand of fiction—the mythologization of the past—is represented in "Childhood. At Grandmother's" by the grandmother's stories. These have a quasi-folkloric quality, hinting at the influence of forces beyond human control, and casting their teller in the archetypal role of the scary old lady with a romantic girlhood only she can remember. Her first tale concerns a Jewish innkeeper suffering harassment at the hands of the town police commissioner. (The evidence of other childhood tales suggests that the details of Shoyl's biography coincide with those of the Jewish innkeeper, making Shoyl the third of Babel's patriarchal forebears to make a discursive appearance in "Childhood. At Grandmother's," albeit not by name.)[54] He takes his problem to the local rabbi, who tells him to go home; the police commissioner "will settle down." When the innkeeper returns to his inn, he finds the commissioner's corpse lying in the doorway.

No more cheery is Grandmother's second tale, about a Polish count on whose revels she had been wont to spy in her girlhood—until "the uprising," when the count, evidently a ringleader, was dragged out and publicly shot by Russian soldiers. Immediately thereafter, Grandmother reports, a messenger arrived bearing—too late—a reprieve for the count from the tsar. This story, like her first one, purports to be not only true, but autobiographical: it is a tale of Grandmother's firsthand brush with History. As such, it provides a kind of model for the young narrator's retelling of his own contact—likewise as witness and chronicler, rather than active participant—with historical events, in "The Story of My Dovecote."

THE "DOVECOTE" THAT SHOYL BUILT

"The Story of My Dovecote," the first-published of the childhood tales, is the longest and most complex story in the cycle, and the one under whose title the whole cycle was theoretically to have been published.[55] The notion that the whole childhood cycle is devoted, in some sense, to the story of Babel's dovecote necessarily invests the dovecote with an intensified emblematic function, which in turn accentuates the importance of the story in which it appears. The dovecote itself does not materialize until halfway through the story (remaining an unrealized longing until then). It thus occupies, literally as well as figuratively, a central position in the narrative, despite the (typically Babelian) lack of ceremony with which it is introduced.

No less crucial than the image of the dovecote is the image of its maker, the protagonist's great-uncle Shoyl. Shoyl is the beloved storyteller whose "inspired lies," as Carden calls them,[56] provide the model for Babel's own historical-autobiographical narrative. His last reported act before dying in the pogrom of October 20, 1905, is the fashioning of his grandnephew's

longed-for dovecote. The specificity about dates—the most notorious pogroms in the Odessa region did indeed rage from October 19 to 22 (O.S.),
1905, following the announcement of Tsar Nicholas II's October Manifesto
on October 17—is a slyly historiographic gesture on Babel's part, designed
presumably to help his readers to their unfounded faith in his veracity. The
making of the dovecote becomes a metaphor for the creation of Shoyl's mar-
velous stories, which are likewise tailored to satisfy the desires of his eager
young listener. Shoyl's stories constitute, in turn, a figuration of Babel's own;
thus, the poetics of the whole childhood cycle is encoded in the image of the
dovecote.

In "The Story of My Dovecote," written some ten years after "Childhood. At Grandmother's," the anatomy of fiction and other counterfactual
discourses (including lies) is explored still more minutely. The very title is a
lie, advertising a narrative focus on the dovecote only to digress from it until
the story is half over, when the dovecote makes a belated appearance only to
be immediately eclipsed by an event of far greater magnitude: the pogrom
in which the narrator's doves, and more importantly his great-uncle Shoyl,
are brutally killed. The narrator himself seems to feel no obligation to deliver the story promised by the title, remarking instead at this halfway point:
"The story about which I am telling you, that is, my admittance to the first
class of the *Gymnasium*, took place in autumn 1905" (2:147, my translation).
This comment, while it appears to be designed to help us readers get our
bearings, has a radically different effect: it destabilizes the reading process
on which we have embarked, first by announcing that the story we are getting is not the promised "story of my dovecote," but another one altogether
(the story of "my admittance"); and second, by disrupting what I have called
"the ordinary readerly activity" of ascribing a provisional reality to the events
of the story. The narrator's slightly odd turn of phrase—not "the story that
I am telling you" but "the story *about* which I am telling you" (*istoriia, o
kotoroi ia rasskazyvaiu*)—might be a product of the peculiar Odessa dia-
lect, but in context it seems to introduce an additional layer of fictionality in
between the events of the story and the narrator, suggesting that the events
form a "story" independently of the narrator's decision to recount them. This
faint but noticeable stress on the "storyness" of the story conflicts with the
impression of historical fidelity created by the main clause of the sentence:
". . . took place in autumn 1905." Thus, instead of orienting the reader, this
seemingly innocuous sentence destabilizes both the strategies of reading
(fictional and autobiographical) between which one would ordinarily choose
in order to interpret the narrative.

The events of the story "about which" we are being told are straightforward enough. The protagonist, who longs for a dovecote, is promised one
as a reward (by, of course, his father) if he succeeds at the entrance exams

for the local gymnasium. Overcome with anxiety, he nonetheless passes with flying colors—twice, for he is cheated of his triumph the first time by the foul play of a fellow student's equally ambitious, but wealthier, Jewish father. (In a typical Babelian move, this minor injustice is played up at the expense of the greater one—the *numerus clausus,* or Jewish quota, which forced the Jewish students into competition with one another.) The protagonist's eventual admittance to the gymnasium is an occasion for great family celebration. Soon thereafter, the boy sets out, despite ominous local stirrings, to buy the long-awaited doves; while he is at the market, the pogrom reaches full force, and when he arrives home—the unfortunate doves having been dashed against his forehead by an enraged cripple—it is to a house devoid of inhabitants, save for the defiled corpse of his great-uncle Shoyl, which the yardsman Kuzma is tending. Kuzma explains the situation to the boy and takes him to his parents, who have sought shelter at a neighbor's house.

This turn of events is horrifying, and on one level it is the sheer impact of the unexpectedly bloody conclusion to the narrator's innocent quest for, of all things, a dovecote—than which no image could be more evocative of peaceful coexistence—that drives the story. On another level, though, the story is "about" something entirely different: counterfactual discourse, in all its glorious variety. Abstracted from its violent context, the story reads as a veritable catalogue of unreliable speech-acts, beginning with the father's promise to buy the doves—a statement whose truth-value cannot be judged until later, at which point it rapidly becomes irrelevant in the light of grimmer events—and continues with his empty threats against Khariton Efrussi, the father of his son's rival. At his second entrance exam, the young protagonist responds to a question about Peter the Great by declaiming Pushkin verses—despite the fact that he has also memorized the relevant section from his history textbook. His gratuitous substitution of *story* for *history* earns him a perfect score on the exam, an honor he immediately describes as "unattainable," despite having just attained it. Flushed with success, he runs home to tell his father, who, he says, "believed my story without hesitation": a highly suspect remark, for his father's willing belief could only be worth mentioning if it were unusual, and yet we know "Babel's" father to be notably "trusting." If his paradigmatic credulity is routinely strained by his son's stories, there must be some reason. Could it be that young Babel has been caught lying before?

The catalogue is interrupted by the narrator's description of his crazy forebears, to which we shall return shortly. It resumes with a description of the ball Babel's father gives in celebration of his success, which is attended by a number of agricultural-machinery salesmen. These are studiously avoided by the rest of the guests, for "those salesmen would sell machines to anyone. The peasants and landowners were afraid of them, it was impossible to get away from them without buying something" (2:145/32). In this case, language not only distorts, but actually alters reality: the commercial rhetoric of the salesmen, the inverse of Babel *père's* imprecations (which threaten an impact on reality that never materializes), creates a "truth" that apparently demands credence, and thus substantiates itself. The word becomes deed. These irresistible sales pitches, which terrorize "the peasants and landowners," are an ironic precursor of the anti-Semitic invective used by Katyusha (wife of Makarenko, the cripple) later on in the story, whose "truth," similarly, is perlocutionary: as she makes the statement, "Their seed ought to be destroyed" (2:149/38), those same "peasants and landowners" are out on the streets doing their best to ensure that very thing.

Celebrating alongside the salesmen at the ball is the venerable "Monsieur" Liberman (his moniker itself paradoxical, or at least Odessanishly heterodox), who toasts the triumphant proto-gymnasiast in ancient Hebrew. The inflated rhetoric of his toast, in which its honoree's academic accomplishments are compared to David's victory over Goliath, represents still another way in which truth may be distorted via language. Liberman's magniloquence, too, has its ironic counterpart later in the text: the pompously euphemistic announcement, by a felt-booted stranger at the hunter's market, of the pogrom: "In town the Jerusalem gentlefolk are receiving a constitution" (2:147–48/35). The same stranger breaks the news of Shoyl's murder: "On Rybnaya they have treated [*ugostili*, a nice irony whose edge is lost in English] old man Babel to death" (2:148, my translation). Poor Shoyl—so recently an exuberant guest at the Babels' ball, as the euphemistic *"ugostili"* reminds us—is now enjoying a grimmer feast.

Against this background of discursive distortions, the Babel men are singled out for their particular susceptibility to fiction, both at the reception level and at the transmission level. Seemingly addicted—as we shall see—to fabrication and falsification, they are also criticized for their naive credulity. The narrator's description of his father in "The Story of My Dovecote" echoes the grandmother's advice in "Childhood. At Grandmother's": "my father was [too] trusting of people; he offended them with the raptures of first love; people could not forgive him this and were always deceiving him" (2:145, my translation). And his father's gullibility is nothing out of the ordinary in the Babel family: "All the men of our breed were trusting of people and quick to unconsidered action" (2:144, my translation). The responsibility of resisting this wholesale confusion of word with deed falls to the women of the family, as the grandmother in "Childhood. At Grandmother's" and the mother in "The Story of My Dovecote" both struggle, against the prevailing winds, to talk some sense into the newest generation of Babel manhood.

Having invoked his heritage of delusion, Babel goes on to establish his pedigree as a falsifier. We have already been treated to his father's penchant for unreliable predictions, in the form of threats and promises. Now it transpires that discursive unreliability is a trait common to the Babel men: the narrator's Grandfather Levi-Itskhok, formerly a rabbi in Belaia Tserkov', is said to have been accused of blasphemy and/or forgery[57]—both forms of "falsification"—and banished; his great-uncle Shoyl tells "lying stories" about his ostensibly adventurous past.

In the Babelian universe of fictions and falsifications, Shoyl's command particular attention, for they are unforgettable: the narrator comments, "Nowadays I know that Shoyl was merely an old ignoramus and a naive liar, but I have not forgotten his stories, for they were very good." It does not take much effort to see in Shoyl a figure for Babel (the real Babel) himself: a storyteller who makes a virtue of the congenital Babelian affinity for fabrication; who tells autobiographical fibs in order to gratify his audience; and whose chief creative act, in the context of this story, is the making of a "Dovecote."

We know that Shoyl's stories are lies because the narrator says so:

> Shoyl differed from ordinary people . . . by virtue of the mendacious stories he used to tell about the Polish uprising of 1861.[58] In the old days Shoyl had been an innkeeper in Skvira; he had seen Nicholas I's soldiers shoot Count Godlewski and the other Polish insurgents. On the other hand, perhaps he had not. (2:145/32)

Shoyl's credentials as a liar are thus firmly asserted from the outset; but the attentive reader will have noticed something fishy about all of this (and not just the odor of Shoyl's fishmonger-hands). The fact is that Shoyl's stories about the uprising are *corroborated* by the grandmother—who, we may deduce, is Shoyl's sister—in "Childhood. At Grandmother's," a story written a decade earlier:

> When I was a girl the Poles rose up in rebellion. Near us there was a Polish count's manor. The tsar himself came to see the count [Godlewski]. . . . Then there was the uprising. Soldiers came and dragged him out to the square. We all stood around and wept. The soldiers dug a pit. They wanted to blindfold the old man. He said, "I don't need one," stood facing the soldiers and ordered, "Fire!" . . . As they were beginning to bury him, a messenger arrived in haste. He had brought a reprieve from the tsar. (1:40–41/26)

The other claim of Shoyl's to which the narrator alludes—that he had been an innkeeper in Skvira—is also intertextually corroborated, in "In the Basement," the fourth of the childhood tales, where we learn that before taking up his controversial career as a rabbi in Belaia Tserkov', Babel's Grandfather

Levi-Itskhok had also lived in Skvira. There seems no reason to doubt that his brother-in-law Shoyl did too, or that Shoyl was, as he says, an innkeeper; and if we accept the latter claim, we must instantly become aware of the resonance with the grandmother's other story, in "Childhood. At Grandmother's," about the "olden days":

> Long ago, many years past, a certain Jew had run an inn. . . . The police commissioner came and harassed him. He began to find life difficult. He went to see the *tsadik* and said, "Rebbe, the police commissioner is vexing me to death. Intercede for me with God." "Go in peace," the *tsadik* said to him. "The police commissioner will settle down." The Jew went away. In the doorway of his inn he found the police commissioner. The latter lay dead with a purple, swollen face. (1:40/25)

If the long-ago innkeeper was actually Shoyl (an assumption less far-fetched than it might seem, given the "Dovecote" narrator's hints that Shoyl too told this story), we can begin to discern patterns in Shoyl's personal narrative that will come to grisly fruition in "The Story of My Dovecote," when he enters the text as a physical character (rather than just an allusion). The familiar structure of the innkeeper story, reminiscent of the fairy tale (naturalized into the Russian canon by Pushkin) about the golden fish who grants the fisherman a series of wishes, leaves us with the impression that the Jew in this story used *his* wish—granted here not by a supernatural fish but by the holy *tsadik*—to kill the unfortunate police commissioner. If the Jew in question was actually Shoyl, then Shoyl's murder (on "Fish Street," no less, and involving the insertion of live perch into his mouth and trousers) may be read as poetic justice, providing a kind of ultimate narrative closure.

There are echoes of Shoyl's death, too, in the story of Count Godlewski's execution. Like the Count, Shoyl, a non-Russian, meets his death at the hands of a hostile Russian assembly, and with fortitude (albeit not with the count's quiet dignity). The soldiers' offer of a blindfold is reflected in the Russian yardsman Kuzma's proposal to cover Shoyl's eyes, after his death, with coins. And, like the count, Shoyl dies untimely: the one person who could reprieve him—Babel, who is writing the story—arrives, in the person of his narrator-protagonist, too late. The fact that Shoyl proceeds, ultimately, to "live out" his stories, lends them additional validity; though the narrator initially presents them as implausible, they acquire the stamp of authenticity by virtue of their subsequent enactment—or to put it more succinctly, they "come true."

So far, my analysis has presumed Grandmother's stories themselves to be "true" (if only within the cosmos of the stories themselves). In fact, however, their credibility remains likewise in question. First, they are literally "grandmother tales," a term which in Yiddish (*bobe-mayses*) refers, like the English "old wives' tales," to preposterous claims, stories one ought *not* to believe.[59] It is easy to imagine that Babel, writing from an eastern European Jewish background, intended Grandmother's stories to be read in the context of this idiom, and thus, in their very essence, to undermine their own credibility. Moreover, the stylized, folktale-like quality of the two stories that are quoted at length casts further doubt on their authenticity as personal reminiscences.

Conversely, however, the details of these particular "grandmother tales" are borne out by biographical details given about the fictional Babel family in "In the Basement" and "Awakening," as well as by their points of concurrence with Shoyl's stories in "The Story of My Dovecote." Moreover, unlike Shoyl, Grandmother is not intrinsically suspect, for the Babel women, in contradistinction to their men, are not explicitly depicted either as liars or as gulls. In fact, as I noted above, their peculiar clarity of vision is stressed throughout the childhood tales. If the grandmother's corroboration does not make Shoyl's stories incontestably true, it does at least mean that they are not incontestably false. Thus, the reader initially inclined to doubt the *veracity* of the stories must, on further reflection, doubt their *mendacity*—an attitude requiring a certain amount of mental contortionism.

This is where the relationship between our two tricksters—Shoyl and Babel himself—gets particularly tricky: if Shoyl's credibility is bolstered by his sister's testimony, the narrator's is commensurately undermined (since it is through his testimony that Shoyl's credibility is compromised to begin with). On the one hand, we can classify the narrator's untruthful designation of Shoyl's stories as "false," alongside the surprise he expresses earlier in the story at being so readily believed by his father, as evidence of his unreliability. On the other hand, to accuse Shoyl of telling the truth is to undermine the narrator's own carefully established "pedigree" as a liar, and thus to *discredit* the notion that he is unreliable. At the least, inasmuch as Shoyl may be read as a representative of the author in the text, Babel's obfuscation of the status of Shoyl's stories signals the ambiguous status of his own authorial project.

And so we find ourselves at an impasse: the more we scrutinize Babel the narrator, the more he changes shape before our eyes, so that finally we are at a loss to say whether or not we should believe him. Babel's ingeniously layered Cretan stories, told by competing autobiographical tricksters, add up to a sticky Cretan paradox: if the narrator is telling the truth, then he must be lying, and vice versa. Although the narrative seems to incorporate Riffaterrian gestures toward its fictional "intentions," centering upon the figure of Shoyl, as these signals are transformed from figures of fictionality or falsehood to figures of potential authenticity, they lose their function of "remind(ing) the reader that the tale he is being told is imaginary," weakening the stories' self-identification as fiction and making them—paradoxically—not more true, but more mendacious. In short, Babel uses these very gestures to do precisely what Riffaterre proscribes: he makes a genre of a lie.

As I indicated earlier, however, the point of Shoyl's stories (as the narrator insists) is not that they are true, or for that matter false, but that they are *good*. Time and again in the childhood cycle we see the narrator address the distinction between good stories and bad: in "Childhood. At Grandmother's," he promises to tell us ("another time") the story of the friendship between his grandmother and her dog, because "it is a very good, touching and tender story" (1:38/23). Shortly thereafter, he presumes to "improve upon" a venerable intertext, Turgenev's *First Love* (a narrative, moreover, that places particular emphasis on the work done by its own narrator to make it "good"),[60] by transferring the site of a whip-lashing from the heroine's arm to her cheek. This rather saucy revision presages a similar move that Babel will make in "The Story of My Dovecote," improving upon a different, specifically Odessan intertext: Alexander Kuprin's "Gambrinus."

"DOVECOTE" AND ODESSAN INTERTEXTUALITY

"Gambrinus," Kuprin's part homage to, part indictment of, the atmosphere of pre-Revolutionary Odessa, is an important part of the "Odessa text" already extant when the Odessans made their first forays into literature, and the role this story plays in works by the Odessans makes an interesting case study in their manipulation of that city-text. Kuprin's story centers on a Jewish fiddler named Sashka, entertainer-in-residence at the Gambrinus tavern. Sashka, an extraordinarily resilient character, survives the rowdy crowd at the tavern, the occasional anti-Semitic barb from a new customer, the Russo-Japanese War (into which he is conscripted, despite being clearly overage), a POW camp, a pogrom, a brawl, and an unwarranted arrest that leads to the mangling of his left arm. Like Shoyl, he is ebullient under fire; unlike Shoyl, he seems indestructible in body as well as in spirit. Sashka's little dog, Belochka, is not so fortunate; she sticks faithfully to his side until—like Babel's doves—she falls victim, as his surrogate, to the anti-Semitic violence that rages in the city.

The destruction of Belochka, set during the same pogroms as "The Story of My Dovecote," those of October 1905, is particularly interesting as an apparent precursor to the one Babel depicts. It begins with a stonemason who, enthusiastically participating in the pogrom, is stopped (by a former Gambrinus customer) in the act of trying to kill Sashka:

He simpered like an idiot, spat, and wiped his nose on his sleeve. But suddenly he noticed a nervous little white dog that snuggled up to Sashka, trembling. He stooped down quickly, grabbed it by the hind legs, lifted it high, dashed its head against the paving stones, and started to run. Sashka stared after him in silence. The man was running along capless, his body bent forward and arms stretched out, his mouth gaping and eyes round and white with madness.

Belochka's brains were scattered over Sashka's boots. He wiped them off with his handkerchief.[61]

Compare the similar scene in "The Story of My Dovecote":

With a fat hand the cripple turned the (bag of) doves upside down and pulled out a cherry-colored female. Its feet thrown back, the bird lay in the palm of his hand.

"Doves," said Makarenko and, his wheels squeaking, approached me. "Doves," he repeated, like an inevitable echo, and struck me on the cheek.

He struck me a swinging blow, his hand now clenched; the dove cracked on my temple, Katyusha's wadded posterior swayed before my eyes and I fell to the earth in my new overcoat. . . . I lay on the earth, and the entrails of the crushed bird trickled from my temple. They flowed down my cheeks, coiling, splashing and blinding me. Soft dove guts crept over my forehead, and I closed a last unstuck eye so as not to see the world that was spreading out before me. (2:149/36)

Babel's version of this structurally similar scenario uses the symbolic potentials of its constituent elements more efficiently: the substitution of doves (the traditional symbol of peace and, in the Noah story, of an end rather than an introduction to hardship) for Sashka's pet dog ratchets up the tension between the action (violence) and its object (a harbinger of peace). Moreover, the elements are more parsimoniously deployed. The narrator and protagonist (and, ostensibly, the author) are the same; the symbolic victim of the murder (Sashka, in the Kuprin story) is also a physical victim; the surrogate victim, or sacrificial animal, is also a weapon; the superfluous paving stones are eliminated; altogether, the number of nouns involved in the attack is reduced from five (assailant, weapon, surrogate victim, symbolic victim, narrator) to three (assailant, weapon/surrogate victim, symbolic victim/narrator).

The identities of the assailant and the symbolic victim also contribute to the immediacy of Babel's drama: the victim, explicitly identified with Babel himself, becomes our direct link to the experience of anti-Jewish violence, and the fact that he is a (future) writer, rather than a fiddler, makes the attack on him implicitly an attack on the very fabric of the text we are reading. Meanwhile, the man shattering Peace upon the face of Literature is no unmotivated thug, but a figure of helplessness in his own right; a cripple, he is too weak to participate in the truly murderous violence taking place downtown, which both supplies his motivation (a frustrated lust for blood and pillage) and underscores the pathos of the scene. Finally, the oozing cerebral matter is moved from the protagonist's boots—the place normally occupied by dust—to his face, where it becomes a virtual surrogate both for the protagonist's blood (trickling from his temple) and for his tears (obscuring his vision, flowing down his cheeks).

It should be noted that one of the few things to remain unchanged about this passage between Kuprin's story and Babel's is the status of the Jew as victim. To be sure, historical accuracy would seem to demand it, but we have seen that Babel is no slave to historical accuracy—and Jewish history could in any event have provided other plots for Babel to pursue. In this story, far from presenting Russian literature with a new, powerful Jewish type, Babel hews close to the traditional imagery of the Jew as a "man of contemplation" who responds helplessly to an unprovoked onslaught from a "man of action." However, unlike Kuprin's Sashka or Chekhov's Rothschild—both downtrodden fiddlers, not fledgling authors—the Jewish protagonist of "The Story of My Dovecote" is able to verbalize his pain. Words, not music, are his art and his preferred medium of expression; words are his power. Where Sashka and Rothschild are largely limited to a wordless form of expression that must be mediated for us by a remote narrator, the "Story of My Dovecote" protagonist controls his own narrative; if he cannot make his encounter with the 1905 pogrom a better experience, he can at least make it a better story. Under attack by *fabula* (story, content), Babel fights back with *siuzhet* (narrative, form).

By writing "himself" (i.e., his autobiographical protagonist) into the Sashka role, Babel rewrites not only a classic text of the "small, bent, weak, and pathetic" Jew genre,[62] but a classic text of the Odessa canon to boot. Konstantin Paustovsky—who, along with Babel, was one of the Odessa school's most devoted mythologizers—offers his own revision of the same Kuprin story in his 1958 memoir, *A Time of Great Expectations* (*Vremia bol'shikh ozhidanii*). Like Babel, Paustovsky (who uses his memoir to insert himself firmly into the canon of the Odessa school and its lore) sets out to dissolve the boundary between "real" and "fictional" events:

> And so one day a death announcement was printed in the "Odessa News" for one Aaron Moiseevich Goldstein. It seems to me that that was the dead man's name. I don't remember exactly. No one would have paid any attention to the announcement if it hadn't said at the bottom, in brackets under the name Goldstein, "Sashka the Musician from 'Gambrinus.'"
>
> Up until then I was convinced that almost all literary heroes were made up. Life and literature never flowed into each other in my imagination. So the announcement about Sashka the Musician's death confused me.

I reread "Gambrinus." Everything in that story was as precise as an official report, and at the same time the story was humane to the point of tears and as picturesque as a summer evening on Deribasovskaya. . . .

Evidently, the noble sensitivity and humanity of Kuprin himself had imparted to this story the characteristics of great art.

I could hardly believe that Sashka the Musician, who had been for me since childhood a literary hero, had really lived just next door, in the garret of an old Odessa house.

I was fortunate. I witnessed the true ending of the story "Gambrinus": the funeral of Sashka the Musician. Life itself wrote this ending in Kuprin's stead.[63]

This passage constitutes nothing less than a conversion narrative: from his initial assumptions that "all literary heroes were made up" and "life and literature never flowed into each other," the narrator travels to a new understanding of the fluid relationship between life and art; an understanding that allows him to make the previously unthinkable statement, "I witnessed the true ending of the story," and to consider "life" as a coauthor of "Gambrinus," where previously he had attributed that story's "great art" to the specific talents of its human author, Alexander Kuprin. This journey, from the complete separation of "life" and "literature" to their complete integration, represents in microcosm the conversion undergone by Paustovsky in *A Time of Great Expectations*—a conversion catalyzed by the interpenetration of "life" and "literature" practiced by Babel.

A Time of Great Expectations, like Babel's childhood tales, narrates Paustovsky's firsthand experience of events in Odessa during a historic epoch (in this case, 1920–21), a setting that allows him to introduce Babel as a main character and to cement in the reader's mind the three-way connection among Babel, Odessa, and Paustovsky himself. As a result, it is largely on the strength of this work that Paustovsky is frequently included among the Odessa school.[64] But, again like Babel's stories, *A Time of Great Expectations* is more than just a document of Paustovsky's life in Odessa: it simultaneously describes and enacts the author's conversion to "Odessanism," which in turn serves to justify his induction into the Odessa school of writers, presided over both implicitly (in the choice of genre and form) and explicitly (in long, "verbatim" speeches) by Babel, who appears as a leading character in Paustovsky's narrative. Paustovsky has, in a sense, picked up the narrative mediation of Babel where the mytholeptic Babel himself left off; he is again transformed into "Babel," a fictional persona, but seen this time from the point of view of a narrator who reveres and longs to emulate him. It seems fitting that Paustovsky uses this fictional persona—as Babel himself did—as a means to insinuate Odessan discourse, and himself along with it, into the Russian canon.

Interestingly, Paustovsky's text also contains an oblique allusion to Babel's revision of Kuprin. In one of the many conversations that Paustovsky quotes verbatim (despite a chronological gap of some thirty-seven years between the conversation and its subsequent narration), Babel remarks: "There are writers, even good ones, who scatter paragraphs and punctuation marks all over the place. . . . Kuprin himself wrote such prose."[65] With this quotation, Paustovsky contrives to hint both at Babel's role in the Odessa discourse, and at his own. Babel, in "improving upon" Kuprin's chapter in the Odessa text, reappropriates that text—originally based on the exoticist objectification of Odessa by mainstream Russians—as a springboard from which Odessan writers can stage a reverse invasion of the Russian canon. Whereas Babel's revision of Kuprin unites the roles of protagonist and author (casting Babel himself as both), Paustovsky inserts himself into Kuprin's narrative as eyewitness and epilogist—a dual title that also describes Paustovsky's modus operandi with respect to Babel in *A Time of Great Expectations*.

In chapter 3, I shall return to the question of Paustovsky's unilateral "collaboration" with Babel on the Odessa discourse, noting the extent to which Paustovsky's life text depends on Babel's, and in particular how it mirrors Babel's concern with the boundaries between "good" and "bad" storytelling—on the ethical as well as on the aesthetic plane. First, however, I shall examine the ways in which the latter concern makes itself felt in the rest of Babel's childhood tales.

Babel's Bildungsroman and Odessan Modernism

GOOD STORY, BAD STORY

The questions Babel raises in "Childhood" and "Dovecote" about the aesthetic qualities, epistemological status, and ethical boundaries of fiction remain on center stage in the three stories that complete the childhood cycle: "First Love" ("Pervaia liubov'"), "In the Basement" ("V podvale"), and "Awakening" ("Probuzhdenie"). In these stories, fiction and falsehood, fantasy and outright delusion are explored in an array of guises and on various narrative levels, both formal and thematic. As in "Childhood" and "Dovecote," the genre and mode of the stories, their rhetoric, characters, and action, all serve to focus the reader's attention upon the nature and teleology of fiction itself. If, as Alice Stone Nakhimovsky has asserted, the stories recount "a past that has an overriding psychological validity, even if the details are made up,"[1] that psychological validity is grounded at least partly in the childhood narrator's ongoing exploration of *what* details to make up, why, and how. The fruits of that exploration are woven into the narratives of the remaining stories in a variety of ways.

"First Love," the third story in the childhood cycle, takes its title from a narrative (Turgenev's eponymous novella) certified as "good" both by Babel's narrator in "Childhood" and by Turgenev's narrator in the original, which itself features—surely not coincidentally—a frame narrative explaining how the story, potentially "bad," came to be a "good" one:

> "My first love really does belong among the not exactly usual ones," answered Vladimir Petrovich with a slight hesitancy. . . .
> "Ah!" said the host and Sergey Nikolaevich simultaneously. "So much the better. . . . Go on then, tell us."
> "If you like . . . or no, I won't start telling you, because I'm no good at telling things. [. . .] If you'll allow me, I'll write down everything I remember in an exercise book and then read it out to you."
> The friends wouldn't agree at first, but Vladimir Petrovich insisted. Two weeks later they gathered again and Vladimir Petrovich kept his promise.[2]

From here on, in Turgenev's novella, the properly prepared Vladimir Petro-vich becomes the narrator of his own autobiographical oddity. His prefatory fastidiousness is particularly interesting because it is perfectly gratuitous to the storyline; one might as well simply begin with the first-person narra-tive. But the frame narrative establishes that there is a difference between "good" and "bad" stories, and that the difference is located in their form, rather than their content: literary value is not immanent in the material, but is produced by the skill of the storyteller (exercised, not incidentally, in the act of writing the story down). We may assume that Vladimir Petrovich has successfully crafted a "good" story by adhering to these values; but what qualities mark a story as "good"? A possible criterion by which to judge liter-ary value is offered later in the novella by Vladimir Petrovich's *First Love*–object, Zinaida: "That's why poetry's so wonderful; it speaks to us of what doesn't exist and of what's not only better than what does exist, but even more like the truth."[3] This emancipation of "truth" from "reality" may be said to have struck a chord with Babel, who adopted it (as we have seen in the last chapter) as a cornerstone of his poetics.

In "In the Basement," the story that follows "First Love," the recur-ring good story/bad story duality is played out by the juxtaposition of Babel (a gripping but mendacious storyteller) with his classmate Mark Borgman (a conscientious but dull one). These two make quite the odd couple with their rival stories about Spinoza, through which, paradoxically, they be-come friends. Mark's primary concern is for the veracity of his narrative; this stands him in poor stead once the audience-hungry Babel arrives on the scene. Whereas Mark's Spinoza stories deal with the religious context of the philosopher's biography, Babel regales his audience with embellished descriptions of what Spinoza got up to in his spare time. The two friends, pitting Spinoza's (life)style against his substance, are in a sense waging a lit-erary battle between content and form over the philosopher's body;[4] unsur-prisingly, Babel wins, although his triumph is confined to the literary (and emphatically not the academic or socioeconomic) arena.

In the fifth and final childhood tale, "Awakening," the young story-teller receives a brisk schooling in naturalism; though he is at liberty to tell stories about "what doesn't exist," he evidently remains under some sort of obligation to make them, in the words of Turgenev's Zinaida, "not only better than what does exist, but even more like the truth." In order to accomplish this, the narrator discovers, he must improve his vocabulary; his stories lack verisimilitude because he does not know the words for "what does exist." This lesson is imparted by a new father figure known as Nikitich, another "good" storyteller whose tales "of fish and animals" make his audience of Jewish children "die with laughter."[5] Nikitich, significantly, is a proofreader by trade: while the lessons he imparts to the young Babel center on knowing the right words for things, we can imagine that he also stands for the importance of good revision—whether it be revision as practiced by Vladimir Petrovich in *First Love* (to perfect the telling of a story), as practiced by Babel on Kuprin in "The Story of My Dovecote" (to make a good story better), or as practiced by Babel in "Guy de Maupassant" (to pinpoint the place where a properly positioned full stop can "enter the human heart" more "chillingly" than a steel blade).

THE TIES THAT BLIND

Among the themes unifying the stories of the childhood cycle are the issues of freedom and confinement, of perception, and of family that made their first appearance in "Childhood." In my analysis of that story, I observed that the three dominant male Babel figures are introduced in absentia: the narrator's great-uncle Shoyl, father Manus, and grandfather Levi-Itskhok proceed to dominate, respectively, each of the three stories that follow. In "Awakening," the fifth story of the cycle, the narrator finally turns to a father-figure outside—and forbidden by—his family, the proofreader Nikitich, whose guidance of and ambitions for the narrator stand in direct opposition to those set out by the latter's father.

The narrator's relationship to his father is problematic in the extreme, at least partly because his father represents his closest link to the troubled male bloodline of the Babel family. In a passage later excised from "Dovecote," the narrator says of his teacher, Karavaev, "The teacher Karavaev was better than a father to me."[6] Karavaev's defining trait, in the sketch of him that follows, becomes his ruddiness; he is thus imbued with the connotations of the red family of colors, associated by Babel with positive action, with the hearty physicality of the (literary-stereotypical) Russian peasantry, and by extension with the liberating "crimson blindness" that comes over the protagonist when, during his oral examinations, he takes flight from his paternally induced anxiety into the verses of Pushkin. The association of Karavaev with the "red" continuum of freedom, blindness, and a kind of delirious autonomy leaves Babel's father, by implication, to represent its counterpart: the "yellow" continuum of unsparing visual clarity, constriction, and oppression, which for the narrator is inextricably linked to the domestic realm, family, and the indoors.

The foregoing brief summary sketches out the web of associations, generated by "Childhood" and "Dovecote," from which the reader approaches "First Love." The appearance, early in the latter story, of a paragraph recapitulating the events of "Dovecote" provides us with an opportunity to look for evidence of Babel's signature technique of prevarication, the exaggeration of trivial details at the expense of significant ones. A close reading of the passage reveals the by-now-expected omission; the narrator skips straight from

> For five years out of the ten I had lived, I had dreamed about doves with all the power of my soul, and then, when I had bought them, Makarenko the cripple had smashed the doves on my temple.

to:

> Then Kuzma took me to the Rubtsovs'. (2:154/42)

The missing event is the child's return home and his horrifying discovery of Shoyl's corpse. Turning to this scene in "Dovecote," we find that it is the site of another, more subtle omission:

> "They gave our grandfather the chop, no one else," said Kuzma. . . . "You should put some five-kopeck coins on his eyes . . ."
> But back then, just ten years old, I did not know what dead people needed five-kopeck coins for. (2:150–52, my translation; concluding ellipsis in original)

The omission of "on their eyes" in the last sentence might appear less significant had not optical imagery proliferated to so noteworthy an extent throughout both "Dovecote" and "Childhood." To make such frequent and prominent references to "eyes" and then suddenly to leave them out in a sentence where mention of them seems to be called for (McDuff's translation here reads ". . . I did not know why dead people needed coins on their eyes" [40]) must occasion some readerly curiosity.

But to what end? In the universe of the childhood tales, images of eyes and visual perception become an extended metaphor—or, at least, analogy—for the act of narration. The metaphor works in counterpoint to the logical connection between seeing and telling forged by the narrator, who functions as the reader's eyes and ears in the text (relaying information that, being fictional, cannot be experienced firsthand), and transforms the evidence of his own eyes into language for consumption by the reader. Babel, apparently at pains to level the playing field between visual mediation ("seeing is believing") and narrative mediation ("don't believe everything you read"), repeatedly makes reference to eyes and eyesight in his depictions of the various "tellers" who appear in the childhood tales, including himself. In "The Story of My Dovecote," the narrator twice describes his mother as follows: "Mother was pale . . . she was experiencing fate (through my eyes)" (2:144, my translation; the phrase "through my eyes" is omitted the second

time, thus receiving a peculiarly Babelian emphasis). The mother's experience of her family's destiny through "Babel's" eyes parallels the reader's experience of their destiny through Babel's prose.

The mother's use of her son as a quasi-narrator is mirrored by the narrator's own attempt to use Kuzma in a similar capacity at the end of the
same story:

> "Kuzma," I said in a whisper, "save us . . ."
> And I went over to the yardkeeper, embraced his old crooked back with
> its one raised shoulder and *saw grand-uncle from behind that dear back.*
> Shoyl lay in the sawdust, his chest crushed, his beard turned up, in rough
> clogs worn on bare feet . . . (2:152/40, my emphasis)

The description of Shoyl's corpse (which, the reader belatedly realizes, has
until now been withheld) follows; the implication is that the child cannot
bring himself to experience Shoyl's corpse except "through the eyes" of another. Unable to confront the death of his former favorite narrator directly,
he turns to Kuzma to fill the void left by the dead storyteller, and, by literally
hiding behind Kuzma, places the latter in a quasi-narrative mediating role.
Conversely, Kuzma's suggestion that coins be laid on the dead man's eyes (a
Russian practice whose purpose is to hold the eyes closed) suggests an end
to Shoyl's role both as a see-er and as a teller.

In "First Love," the opposition of outdoor to indoor space and the
theme of visual perception are further integrated to produce a spatial figuration of objectivity and illusion. Whereas "Dovecote" catalogued various kinds of fabrications, crowned by Shoyl's "inspired lies," "First Love"
explores another, equally important aspect of fiction: fantasy. Nakhimovsky
characterizes the prevailing aesthetic of the story as "ironic and misplaced";
that sense of ironic mis- or displacement stems in part from the febrile,
overimaginative quality of the narration.[7] From the dragons on Galina's robe
at the beginning of the story, to the narrator's extraordinary illness at the
end, everything depicted in the story seems surreal, illusive.

The story opens with the narrator's description of his fantasies about
Galina Rubtsova, the wife of the neighboring tax collector in whose home
the (fictional) Babels will seek refuge from the pogrom introduced in "Dovecote." The narrator watches Galina covertly from his window, establishing
the antecedent from which we may extrapolate a mechanism for reading the
story on a metaphorical plane: the window opens a view into a land popu-
lated by objects of the narrator's fantasy. Marc Chagall, Babel's near contemporary and arguably his artistic fellow traveler, espoused a similar relationship between the window and the imagination, which he exploited in his
many window paintings, including *The Window* (1908), *Paris Through the*

Window (1913), *View from the Window, Vitebsk* (1914–15), and *View from the Window, on the Olcha* (1915).[8] For Chagall, the window in a painting looked not into the objective realm outside, but into the painter's fantasy of that realm; thus, in *Paris Through the Window*, he offers a glimpse of "his own private, imaginary world, which he here projects onto his vision of Paris. . . . an upside down train chugs past and a parachutist drifts slowly down toward a couple who float horizontally in the sky."[9]

Though characters glimpsed through windows by Babel's narrator do not float through the air, they do behave in ways that seem unlikely, if not—as Nathalie Babel somewhat acerbically observes—downright impossible:

> [Babel's] father would not have had to kneel at a Cossack's feet and beg that his store be spared, for the simple reason that Babel's father did not own a store. He owned a warehouse, which was neither broken into nor plundered during the pogrom. I must add (and this may be a disillusionment to readers of "First Love") that no member of the Babel family was redheaded, that my grandmother's name was Fanny, not Rachel, nor would she ever have thought of addressing her husband in the terms used by the woman in the story; she was a modest, sensitive woman. It is, of course, not impossible that there was a charming girl named Galina who wore a Chinese peignoir, and who inflamed my father's passions at the age of ten. But if she did exist, then my father was the only member of the family who had the privilege of knowing her.[10]

In "First Love," we are led from the narrator's voyeuristic surveillance of this imaginary siren and her (possibly just as imaginary) husband into the one-paragraph summary of the events of "Dovecote" examined above, and thence into a description of the protagonist's arrival at the Rubtsovs' on the day of the pogrom. The bulk of the Rubtsovs' domestic activity appears to take place in the "glass veranda" that "usurp(s) part of (the Babels') land," which has a destabilizing effect on the action of the story as a whole, for events that take place behind glass cannot help but take on, especially in this context, a certain aura of unreality. As a result, there is no truly stable narrative ground in "First Love"—hence its general atmosphere of delirium—but events glimpsed by the protagonist through a window remain the least anchored in "reality."

Upon his arrival at the Rubtsovs', the narrator finds the women—his mother and Galina, neatly embodying the archetypal feminine division of labor between Mary and Eve—within the glass veranda, in a "green rotunda" (the color green, especially prominent in "First Love," is associated in Babel's universe not with growing things but with death and decay).[11] Women, in the fictional Babel family, are the pragmatic ones (see chapter

2), and accordingly they occupy here the relatively stable territory of indoor space, while all around them are windows. Galina explains that the narrator's father is wandering the streets outside, "upset," and urges the boy to "call him home." The boy looks out through the window at a scene that possesses a distinctly fantastic quality:

> And through the window I saw the deserted street with an enormous sky above it and my red-haired father [*ryzhego moego otets*] walking along the roadway. He had no hat covering his lightly ruffled red [*ryzhikh*] hair; his cotton shirtfront was turned askew and fastened by some button or other, but not the one it ought to have been fastened by. (2:154–55/43)

The insistence on the father's redheadedness—a detail discredited at the biographical level by Nathalie Babel—has a number of literary resonances. It recalls the similarly "*ryzhii*" Rudy Panko, narrator of Gogol's *Evenings on a Farm near Dikanka,* who is himself both a purveyor of fantastic stories and, arguably, a "father" of Babel's Odessa narrators, who would similarly seek to make their mark on Russian literature through a combination of local color, stories of "deceptions and transformations," and "plots . . . presented by turns in a comic and in a horrific key."[12] The father's red hair also, however, places him in a line of pathetic Jews from Russian literature, a group that includes the "red-haired Jew, with freckles all over his face that made him look like a sparrow's egg" encountered by Gogol's Taras Bulba; "Girshel," the title character of Turgenev's *The Jew* (*Zhid,* 1846); one of the heavily stereotypical Jews in Leskov's "Jewish Somersault" ("Zhidovskaia kuvyrkolegiia," 1882); and the "red-haired, skinny" title character of Chekhov's "Rothschild's Fiddle" ("Skripka Rotshil'da," 1894).[13] These characters embody the quintessence of Russian literature's assumptions about Jewish weakness, a canon to which Babel is about to contribute.

Still watching through the window, the boy witnesses the famous scene of his father's kneeling before the mounted Cossack, pleading for the salvation of his family store. The scene over, the father's supplication refused, the boy sticks his head out of the window—into the imaginary realm—and calls to him.

> Father turned around when he heard my voice.
> "My little son," he mouthed with inexpressible tenderness, and began to tremble with love for me. (2:156/45)

This moment is particularly poignant given that such tenderness from the normally authoritarian father—whose chief role in "Dovecote" and "Awakening" is to enforce his own ambitions for the narrator's education—is apparently forthcoming only in the boy's own imagination.

The father's transition from the otherworld behind the window into the more certain territory of domestic space is accompanied by the onset of his son's mysterious hiccupping disease, which afflicts him until the end of the story. His symptoms escalate into a (latterly heavily censored) bout of convulsions, a highly Freudian "swelling, pleasant to the touch" that rises from the boy's throat, and copious quantities of green vomit.[14] Experienced by the narrator as a rite of passage ("towards night I was no longer the lop-eared boy I had been all my life"), and as a demonstration of his mastery over Galina ("Fear was shaking the woman and making her writhe"), the illness has unmistakably sexual overtones:[15]

> I snarled in triumph, in exhaustion, with the ultimate exertions of love.
>
> Thus did my illness begin. I was ten at the time. In the morning I was taken to see the doctor. The pogrom continued, but we were left alone. The doctor, a fat man, found that I had a nervous illness. . . .
>
> Now, when I remember those sad years, I find in them the beginning of the ailments that torment me, and the causes of my premature and dreadful decline. (2:159/48–49)

The "ailments" in question undoubtedly include the "unbridled fantasies" that "torment" the young voyeur earlier in the story, as well as the pangs of "first love" (which we must interpret, following the narrator's use of the phrase in "Dovecote," as a reference not only to the boy's crush on Galina, but more globally to the self-destructive credulity of the Babel men) and the mysterious hiccupping illness, possibly a metaphor for puberty. Jerome Charyn diagnoses it as follows:

> The pogrom winds around the boy with such ferocious ambiguity that we can't help but read it as a focal point of his fiction. The pogrom punishes him and rewards him. . . . If he hadn't been sullied by the cigarette boy, would he have been able to lean against Galina's hip, "her hip that moved and breathed," and would she have washed off the "smear of pigeon" sticking to his cheek like sexual matter, and kissed him on the mouth? It's as if the pogrom itself had aroused him, and sexuality is seen as a form of violence, with the Cossack officer riding as erect as a penis with "a tall peaked cap." Unable to unravel his own crisis of pleasure and pain, the reality that he's been eroticized by the pogrom, [the narrator] develops a nervous disorder that covers up his confusion and guilt.[16]

Curiously, however, in a passage censored from most Soviet editions, the doctor who diagnoses Babel's "nervous illness" in "First Love" emphasizes that the illness occurs "only in Jews and among Jews only in women."[17] This strangely gendered nervous illness, providing the newly eroticized young

Babel with female symptoms, may suggest that he is struggling, either to remain in the comparatively sane female-dominated sphere, or—given the association of outdoor space with both fantasy and freedom—to escape it. Increasingly, throughout the childhood tales, the narrator's impulse is to escape from the tyranny of domestic expectations into fiction and fresh air—the world beyond the window.

It is tempting to see here also some prescience of the genuinely "premature and dreadful decline" suffered by Babel in the 1930s, as his output tapered off and the political landscape grew more treacherous. It is not unlikely that even as early as 1925, with the *Odessa Tales* and most of *Red Cavalry* behind him, Babel had some inkling of the difficulties he faced, both politically and poetically. In the confession that would later swell his secret police file, Babel would use similarly pathological language to describe his supposed crimes: "Artists who came into contact with me felt the fatal influence of [my] emasculated and sterile view of the world."[18] An alternative, more innocent interpretation of Babel's "ailments" is that they refer to the adult Babel's crippling perfectionism, which according to the (admittedly tendentious) testimony of Paustovsky, was in evidence as early as 1921:

> Babel . . . took from the desk drawer a thick typewritten manuscript. The manuscript was at least a hundred pages long.
>
> "You know what this is?"
>
> I wondered. Surely Babel couldn't have written a long novella at last, and kept it a secret from everyone? . . . Looking at the first page, I saw the title "Liubka the Cossack" and wondered even more. "Permit me," I said. "I understood that 'Liubka the Cossack' was a small short story. Not yet printed. Have you really turned this story into a novella?" . . .
>
> "Yes," [Babel] said, blushing with embarrassment, "this is 'Liubka the Cossack.' The short story. It's no more than fifteen pages, but here are all the drafts of the story, including the final one. . . . And I'm not even sure yet that the final draft is fit to print!"[19]

This anecdote, as is so often the case in Paustovsky's reminiscences of Babel, contains disconcerting echoes of Babel's own stories, including a reference by Babel to the "mysterious disease" (*neponiatnyi nedug*) that afflicts him:

> "I age several years after every story. . . . I wrote somewhere that I am aging fast from asthma, from a mysterious disease that was installed in my weak body when I was just a child. All that is a lie! Writing even the smallest short story, I work on it like a navvy, as if I had to raze Everest to its foundations all on my own. Beginning work, I always think that I won't have the strength for

it. Sometimes I even weep from exhaustion. My blood vessels ache from this work. If some phrase or other won't come out, a spasm grips my heart. And they so often won't come out, these accursed phrases!"[20]

By Paustovsky's account, then, fiction itself (characterized by Paustovsky's Babel not as an irresistible impulse but as a punishing craft) constitutes Babel's "illness," a reading that is not inconsistent with the overtones of sexual transition associated with the disease of "First Love." After all, for a Babel male, puberty means induction into the Babel family's tortuous version of manhood, the province of fiction and delusion.

COMPLETING THE CIRCLE—AND ESCAPING IT

Mark Antony in the Basement

In the fourth childhood tale, "In the Basement," Babel returns both to the theme of confinement (with a title that cannot help but evoke the self-imposed cage of Dostoevsky's narrator-*chudak* in "Notes from Underground") and to a consideration of lying, which he links immediately to the practice of literature: the story opens, "I was an untruthful little boy. This came from reading" (2:179, my translation). Here Babel turns the concept of "book learning" on its head, arguing that his character has learned from books not useful knowledge, but the art of spinning yarns, which proves both a liability and an asset, especially at school. Through the rather naive voice of his narrator, Babel appears to satirize Plato's contention that "poetry . . . has a terrible power to corrupt even the best characters, with very few exceptions."[21] (We will see a further sly reference to this argument later in the story, when the narrator launches into a recital of precisely the kind of poetry most censured by Plato—dramatic verse, here represented by Shakespeare's *Julius Caesar.*)[22] In *The Republic,* Plato goes on to argue that "the only poetry that should be allowed in a state is hymns to the gods and paeans in praise of good men,"[23] a formula that, mutatis mutandis, would be institutionalized by the Soviet regime a few years later, in the form of Socialist Realism. This political subtext cannot, of course, be discounted in reading Babel, who was (as his speech at the 1934 All-Union Congress of Soviet Writers indicates) acutely conscious of the burden placed on writers by the institution of a state-mandated program for literature. Here, as so often with Babel, his treatment of this serious theme is ambiguous; it is hard to say whether his conceit of the fiction-infected reader/narrator supports or undermines the founding theses of Socialist Realism. On the one hand, the narrator's addiction to fiction appears to impair his ability to negotiate reality (whatever "reality," in these stories, may be said to mean); on the other, it is in this story that we really observe the childhood narrator *exploiting* his imagination for the first time; he uses it, literally, to win friends and influence people.

I have already discussed, earlier in this chapter, the competing versions of Spinoza rendered by the rival narrative philosophies of this narrator and his classmate Mark Borgman, and the triumph (with a playground audience) of Babel's inventions over Borgman's more sober testimony. Inside the classroom, however, the signs are again ambiguous, as Babel both suffers and profits from the exercise of his imagination:

> That year we moved up to the third class. My transcript was covered with three-minuses. I was so strange with my carryings-on that the teachers, on reflection, could not bring themselves to give me twos. (2:180; my translation)

It is interesting to speculate on how the "five-plus" pupil of "The Story of My Dovecote" has sunk to such new academic lows: is it the move from suburban Nikolaev to urban Odessa (prompted, if the stories may be read as a coherent arc, by the 1905 pogroms and the onset of the narrator's mysterious illness)? Is it the narrator's inability, as he says, "at twelve years of age . . . to get along with truth in this world" (2:181/53)? Or is it that Pushkin's verses, however inappositely declaimed, garner maximum acclaim, whereas the narrator's own literary efforts are still worth only half as much? The narrator seems to invite a combination of the second and third explanations: on the one hand, his book-fueled fictionalizing is not an acceptable substitute for conventional academic performance, as represented by young Borgman; on the other, it *might* be an acceptable substitute if it were good enough—if, for example, the fictional Babel's storytelling were equal in quality (or, perhaps, merely in canonicity) to Pushkin's.

One thing is for certain: the narrator has traded in the extraordinary, desperate rote learning—the "crimson blindness"—that served him so well in "The Story of My Dovecote" for a new academic, and narrative, strategy. Having gained a degree of mastery over the "unbridled" fantasy that plagued and delighted him in "First Love," he now wields this fantasy in the service of "good" stories like those formerly told by Shoyl; in short, he has learned to lie for aesthetic effect. While the results may yet be mixed, we can perceive that slowly but surely, this narrator is gaining in skill.

This skill is not enough to overcome the real disparity in material circumstances between Babel and his new friend, the investment banker's son Mark Borgman, although the narrator deploys all the invention at his disposal to bridge the gap, even furnishing his unrelievedly eccentric male relatives with new pasts that, he hopes, will the better equip them to bear comparison with the exotic, sumptuous lifestyle of the Anglicized investment banker's family:

> I told Mark that even though everything in our house was different, Grandfather Levi-Itskhok and my uncle had travelled the world and had thousands of adventures. I described these adventures in order. My sense of the impossible instantly left me. (2:181/52)

These stories represent another of the narrator's attempts to use fiction to improve upon reality—to answer the call of Turgenev's Zinaida in *First Love* for "what's not only better than what does exist, but even more like the truth." Even as he admits (2:182/53) that "the story about my uncle's kindness and strength was a false one" (*lzhivyi rasskaz*—precisely the term used to describe Shoyl's stories in "The Story of My Dovecote"), the narrator goes on to note:

> Conscientiously speaking, if one considered with one's heart, this was the truth [*pravda*] and not a lie [*lozh'*], but on a first glance at the dirty and raucous Simon-Volf, this incomprehensible truth [*istina*] was impossible to perceive. (2:182, my translation)

Whether Babel intends a subtle distinction between *pravda* and the more Church-Slavonic *istina* (perhaps something along the lines of "a truth" versus "The Truth") is unclear, but like Shoyl's "*lzhivye rasskazy*," this "lying story" represents a case in which the narrator's stated project seems to parallel (if not precisely coincide with) Babel's own: an effort to tell stories that surpass reality as much in credibility as in invention.

Unfortunately, the very success of his "lying" strategy means that the narrator eventually has to confront the incompatible facts of his situation: "The following day, little Borgman was coming [to visit]. Nothing of what I had told him existed" (2:181/52). He engineers a fragile semblance of domestic tranquility by banishing his problematic male ancestors from the house for the day, but, inevitably, the home front erupts into a state of exuberant, absurd, and (for the narrator) exasperating bedlam upon these inconsiderate relatives' untimely return. A drunken Uncle Simon-Volf appears with kitschy animal-themed furniture—perhaps a distant echo of the mania for bringing home live animals (and other improbable objects) shown by the possible Gogolian ancestors of Simon-Volf, such as *Dead Souls*'s Nozdrev. In response, Grandfather Levi-Itskhok, eluding his minders, "cre[eps] up to the window and beg[ins] to saw away on his violin, probably so that Simon-

Volf's foul language should not be audible to passersby" (2:185/58)—certainly a travesty of the literary and historical stereotype of the Jewish fiddler (Chekhov's Rothschild; Kuprin's Sashka; real-life superstars Jascha Heifetz and the Odessan David Oistrakh, to name a few) which is also satirized in "Childhood. At Grandmother's" and "Awakening." That Grandfather is located just *outside* the window again hints at his status as an imaginary figment; Uncle Simon-Volf, too, though he eventually enters the house, is first spotted, in all his vulgar glory, "through the window" (*v okne*, 2:184). The story culminates in another travesty of famous literary scenes, as the boy, despairing of his situation, attempts to take "Poor Liza's" way out and drown himself, but fails ignominiously:

> In the corner, as always, stood the water butt. I lowered myself into it. The water cut me in two. I let my head go under, choked, came to the surface again. From above, on a shelf, a cat looked at me sleepily. . . . Again I did not have enough strength, I came to the surface. Beside the barrel stood Grandfather in his bed jacket. His only tooth rang out.
>
> "My grandson." He spoke the words contemptuously and distinctly. "I go to take castor oil, that I should have something to put on your grave." (2:185–86/58–59)

The boy's humiliation is complete.

The narrator's idea of committing suicide may have been inspired by the example of Shakespeare's Brutus, since the high point of his day has been reciting Mark Antony's funeral oration from *Julius Caesar*, in a fit of declamatory berserkism that recalls the "crimson blindness" of the oral exam scene in "The Story of My Dovecote." Initially just reciting his favorite Shakespeare speech for his friend, the narrator once again finds himself fleeing from unbearable anxiety into the realm of poetry. As his own anxiety dissipates (or is drowned out), the dramatic tension supplied by Shakespeare escalates: "I attained a happy state of mind, assumed a pose and began to declaim the lines of poetry I loved more than anything else in life"; "Before my eyes, in the mist of the universe, hung Brutus's face"; "In order to suppress my anxiety, I began to shout in Antony's words"; "I tried to shout down all the evil of the world. . . . I was dead, and I was shouting. A wheezing rose up from the bottom of my existence" (2:183–85/55–56). The beloved speech of Mark Antony's in which the narrator loses himself has probably earned his favor by virtue of its status as the most literary of lies—"literary" because it bears the imprimatur of Shakespeare, and a "lie" for reasons that Babel will soon bring to our attention. Babel highlights the mendacity of the speech by interrupting it, for narratorial commentary, after the first two (in Russian, four) lines:

Friends, Romans, countrymen, lend me your ears;
I come to bury Caesar, not to praise him.
Thus does Antony begin his performance. I choked and pressed my
    hands to my chest.
He was my friend, faithful and just to me. (2:183/55)

Significantly, Babel points out that Mark Antony's famous oration is a "performance," a kind of play-within-a-play; it is a histrionic rather than an authentic utterance—but one that changes, through the power of words alone, the course of events in Rome. By breaking the speech where he does, Babel also catches Antony in a lie: he disclaims any intent to praise Caesar immediately before launching into praise of him. Like Shoyl in "The Story of My Dovecote," Antony provides a possible model for the young narrator, and for Babel himself: he is a teller of lies that end up being worth more than the truth.

Awakening to Verisimilitude

The last of the childhood tales, "Awakening," contains echoes of all four of its predecessors; it also completes the young storyteller's progress toward a working control of his imaginative powers, the exercise of which is posited as a solution to the insupportable constriction that dominated the atmosphere of "Childhood. At Grandmother's." In "Awakening," we see the act of writing reach its full potential as an act of freedom: the circle is completed (the narrator acquires the last skill he needs to become a writer) and broken (the narrator escapes the confinement of his crazy family and learns about the outside world).

The opening of "Awakening" carries strong reminders of "Childhood. At Grandmother's": a similar atmosphere of imprisonment is felt, as the narrator's ambitious and authoritarian father is depicted as a hapless tyrant who forces his unmusical son to learn to play the violin. The young narrator pretends to practice, but instead reads the works of Dumas and (again) Turgenev while going through the motions of practicing. When not chained to his music stand, he is telling or writing stories, consciously following in the footsteps of his brilliant, insane, and graphomaniac grandfather—who, as we have witnessed in "In the Basement," is like the narrator a violinist of dubious gifts.

The use of literature as a means of escape leads to the protagonist's surreptitious abandonment of his musical education, and his adoption of new mentor figures to supplant the violin teacher. The first of these is the English pipe-maker and seaman, Mister Trottyburn (*Trottibern*). Instead of duly making his way to the "*Wunderkind* factory" where Mr. Zagursky turns "Jewish dwarfs in lace collars and patent-leather shoes" into "renowned virtuosi," the narrator "finds himself" at the port, where a different theory of child manufacture holds sway. Trottyburn, who sells smuggled handmade pipes carved by his brother in Lincoln, refers to the pipes as "children"; he insists to the real children following him around, "children must be made by one's own hand" (2:173–74/61–62).

All this talk of "factories" and "handmade children" seems designed to evoke two separate, but complementary, theories of literature, both with Platonic roots (though thoroughly naturalized in Russian literature by the 1920s). The first of these, emanating from Plato's arguments in the *Republic* about the power of poetry to corrupt or reform a human character, finds a parallel in the Soviet theory of the 'industrial" production of the socialist citizen, most vividly captured by Stalin's famous speech in which he called writers "the engineers of the human soul" (an expression possibly of Odessan origin, since Stalin allegedly borrowed it from Olesha!) and argued that "the production of souls is more important than the production of tanks."²⁴ The second, emanating from Plato's *Symposium,* consists in the idea that intellectual (and artistic) "children," produced by those who, through "love of beauty," become "pregnant in soul," represent a greater immortality than mere physical progeny; or in other words, creation is higher than procreation. "Awakening" is, on one level, the story of a struggle between these two opposing theories: the Babel parents, keen to manufacture a "renowned virtuoso" from the unpromising human material of their son, have placed their faith in the power of art to shape human character; their son, meanwhile, is desperate to create the conditions whereby he, too, can become capable of "creating children with his own hands." (Perhaps we can even find here a retrospective interpretation for Babel's mysterious "nervous illness . . . found only in women": at the end of "First Love," the narrator is preparing to undergo the equally mysterious process of becoming "pregnant in soul.")

To "create with one's own hands," one must be capable of practical action, of participating in the physical world, but as we have seen from "Childhood. At Grandmother's" on, our narrator is trapped in the spectatorial relationship to the world associated with the intense scrutiny and claustrophobic, intellectual environment of his Jewish upbringing. The truanting boy seems not to *act on* reality but to *read* it. *Things*—the "forbidden" things associated with his escape to the outdoors—appear to him as *words:* "The pipes of the Lincoln master [Trottyburn] breathed poetry. Into each one of them had been inserted an idea, a drop of eternity" (2:174/62). In this same passage, though, lies the germ of the narrator's longed-for immortality, the means by which he will effect his escape and seize power over the levers of his world. Each of these "children," "breathing poetry," containing "an idea, a drop of eternity," represents to the young Babel a sememe—the "inchoate or future text" contained within any single word, which, according to Michael Riffaterre, holds the key to narrative verisimilitude:

> The nuclear word can at any time generate a story simply by transforming its implicit semes into words and letting them be organized by narrative structures. . . . Any (such) agreement between the narrative model and the sememic model will produce . . . an ironclad verisimilitude.[25]

In other words, realism is produced by *really knowing words:* a narrative that fully realizes the sememic potential of the words from which it is made will attain Zinaida's standard of being "not only better than what does exist but even more like the truth." Seen in this light, "Awakening" can be read as, above all, a war between the young (fictional) Babel and his (fictional) parents to realize opposing stories from competing vocabularies. From the sememes "small," "frail," "Jewish," and "violin," the parents hope to generate their own sequel to the "Jascha Heifetz" text, which to them represents the ultimate model of Jewish success. Their son, rejecting that text (and perhaps sensing in it a subtext of victimhood imprinted by Kuprin and Chekhov), seeks to create for himself an alternative text, to be generated from the sememes "port," "smuggler," "sea," and "sun," and consummated—he vainly hopes—by his finally learning to swim.

The latter skill—part of the larger project of learning to act in the world rather than watch it, to create with hands rather than eyes—is one he will pursue under the tutelage of his second mentor, the athletic storyteller and professional proofreader Yefim Nikitich Smolich. It is this "Nikitich" who undertakes the final step in the child's education as a writer: the introduction of verisimilitude. From his fictional, and fantastical, family, the narrator has learned to generate fantasies about "what doesn't exist," and to articulate these as fiction; through an apprenticeship with Nikitich, the boy will learn how to make his new fictions as viable, or "real," as real life.

To accomplish this, the narrator must learn how the natural world works, information he portrays as being inaccessible from within the indoor world of desks, bookshelves, and music stands that has been prescribed for him, and in which the outdoors functions only as a corridor between worthy indoor destinations. His "escape" from this oppressive domestic sphere is thus directly linked to his achievement of "realistic," or verisimilar, prose, metaphorically represented by the task of learning to swim. Grasping that, as the narrator puts it, "the ability to swim proved to be beyond my reach" (2:174/63), Nikitich correctly diagnoses the problem: "What is it you lack? . . . Your youth is no problem, it will pass with the years . . . What you lack is a feeling for nature" (2:175/64, ellipses in original). Nikitich under-takes to teach the boy the vocabulary—the sememes—he lacks: the names and particulars of the flora, fauna, and other natural phenomena that make up the world of "fresh air" he longs to command.

Before the narrator has time to make much progress, however, the jig is up: Zagursky, the violin teacher, comes to inform on his neglectful pupil, who, anticipating his father's reaction, is forced to flee ignominiously to the lavatory and lock himself in. The scene is reminiscent of the narrator's at-tempted suicide at the end of "In the Basement," with the narrator again seeking refuge from a crazed patriarch in a confined space, but where that scene lightly resembled a farcical travesty of sentimental literature, this one contains echoes (albeit, again, farcical ones) of a familiar and chilling Soviet pattern. Denounced by a favored authority figure, the child is incarcerated in the water closet (which he describes as a "fortress," 2:178/67), under threat of execution by a vengeful father figure, with women (his aunt Bobka and unspecified others) interceding for mercy. At least in this case, they are successful: the father retreats, and the boy waits till dark to creep out of his refuge.

The final paragraph in "Awakening" resembles a color-reversed nega-tive of the opening paragraph in "Childhood. At Grandmother's." The latter story, which begins the childhood cycle, starts with a walk to Grandmother's house:

> On Saturdays, I returned home late, after six lessons. Walking along the street did not seem to me an idle occupation. As I walked, I had remarkably good dreams and everything, everything was native and familiar. I knew the signboards, the stones of the houses, and the windows of the shops. I knew them individually, only for myself [and] was firmly convinced that in them I could see the principal thing, the secret thing, what we grown-ups call the es-sence of things. . . . And from the shops, the people, the air, the theatre play-bills, *I created a city of my own.* (1:37/21; my emphasis)

"Awakening," which closes the childhood cycle, ends with a walk to the same destination:

> When everyone had gone to bed, Aunt Bobka took me to Grandmother's. We had a long way to go. The moonlight froze on unknown bushes, on trees that had no name. An invisible bird gave a peep and was silent—perhaps it had fallen asleep. What kind of bird was it? What was its name? Is there dew in the evening? Where is the constellation of the Great Bear situated? In what direction does the sun rise?
>
> We walked along Pochtovaya Street. Bobka held me tightly by the hand, so that I should not run away. She was right. I was thinking of escape. (2:178/67)

Where the overture to "Childhood" displays a narrator conversant with the elements of his world, the coda to "Awakening" shows us the same narrator, on the same stretch of road, in a state of radical disorientation. The sememes from which he generates his city-text in "Childhood"—and it is significant that Babel, the father of literary Odessa, describes himself as "creat[ing] a city"—are man-made things, like Trottyburn's pipes; he is utterly blind to the "natural" text that lurks behind this synthetic world, which is made up of words absent from his vocabulary. His familiarity with the man-made world—the "Jewish" world of culture, books, violins, and domestic interiors—is borne out by his ability to *tell* it, which is what the childhood tales have done. To escape from this fictional plane to the broader "Russian" canvas of the natural world—the canvas that will launch Babel, like Gogol before him, into the Russian canon—he must master the new vocabulary to which Nikitich has alerted him. Only by so doing can he make his stories about this newly discovered world "good" enough to supplant the story he already knows by heart: the oppressive text of his childhood.

BABEL'S BILDUNGSROMAN

Viewed as a complete cycle, the childhood tales have a pleasing symmetry, visible in the respective opening and closing sections of "Childhood. At Grandmother's" and "Awakening," above. They also appear, as I have taken pains to demonstrate, to follow a single unifying story arc: the formation of Babel as a writer, and specifically as the kind of writer whom critics would later perceive as palpably Odessan. Taking the stories in the order I have suggested, we see the narrator, first, absorbing intertexts and arguments about what makes a story "good"; second, absorbing different kinds of counterfactual discourse and learning that a lie can supersede the truth; third, indulging his fantasy; fourth, marrying his fantasy to canonical texts; and finally, joining the world of fantasy and books to the natural realm. In the process, we also see the nascence of certain attributes I have assigned to Odessan discourse: the refutation of the Chekhov-Kuprin "frail Jew" text, the reconciliation of the seemingly irreconcilable (for example, the narrator's contraction, in "First Love," of a disease supposedly found "only in women"), the use of autobiographical discourse, and the interpenetration of "life" and "literature."

The reception of the stories as a cycle is, then, satisfying on a number of levels, including both content and form. It is, however, not without problems. Most obviously, "Childhood. At Grandmother's" was never published; we cannot say for certain what Babel's intentions were for the story. The symmetries between that story and "Awakening" may reflect not an architectural design but a comprehensive rewriting in which material was pillaged from the earlier story and retooled for the later, better one. Moreover, while the protagonist's age is not indicated in "Childhood," the setting of that story is more akin to the Odessa of "In the Basement" and "Awakening" than to the Nikolaev of the earlier childhood tales. Finally, it is difficult to justify the exclusion of later stories in the "bildungsroman" series, particularly "Di Grasso," in which the narrator's age is the same as in "Awakening," fourteen.

And yet the stories are what they are, and our lack of information about Babel's final intentions for them must allow us some leeway in reading them as the stories themselves seem to dictate. As I have conceived of them, the childhood tales have an integrity of theme and language that makes good readerly sense; "Di Grasso," while similar in setting and spirit, is, as Gregory Freidin has observed,

> rather different from Babel's other childhood reminiscences. . . . First of all, it is much shorter both in the amount of time that it covers and in its actual length. Secondly, its thematic content, packed into a compact frame, possesses an unusual depth, since the main narrative incorporates within itself another narrative, a play performed by a travelling troupe of Di Grasso [the lead actor's name].[26]

Perhaps most important, "Di Grasso" presents the narrator not as a writer in the making—the unifying trope of what I have termed the "childhood tales"—but as a spectator, indeed, as a critic; the insights into art that he offers here from a spectator's perspective seem of a different order from the narrator's more diffuse epiphanies (and sly arguments) about the nature of literary language in the childhood cycle.

The title of "Di Grasso," with its evocation of carnival (the eponymous character's name is derived from the Italian for Shrove Tuesday, *martedi grasso*) does, however, capture the most celebrated—and most Odessan—feature of Babel's style, the "reconciliation of opposites" noted by Shklovsky, Markish, Erlich, and others.[27] This invites us to consider other ways in which the poetics of the childhood cycle extend to Babel's oeuvre more generally. It is impossible not to notice the predominance of autobiographical discourse in Babel's stories—it is used even in the *Odessa Tales,* though more subtly there than in the "lying" autobiographical stories of the childhood cycle, or the thinly veiled "pseudoautobiography" of *Red Cavalry*—and the accompanying interpenetration of literature and life. And, noting this, we cannot help but remark further that the first-person narrators in each of the sequences listed above (the *Odessa Tales,* the childhood tales, and *Red Cavalry*) are remarkably similar; while they do not all share a name, they are all observers, intellectuals, and "outsiders," uncomfortably aware of their own incongruity both among the groups they seek to join (always, physically powerful and decisive groups: the gangsters, the Russian urchins, the Cossacks) and among a posited "own kind" (the family of the childhood tales, the Jews of *Red Cavalry*).

As Barry Scherr points out, the Odessa of the childhood tales and the Odessa of the *Odessa Tales* are geographically distinct entities; the childhood tales, described above, are set in the more bourgeois areas of the city, whereas the *Odessa Tales* immortalize the "less savory side streets" of the Moldavanka district, the lair of the Jewish gangsters who became, through these same stories, irrevocably linked with Odessa.[28] Yet the two sets of stories have more in common than Scherr goes on to propose. The cumulative effect of the two cycles is to delineate two contiguous, yet mutually exclusive, fields of Jewish experience, both distinctively Odessan, both radically different from the Yiddish world of the shtetl and (despite the inclusion of the 1905 pogrom) from the dreary alternatives of half-digested assimilation and political victimization portrayed by Chekhov, Kuprin, and others. Located at opposite ends of the same tramline, these two worlds are united by the Black Sea; by at least one emblematic character (the mysterious Mister Trottyburn, who appears in the Odessa tale "Liubka the Cossack" as well as in "Awakening"); by the carnivalesque reconciliation of opposites; by a preponderance of "abundant" female characters;[29] by a certain flair, on the part of the characters who populate them, for aphoristic pronouncements; and—crucially—by the narrator's uneasy distance from the milieu he is describing (a quality Scherr ascribes to *Red Cavalry* and the *Odessa Tales* but not to the childhood tales). Moreover, the "two Odessas" actually meet in "Awakening," when the narrator attempts to flee the bourgeois milieu of the earlier childhood tales for precisely the muscular and lawless environment presided over by Benya Krik in the *Odessa Tales*.

The *Odessa Tales*, like the childhood tales, constitute a somewhat disputed, and disputable, entity: from the strict constructionist's point of view, they consist of the four stories republished by Babel in 1927 as a single volume, under the title *Odessa Tales*: "The King" ("Korol'," 1921), "How It Was Done in Odessa" ("Kak eto delalos' v Odesse," 1923), "The Father" ("Otets," 1924), and "Liubka the Cossack" ("Liubka Kazak," 1924). Other stories, drawing on the same cast of characters and set in the same milieu, are often considered alongside the core four: most notably, "Justice in Brackets" ("Spravedlivost' v skobkakh," 1921) and "The End of the Almshouse" ("Konets bogadel'ni," 1932), which also bear the subtitle "From the Odessa Tales," but were not published in that original volume.[30] For the purposes of the current discussion, namely the underlying consistency of Babel's narrative voice and his vision of Odessa between the childhood and Odessa tales, my analysis will focus on just one of these stories: "How It Was Done in Odessa." However, my conclusions are intended to bear on Babel's other stories of the Moldavanka as well.

In "How It Was Done in Odessa," the gap between the narrator and the milieu he is describing is underlined by the narrator's decision, early in the story, to hand over the narration to a third party, the old man Arye-Leib (the name, with typically Babelian irony, means "lion-lion"; the old man uses "lion" as an epithet for the young, sexually and generally potent Benya in his story). Arye-Leib's portrayal of Benya Krik coincides with what we learn from the other Benya stories, but we get the bonus of Arye's outside perspective on the main narrator (Babel's narratorial persona). It is from this story that Babel criticism inherits the famous description so often applied to Babel himself: "you have glasses on your nose, and autumn in your soul."[31] Time and again, Arye-Leib stresses the discrepancy between the narrator, who "brawl[s] at his desk and stutter[s] in the presence of others," and Benya Krik, who does his "brawling on the squares and [his] stuttering on paper" (1:127/244).

These asides frame an internal narrative in which Benya the drayman's son becomes the larger-than-life Benya Krik. Finding that his strength and drive exceed the possibilities of his lowly position, Benya establishes himself in the Moldavanka underworld by performing, with flair, a task (mounting an extortion raid against an oft-robbed Jewish businessman, Tartakovsky) set him by its ruling cartel. There are many parallels between Benya Krik's coming-of-age story and Babel's "autobiographical" one: both struggles pit the son against the father ("Babel's" father actually threatens to kills him in "Awakening," while Benya's father "compels [him] to die twenty times a day"). Both are propelled by the son's urge to become an integral part of the seedy, but fabulously profitable, life of the port (Benya asks to be apprenticed to Froim Grach; the young Babel marvels at the 100 percent profit turned by his eleven-year-old friend on each one of Mister Trotty-burn's pipes). Prowess, physical and sexual, is an important component of each son's self-realization: young Babel fantasizes about the Russian Galina and ditches violin lessons for swimming ones; Benya, "the lion," "can spend the night with a Russian woman and satisfy her." It will be noted that while these rites of passage are expressed in similar terms, Babel (both in the childhood tales and in the *Odessa Tales*) remains a spectator, while Benya is the man of action; the same dichotomy obtains, famously, in *Red Cavalry*.

The consistency of Babel's first-person narrative voice across his oeuvre has led Freidin to hypothesize, intriguingly, that Babel

> had in mind a larger autobiographical frame designed to incorporate his known and future work and enclosing the entire life span of the boy who grew up to be the author-narrator of *Red Cavalry* and, finally, a major Soviet writer. The great success enjoyed by the autobiographical fiction of Maksim Gorky—Babel's acknowledged protector and mentor—its elevation to the status of a national epic in the 1930s, lends support to this conjecture.[32]

This overarching autobiographical frame is Freidin's best guess as to the meaning of Babel's famous last words upon being arrested: "They didn't let me finish" (*Ne dali mne konchit'*). No evidence having emerged either to support or to confirm the widespread speculation about Babel's being engaged in work on a novel at the time of his arrest, and the novelistic form being otherwise unrepresented among Babel's works, Freidin's conjecture seems a highly plausible one. Precisely how the *Odessa Tales* would have been fitted into this autobiographical scheme is unclear, but their consistency with the narrative voice of Babel's more obviously "autobiographical" works,[33] as well as their value as a counterpoint to Babel's other "Odessa tales"—that is, the childhood tales—suggests that they could have contributed a great deal to this hypothetical project.

THE BABEL TEXT

One further point of convergence between the "Odessa" and "childhood" tales on which I have not yet commented is the double-edged Anglophilia that marks the yearnings of Babel's narrative persona(e) toward the two poles of Odessan-Jewish success: that is, the black-market magic represented by Mister Trottyburn ("Liubka the Cossack"; "Awakening") and the bourgeois bliss represented by Mark Borgman's father ("In the Basement"), the prosperous bank director who "expresse[s] himself in the coarsish, abrupt language of Liverpool captains" (2:180/51), plans to educate his son in England, and celebrates his arrival home from work by settling down with the *Manchester Guardian*. These characters make up part of the glamorous, outlandish fabric of the stories—what Scherr calls their "exotic foreign quality, usually accompanied by the motif of the sea"[34]—to which the Italian thespians of "Di Grasso" and "In the Basement" also contribute. They also represent an important component of the Odessa text more broadly speaking: that is, the influence of the West, which Shklovsky characterized, approvingly, as a source of "new themes" in the work of Odessa writers. (This portion of his "South-West" hypothesis Shklovsky was forced to recant, calling it "politically and methodologically wrong, and therefore harmful," since it contravened the official stipulation that Soviet literature be based on the homegrown literary heritage.)[35]

For Babel, the most desirable Western influence—the one to which he would most insistently allude and return, notwithstanding the Anglophilia on display in the childhood stories—was not English but French: the nineteenth-century French master of the short story, Guy de Maupassant, who appears in Babel's works first in the 1916 sketch "Odessa," and later as the title and subject of Babel's 1932 story "Guy de Maupassant." The latter story, the last one I will touch upon here, is of interest for the same reasons as the other stories I have treated in this and the previous chapter; it has transgressed the boundary between "fiction" and "fact" to become firmly ensconced in the generally accepted Babel lore, and now enjoys more widespread dissemination and educated belief than most of what is "factually" known about Babel. A number of important aspects of this story have been commented upon by earlier scholars. For example, as Freidin notes, "Guy de Maupassant," which ends with a lurid (and largely fictional) account of Maupassant slitting his own throat, participates in the "decapitation" theme that is also on view in "First Love" (with its lurid description of the boy's "swollen neck" and "lacerated breath"). This "decapitation" thread, with its obvious Freudian links to castration and patricide, runs through all three of the major story cycles (childhood, *Odessa*, and *Red Cavalry*).[36]

A second important aspect of "Guy de Maupassant" that links it to the "childhood" stories is its incorrigible mendacity. His autobiographical narrator borrows from the fabricated life story Babel gives in "Autobiography," beginning "In the winter of 1916 I found myself in St. Petersburg with a forged passport and without a copeck" (2:217/71). This lie is at least consistent (as is Babel's persona, across all the "autobiographical" texts), but as Charles Rougle points out:

> First, as a student at the Neurological Institute, Babel had a residence permit and had no need to hide from the police. Second, he was not destitute; he received an adequate allowance from his father. . . . The rootless bohemian in the "official" autobiography fits suspiciously well the stance of the alienated outsider who is a hallmark of Babel's mature narratives and exemplifies the theatrical mysteriousness in which he was fond of enveloping certain aspects of his life.[37]

From this promising beginning, Babel goes on to concoct a story that literally acts out a series of connections between himself and Maupassant: engaged to help a barrister's wife translate the complete works of Maupassant, the narrator is nearly seduced by prose and wine into reenacting the central affair from Maupassant's "Confession" ("L'Aveu") with her. After this awkward encounter, he goes home and reads a book *about* Maupassant, Édouard de Maynial's *La Vie et l'oeuvre de Guy de Maupassant*. And here, as in his deliberate miscitation of *First Love* in "Childhood. At Grandmother's," Babel lies in plain view, mendaciously citing Maynial's biography for a scene of his own invention in which Maupassant is found "crawl[ing] about on all fours and [eating] his own excrement" (2:223/80). As Elif Batuman explains, this scene is not only not in Maynial, but appears in no known biography of Maupassant:

The image appears to be borrowed from either [Zola's] *Nana* (Count Muffat crawls at Nana's feet, thinking of saints who "eat their own excrement"), or [Flaubert's] *Madame Bovary* (a reference to Voltaire on his deathbed, "devouring his own excrement"). In "Guy de Maupassant," Babel mentions neither Voltaire nor Zola nor Flaubert—except to claim that Maupassant's mother is Flaubert's cousin: *a false rumor explicitly controverted by Maynial.*[38]

Babel's lies here have the purpose not only of establishing a connection between himself and Maupassant (and perhaps, obliquely, to Flaubert, the French writer whom most critics, for good or ill, believe Babel more nearly resembles), but also of getting the upper hand in the relationship. Not only does he rewrite Maupassant's life (and, most would argue, considerably for the worse), but he also rewrites his prose: in "Guy de Maupassant," we see Babel at work as a proofreader and copy editor, inheriting the mantle of his old mentor Nikitich and enforcing his own ideas about style on Maupassant.

The narrator's programmatic statements about literary style in "Guy de Maupassant" have been read and reproduced ad infinitum as a bona fide articulation of Babel's poetics—much as Arye-Leib's phrase "spectacles on your nose and autumn in your soul" has become the defining interpretation of Babel's authorial personality. The key passage, in which the narrator "repairs" a Russian translation of Maupassant done by a lady of leisure, is worth reproducing in full, because of its influence on the cumulative narrative of Babel:

> I took the manuscript home with me, and there, in Kazantsev's attic—among the sleepers—cut clearings in someone else's translation. This is not such unpleasant work as it might seem. A phrase is born into the world good and bad at the same time. The secret lies in a barely perceptible turn. The lever must lie in one's hand and get warm. It must be turned once, and no more.
>
> In the morning I took back the corrected manuscript. Raisa had not been lying when she had spoken of her passion for Maupassant. She sat immobile during the reading, her hands clasped: those satin hands flowed to the floor, her forehead was pale, the lace between her downwards-crushed breasts moved aside and trembled.
>
> "How did you do it?"
>
> Then I began to speak of style, of the army of words, an army in which all kinds of weapons are on the move. No iron can enter the human heart as chillingly as a full stop placed at the right time. (2:217/74)

In a textbook example of the interpenetration of "fiction" and "reality" that I have characterized as central to the Odessan literary identity, and which emanates above all from Babel, Paustovsky narrates a breathtakingly similar episode—set in Odessa, during his sojourn there—in *The Golden Rose*. In this case, the story in need of repair is not a translation, but an original work submitted to *The Seaman*, an Odessa newspaper of which Paustovsky was managing editor. Written by one Andrei Sobol, the story was, Paustovsky reports, "disorderly and all mixed up, but undoubtedly a work of talent and dealing with an interesting subject." An editor, Blagov, offers to make the story fit for publication without changing a word, and does so—by correcting all the punctuation and paragraphing. Sobol's gratitude is comparable to that of a freshly redeemed Dostoevskian hero:

> Sobol dashed up to Blagov, seized both his hands and shook them heartily. A minute later he was hugging Blagov and kissing him three times in the Moscow fashion.
>
> "Thanks," he said, very much agitated. "Thanks for the lesson you have taught me—a little too late in the day, I'm afraid. I feel like a criminal when I think how I used to mutilate my writings."[39]

The reminiscence ends with Paustovsky, Blagov, a local militiaman, and Eduard Bagritsky drinking together

> to the glory of literature in general and punctuation marks in particular. *We all agreed that a full stop in the right place may work wonders.*[40]

This near-verbatim echo of Babel's oft-quoted maxim is just one of the many ways in which Paustovsky conjures Babel as the presiding spirit over his (Paustovsky's) conversion to Odessanism, and Maupassant as the presiding spirit over Babel's art.[41]

Babel first materializes on Paustovsky's horizon in 1921, in the form of a story, "The King"; shortly thereafter, already a celebrity (at least according to Paustovsky), he appears at *The Seaman*'s offices in the flesh. Paustovsky tends to the mythology of Babel—Odessa's "literary messiah"—as zealously as Saint Paul to that of Jesus, fluently couching his first impressions of Babel (as a reader of "The King") in the terms deployed by Babel himself in the 1916 "Odessa" manifesto:

> Everything in "The King" was *completely unaccustomed* for us. . . . Suddenly, *like an unexpected burst of sunshine* through the window, some exquisite fragment or melody of a sentence, *like a translation from the French*, would invade the text.[42]

The echoes of Babel's own writing grow still stronger when the man himself enters the text. Paustovsky, writing in the late 1950s about conversations that took place in the early 1920s, wields dialogue like a latter-day Thucydides—which, incidentally, is one of the techniques (under the heading of "mimetic excesses") listed by Riffaterre as a "sign pointing to the fictionality of fiction"[43]—so that the reader involuntarily wonders whether Babel knew he was being recorded. Babel's first line of direct speech is drawn, again, straight from the pages of "Odessa"—and returns us, again, to the contemplation of Maupassant:

> "Here in Odessa," [Babel] said with a mocking twinkle, "we will not have our Kiplings. We are peaceful lovers of life. But we *shall* have our Maupassants. Because we have plenty of sea, sun, beautiful women, and plenty of food for thought. I guarantee you some Maupassants."[44]

Looking again at the parallel scenes from "Guy de Maupassant" and Paustovsky's memoir, one might be struck by the addition of Eduard Bagritsky to the drinking party following Blagov's successful conversion of Sobol's story to Babelian standards of punctuation. In addition to providing local Odessan literary color, Bagritsky's presence in this scene could be interpreted as a wink to the reader, since such wholesale appropriation of Babel's ideas and phraseology is mockingly ascribed to Bagritsky in A *Time of Great Expectations*. In one episode, Babel (according to Paustovsky) compares the poetry of Alexander Blok to "the ringing of a thousand harps"; Bagritsky, in a subsequent conversation, muses, "You understand, just the melody on unison harps with the muted voice of the poet. That was the voice Blok had," and is abruptly cut off by Isaac Livshits:

> "Edya!" said Izya Livshits, "don't parrot and distort Babel. What I'm hearing is an outlandish jumble of things he has said."
> "This is what I think myself," said Bagritsky modestly.
> "Oh yes?" Izya feigned surprise. "Since when have you been so eloquent?"[45]

Bagritsky becomes something of a symbol for the confusion of factual and fictional discourses in Paustovsky's narrative; in The *Golden Rose,* Paustovsky writes of him:

> We might as well warn Eduard Bagritsky's biographers that they will have a hard time establishing the facts of his life. The reason for this is that the poet was in the habit of spreading the most fantastic stories about himself. These became so inseparably linked up with his life that it is now impossible to distinguish fact from fiction. . . . The stories he told about himself became woven into the texture of his life.[46]

Paustovsky here might as well be talking about Babel—or even about himself; for that matter, Paustovsky himself is at least partly responsible for "spreading fantastic stories about" Bagritsky, as well as about other Odessa writers. His stories about Babel, though, bear the particular distinction of being themselves Babelian, both in subject matter (Paustovsky recounts amusing tales of Moldavanka organized—or rather, *dis*organized—crime, and of Babel's family) and in the ambiguous territory between "fact" and "fiction" that they occupy. In one, Babel puts an end to a protracted visit from his in-laws by insisting that they return in haste to Kiev to see a "world-famous" otolaryngologist by the name of Greenblatt—the only one who can be entrusted with the mysterious ear ailment of Babel's nephew. The humor of the story resides in the fact that, as Paustovsky subsequently realizes, "that whole business with the eminent Kiev specialist had been pure improvisation. Babel had played it like a first-class actor."

But the ending of the story, much like the Grandmother's stories in "Childhood. At Grandmother's," introduces a competing reality:

> After a week a letter came from Babel's mother-in-law.
> "What do you think?" she wrote indignantly. "What did Professor Greenblatt establish? Professor Greenblatt established that that rascal stuck a piece of indelible pencil into his ear, nothing more. Nothing more, not a single speck. How do you like that?"[47]

So, while Babel on the one hand "improvised" the entire story of the eminent specialist, it turns out on the other hand to be true (there *is* an eminent Professor Greenblatt practicing otolaryngology in Kiev)—just like Shoyl's stories. Elsewhere, Paustovsky quotes Babel as lamenting,

> I have no imagination. . . . I don't know how to make things up. I have to know everything down to the last wrinkle, or else I can't write anything. On my shield is inscribed the motto "Authenticity!"[48]

Yet every story simultaneously suggests that Babel might just be "improvising."

In summary, Paustovsky supports his claim to be an "Odessa writer" by saturating his prose with implicit and explicit references to Babel; promoting Babel's own mythology both of himself and of Odessa; presenting Babel paradoxically as a storyteller who drew all his tales from life, yet might also have "made the whole thing up";[49] drawing parallels among the autobiographical practices of Babel, Bagritsky, and himself; and using Babel's own language to associate all the above features with Odessa itself. I contend that these practices exactly coincide with what Babel himself intended. Indeed, what has been demonstrated repeatedly over the course of the last two chapters is that Babel, in his works, continually seeks to *invade* and if possible even to *supersede* "real life" ("what does exist," in the words of Turgenev's Zinaida) with stories.

The success of this gambit seems in keeping with the privileged position Babel consistently awards to fiction over all other forms of artistic creation (one need only think, for example, of the treatment meted out to music in "Childhood" and "Awakening"). Only in prose—the stuff of our everyday communication, a humble yet infinitely malleable clay, as Babel has shown—can an artist construct and mediate a reality capable of competing with "real-life," extratextual reality (which is itself, after all, subject to representation by precisely the same sorts of text) in viability and depth. Babel's works, with their emphasis on the pursuit of "liberation" and autonomy, seem to equate "real life" with a sort of determinism; the seductive aspect of fiction is precisely its total submission to the will of the author.

It is possible to see in this project a kind of parody of the Neoplatonic assumptions about the relationship between art and life underlying Socialist Realism, to which Babel seems to allude repeatedly in his stories; it is also possible to see, as some critics have done, an attempt "to present an appropriate past for a young Soviet writer who was not a member of the Communist Party."[50] It is unlikely that such conjectures can ever be resolved fully one way or the other, nor does the "real" answer much matter; "reality" consists, now, in the narrative Babel has bequeathed to us. As it happens, Babel's "lying stories" about himself, his fictive autobiography, have proven far more authoritative than any authentic biography is ever likely to be—and have insinuated themselves into our contemporary perception not only of Babel himself, but of his fellow Odessan writers, and even of his native city. Thus, through narrative roguery, Babel has contrived to make reality conform to his stories, rather than the other way around; and his version has been, for more than three-quarters of a century, the definitive one.

Reinventing the Self: Valentin Kataev and Yury Olesha

ALTHOUGH IT WAS Isaac Babel who, in his essay "Odessa" and the fictional works that followed it, defined the idea of an Odessa writer, his trajectory was actually not a typical one for writers of the Odessa or "South-West" school. Other Odessa writers of Babel's generation regularly foregathered in the poets' club "The Green Lamp" (*Zelenaia lampa,* modeled on the eponymous group to which Pushkin had belonged), where they read and criticized one another's works, held public readings and discussions, and sometimes hosted visiting scholars or literary luminaries such as Alexei Tolstoy. Members of the "Green Lamp" society included Eduard Bagritsky, Ilya Ilf, and Semyon Kirsanov, as well as the two writers on whom this chapter focuses, Valentin Kataev and Yury Olesha.

The younger of the two, Yury Karlovich Olesha was born in 1899, making him two years younger than Kataev and five years younger than Babel. His family, middle-class Polish Catholic aristocrats, moved to Odessa from Elizavetgrad in 1902, when Yury was three years old. Here his father, a former landowner (who, according to "a dark family legend . . . had lost all his money at cards"),[1] worked as a government inspector in a vodka distillery and indulged "his favorite pastimes of cards and alcohol."[2] Yury began his education at home, studying Russian and arithmetic with his grandmother— a point in common with Babel—and subsequently enrolled in Odessa's Rishelievsky Gymnasium and Novorossiisky University (from which Babel, as a Jew, was excluded). During his student years, he began writing poetry, most of which is now lost, and joined the "Green Lamp" society, where he met and formed a fast friendship with Valentin Kataev.

Valentin Petrovich Kataev, born in 1897, enjoyed a more purely "Russian" childhood than any of the other Odessa writers, with the exception of his own brother Evgeny (born in 1903), who would later adopt a shortened version of his patronymic as his nom de plume and team up with the also-pseudonymed Ilya Fainzilberg to become the satirical literary double act Ilf and Petrov. The Kataev brothers, both born in Odessa, received from their parents (a Russian schoolteacher and a Ukrainian woman from a military family) what would come to be seen as a politically correct literary education at home, reading the works of canonical authors such as Lermontov and Tolstoy.[3] Young Valentin began writing poetry while still a child—his first published works were patriotic verses, printed in Odessa and St. Petersburg newspapers—and acquired an influential literary mentor in the person of Ivan Bunin in 1914.[4]

After Russia's entry into World War I, Kataev volunteered for the army, serving as an artillery officer from 1915 to 1917, when he was returned to Odessa for medical treatment. The Bolshevik Revolution found Kataev in the Odessa Military Hospital, and thus temporarily constrained from actively taking sides (an experience he would later use in chronicling the adventures—and ideological ambivalence—of his hero Petya Bachey in the *Waves of the Black Sea* tetralogy).[5] Thereupon followed what his biographer Robert Russell has called "three of the most complicated years of Kataev's life—the years of the Civil War." Having founded the "Green Lamp" in 1917, Kataev alternated his literary activities with service in the Volunteer White Army in Odessa; in 1919 he was imprisoned by the Cheka for eight months for counterrevolutionary activities.

Only thereafter does Kataev's biography rejoin the collective path of the Odessa writers: like Olesha (who had to break with his monarchist parents to do it), he joined the Red Army in 1919. (Babel had joined up in 1917.) During the Civil War, Babel, Olesha, and Kataev all served as propagandists for one or another branch of ROSTA, the Russian Telegraph Agency of the period, whose "purpose was to travel around the Soviet Union to communicate Soviet ideology, educate people, and promote the Soviet way of life";[6] it was in the context of their work for this organization that Babel accompanied the Red Cavalry and Olesha published his first story ("Angel," 1922). By 1923 all three writers were in Moscow (Kataev and Olesha having moved there in 1922, Babel in late 1923), working alongside fellow Odessans Ilya Ilf and Lev Slavin on the staff of *The Siren* and beginning to establish what would become their collective myth.

The NEP years (1921–28) were ones of peak productivity for all the Odessa writers, and Kataev and Olesha were no exceptions. Kataev published numerous stories and sketches in *The Whistle* as well as two adventure novels, *Erendorf Island* (*Ostrov Erendorf,* 1924) and *The Master of Iron* (*Povelitel' zheleza,* 1925), before producing his satirical novel, *The Embezzlers* (*Rastratchiki,* 1927), "one of the most popular Soviet works of the period."[7] He then turned to writing for the stage, delighting audiences with his comedy about the housing shortage in Moscow, *Squaring the Circle* (*Kvadratura kruga*), in 1928. Olesha's satirical poetry in *The Whistle,* published under the pseudonym "The Chisel" (*Zubilo*), earned great popularity among the paper's readership, and two collections of his verses were published in 1924 and 1927, respectively. His prose masterpiece, *Envy* (*Zavist'*), was published in 1927, to instant acclaim (though critics would later discover political flaws in it); his children's book *Three Fat Men* (*Tri tolstiaka: Roman dlia detei*) followed in 1928.

But with the advent of the First Five-Year Plan in 1928, followed by the formulation of Socialist Realism in 1932 and its official adoption as artistic policy by the First All-Union Congress of Soviet Writers in 1934, the age of Odessan modernism appeared to draw to a close. After 1932, "Olesha's activity as a literary artist diminished in both quantity and quality—indeed, it virtually ceased to exist."[8] Babel, too, by the early 1930s had virtually ceased to produce major fiction, leading him to pronounce himself a "great master of the genre" of silence.[9] His famous Odessan gangster-hero, Benya Krik, had by then been exposed as a counterrevolutionary and shot by a Red Army soldier in Babel's film scenario for *Benya Krik* (1926).[10] Following in his hero's footsteps—another, profoundly macabre "story that came true"—Babel himself would be arrested and executed in 1939. Bagritsky was silenced by death in 1934. Ilf and Petrov published their final work together in 1936, having disappointed, bedraggled, and finally assimilated to Soviet bureaucracy (as an *upravdom*, or apartment-building administrator) their picaresque Odessan hero, Ostap Bender, in 1931.[11] Ilf died of tuberculosis in 1937; Petrov was killed in a plane crash in 1942 while serving as a war correspondent. Heralded by the title (surely not accidental) of Babel's 1926 play *Sunset*, the "bright, clear depiction of the sun" promised by Odessan modernism seemed to have vanished beyond the horizon.

Of the major writers associated with the Odessa school, only Kataev continued to thrive, repeatedly adjusting his style and content to suit the latest Party directives about literature with remarkably consistent success. His novel *Time Forward!* (*Vremia, vpered!*, 1932) became an instant classic of Five-Year Plan literature. *I, Son of the Working People* (*Ia, syn trudovogo naroda*, 1937), which chronicled the return of a Ukrainian soldier from World War I and his subsequent heroic efforts to save his village and sweetheart from invading Germans, was made into a popular play, an action film, and Prokofiev's first Soviet opera. (Kataev's timing was, as always, better than Prokofiev's: before the opera could be staged, the Molotov-Ribbentrop Pact was signed, making anti-German propaganda suddenly no longer in official vogue.)[12] A World War II novel, *Son of the Regiment* (*Syn polka*, 1945), garnered Kataev the Stalin Prize; he had already been awarded a Lenin Prize in 1939 for his services to Soviet literature. By the time he completed his *Waves of the Black Sea* tetralogy (*Volny chernogo moria*, 1936–61), tracing "the participation of two Odessa children in the major historical events of the Soviet era,"[13] Kataev had managed both to outlive Stalinism and to accrue enough credibility as a Socialist Realist classic that he was able to begin gently reintroducing the themes of Odessan modernism—paradox, roguery, nostalgia, sunlight, and self-invention—into Soviet literature.

THE RETURN OF THE SELF

As we have seen, Odessa's most famous literary son, Isaac Babel, seemed to gravitate almost exclusively toward a first-person narrative voice that was widely understood to be autobiographical, even when the content or form of his works did not fully authorize their reception as autobiography. A similar attraction to the autobiographical mode, with similar implications for the reception of the texts in question, can be seen in the works of the other Odessan prosaists, especially Yury Olesha and Valentin Kataev. Olesha, in his speech to the first All-Union Congress of Soviet Writers—itself a highly autobiographical exercise—endorsed the conclusions reached by unnamed "people" that the protagonist of *Envy* (*Zavist'*, 1927), Nikolai Kavalerov, was in many ways "an autobiographical portrait."[14] In Olesha criticism, Elizabeth Beaujour has shown how close Kavalerov's narrative voice is in some respects to that of Olesha's autobiographical narrator in *No Day Without a Line* (*Ni dnia bez strochki*, 1965).[15] And when Kataev, in the 1960s, developed his doctrine of "Mauvism" (*movizm*), which centered on the subjectivity of the narrating author, his "Mauvist" works were repeatedly interpreted as memoirs despite explicit disclaimers such as the following:

> In general I do not vouch for the details in this work. I implore readers not to perceive my work as memoirs. I can't stand memoirs. I repeat. This is a free flight of my fantasy, based on real events, which might not even be quite accurately preserved in my memory.[16]

The work from which this disclaimer is drawn, *My Diamond Crown* (*Almaznyi moi venets*, 1977), explicitly disavows membership in any of the usual Russian genres: "Not a novel, not a story, not a novella, not a *poema*, not reminiscences, not memoirs, not a lyrical diary . . . But what then? I don't know!" (67). The only genre to which Kataev, following Tiutchev,[17] can reliably assign his narrative is that of the lie. However, in true Odessan fashion, he immediately pushes the definition of "lying" into the realm of paradox, using words that remind us of Zinaida's pronouncement about poetry in Turgenev's *First Love:*

Yes, this is a lie. But the lie is *even more like the truth* than truth itself. A truth born in the mysterious coils of the mechanism of my imagination. . . . In any case, I swear that everything written here is the purest truth and at the same time the purest fantasy.[18]

In an additional effort to unsign the autobiographical pact, Kataev declines to refer to any of the contemporaries (including all the major Odessan writers) who people his narrative by their real names, instead substituting lowercase epithets, a move that could be variously interpreted as whimsical, protective, or dismissive. Among the Odessans, Olesha is referred to as *kliuchik* (little key),[19] Bagritsky as *ptitselov* (birdhunter), Ilf and Petrov as *drug* (friend) and *brat* (brother), and Babel as *konarmeets* ([Red] cavalryman). Paustovsky does not appear.

My Diamond Crown was written and published long after the deaths of all the other Odessa writers whose careers, in the 1920s, had seemed so promising. Yet, like all Kataev's major works of Mauvist quasi-autobiography, it reaches back to a time when they were not only still alive, but thriving: a time before that troublesome watershed year, 1934, when Babel and Olesha gave the speeches at the first Congress of Soviet Writers that, in retrospect, seemed to mark the end, not the pinnacle, of their renown. Thus, in the years following the Thaw, the writer of *Time, Forward!* makes it his project to turn time backward again.

VALENTIN KATAEV AND THE PROBLEM OF LONGEVITY

As we have seen, by 1934, all the Odessan writers except Kataev had published the works for which they are remembered; alone among them, Kataev adopted the artistic principles of Socialist Realism as his own, and continued his literary career with a minimum of inconvenience. Paradoxically, Kataev's success as a writer has almost automatically disqualified him, until relatively recently, from serious critical study. It also makes him a total anomaly among the Odessans, with only Lev Slavin and Paustovsky—the latter of whose Odessan credentials Kataev, in a conversation reported by Arkady Lvov, roundly dismisses[20]—surviving long enough to compete with Kataev in memorializing the Odessan moment in Russian literature.

Kataev's long life in Russian letters raises the specter of an ancient dilemma, immortalized by Homer: the "choice of Achilles" between a long life and great renown. The dilemma is sharpened by Kataev's position as a Russian, and a Soviet, writer. Thanks only in part to the early canonization of Pushkin as Russia's greatest poetic genius, longevity and greatness were, if not mutually exclusive (Leo Tolstoy alone would be sufficient to refute that possibility), at least not often correlated in the Russian canon. In tsarist Russia, a striking proportion of notable writers died young of dueling, drink, or disease; in Soviet times, political incorrectness was added to the list of mortal perils besetting writers whose talents set them apart from the common. For the writers who perished in Stalin's purges, posterity provided one tiny, ironic consolation: their literary reputations would be neither tarnished by political conformity, nor dissipated by a gradual decline from excellence.[21] To survive, one had to compromise, and literary activity that satisfied Party watchdogs attracted suspicion from a different quarter, that of the intelligentsia.

For Kataev, longevity encumbered him with two problems: first, how to sustain a literary reputation commensurate with the length of his career, as Tolstoy had; and second, how to cope with the burden of survival itself, and in particular with being the sole survivor of the group of writers—chiefly Odessans—with whom he had begun his career. To solve these problems, he had to demonstrate that his survival was justified on literary grounds, or in other words that he "deserved" to stand as a successor to Pushkin and the other writers of the "great" nineteenth-century tradition. He had to prove that he was more than just a political shill writing to the Party formula. And he had to authenticate himself as a true representative of his own, largely ill-fated, generation in Russian letters. In *My Diamond Crown,* Kataev tackles these problems in a variety of ways.

KATAEV AND PUSHKINIAN TRADITION

"My love, forgive me this apostasy," writes Vladimir Nabokov in a poem addressing the poet's grief at being exiled from his literary mother tongue,[22] and it is the charge of apostasy that Kataev, like his contemporary Nabokov, must answer in order to take a place in the Russian canon. While these days the nineteenth century seems relatively distant, for both Kataev (born in 1897) and Nabokov (born in 1899) it was the era into whose twilight they were born. Both are of the generation whose task it would be to determine what the twentieth century was, in literary terms. Thus, they look back to the nineteenth century not only as the "great" century of Russian literature but also as the epoch immediately preceding their own—making the question of continuity, of membership in this tradition, a genuinely urgent one. Where Nabokov must compensate for his linguistic estrangement from the wellsprings of "great" Russian literature, the disjunction for which Kataev must compensate is ideological and, metaphorically speaking, temporal: by urging time forward he has opened a potentially prejudicial gap between himself and the nineteenth-century writers who represent the immortality of "tradition." Like Nabokov's—and like the Odessa myth itself, which Kataev outwardly rejects—Kataev's claim to canonicity is established on the fringes of Pushkin's most canonical works, or what might be termed "Pushkin's cutting-room floor."[23]

The novel in which Nabokov "appropriates" the canon of nineteenth-century Russian literature famously ends with a paragraph that evokes Pushkin's *Eugene Onegin* both in form and in content:

> Goodbye, my book! Like mortal eyes, imagined ones must close some day. Onegin from his knees will rise—but his creator strolls away. And yet the ear cannot right now part with the music and allow the tale to fade; the chords of fate itself continue to vibrate; and no obstruction for the sage exists where I have put The End: the shadows of my world extend beyond the skyline of the page, blue as tomorrow's morning haze—nor does this terminate the phrase.[24]

Here Nabokov, underscoring his implicit argument throughout the novel that the line of succession to Pushkin's throne ran now through the fragile émigré literary community, not the Soviet establishment, "inherits" from Pushkin an artifact crafted by the great poet but subsequently fallen into disuse: the Onegin stanza, here cunningly disguised as a paragraph of lyrical prose. That is the formal allusion. The content of the passage similarly invokes a kinship between Nabokov's novel and Pushkin's, one based less on the texts of the novels themselves than on the imaginary plane on which the stories coexist, the world into which the author-narrator "strolls away" when it is time to say "The End." This idea, of a validating encounter with Pushkin that takes place just outside the gates of Pushkin's published texts, is also used by Kataev in *My Diamond Crown*, as is the ploy of "inheriting" a disused Pushkin artifact.

The artifact in question, which forms the title of Kataev's book, itself exists only outside Pushkin's finished text, on the great poet's cutting-room floor. It is a diamond crown fashioned for Marina Mnishek to wear in *Boris Godunov*, but left out of the final published version of Pushkin's verse drama,[25] as Kataev explains:

> I shall probably name my book . . . *My Diamond Crown,* from the scene of *Boris Godunov* that Pushkin crossed out, in my view wrongly.
>
> It's a charming scene: in preparation for her decisive meeting with the Pretender, Marina consults her maid Ruzia about what adornments to wear.
>
> "Now then, is it ready? Can't you make haste?"—"By your leave, first make the difficult choice; what will you put on, the strand of pearls or the

emerald crescent?"—"My diamond crown."—"Splendid! Do you remember? You wore it when you deigned to go to the palace. At the ball, so they say, you shone like the sun. Men sighed, beauties whispered . . . At that time, it seems, young Khotkevich saw you for the first time, he who afterward shot himself. And indeed, so they say, whoever looked on you fell in love on the spot."—"Can't you be quicker?"

No, Marina can't be bothered with reminiscences, she is in a hurry. Away with the strand of pearls, away with the emerald crescent. You can't put on everything. A genius must know how to limit himself, and most of all, how to choose. Choice is the soul of poetry. (12–13, ellipsis in original)

Of course, not only the ornaments rejected by Marina are cast aside by the poet's "choice": the diamond crown she does select falls by the wayside too. Kataev, following the example of the Pretender (*samozvanets*) in *Boris Godunov* who crowns himself tsar of Russia, picks up Marina's lost diamond crown and puts it on, thus crowning himself, as Borden says, "the Pretender, the Tsar of Russian culture of the 1920s."[26]

Marina already made her choice. Me too: everything superfluous is rejected. What's left is "My Diamond Crown." Hastening to the fountain, I am ready to put it on my own balding head.

Marina is my soul before a decisive meeting. But where is that fountain? Isn't it in the Parc Monceau, whither I was once summoned by a mad sculptor? (13)

As the reader learns in *My Diamond Crown*'s final tableau, to which I will return presently, it is indeed in the Parc Monceau in Paris that the fictional Kataev finally dons his diamond crown. By then, however, the "crown" has acquired additional symbolic resonances from the various uses to which Pushkin is put in the course of Kataev's narrative.

After *Boris Godunov* (which also, in *My Diamond Crown*, provides the basis of an anecdote connecting Pushkin to Olesha),[27] the most important Pushkin intertext for *My Diamond Crown* is his 1836 poem "Exegi Monumentum," which begins with the famous line "I raised to myself a monument not made by hands" ("*Ia pamiatnik sebe vozdvig nerukotvornyi*"). Kataev takes Pushkin's metaphorical "monument not made by hands" and "realizes" it in his own text as a monument that only Kataev, as the sole surviving writer of his original circle, can see: the ghostly afterimage of the Pushkin monument that, sometime in the five decades between the time being written about and the time of writing, had been moved from its "lawful place, at the head of Tverskoy Boulevard" to a position across the street. Kataev explains:

For people of my generation there are two monuments to Pushkin. The two identical Pushkins stand opposite each other, separated by a noisy square, streams of automobiles, traffic lights, the batons of traffic wardens. One Pushkin is ghostly. He stands in his old, lawful place, but only old Muscovites see him. To others he is invisible. In the unfilled emptiness at the beginning of Tverskoy Boulevard, they see the real Pushkin, surrounded by streetlamps and a bronze chain, on which, sitting in a row and rocking slightly, in the early 1920s conversed two poets [Bagritsky and Esenin] and a third party—I, their contemporary.

And the Pushkin of today is for me just a ghost. (30–31)

The theme of the monument "not built by hands" (*nerukotvornyi*) unites with the theme of the crown not worn in the final stanza of Pushkin's poem, and in the final paragraphs of Kataev's "unmemoir." Like Marina on the cutting-room floor, Pushkin's muse is ultimately forced to forgo her crown:

> Be obedient, O Muse, to the divine commandment,
> Fearing no offense, *demanding no crown;*
> Receive flattery and slander with indifference,
> And do not argue with a fool.[28]

These two Pushkinian crowns-not-worn—Marina's diadem and the Muse's laurels—will merge and reemerge at the end of *My Diamond Crown.*

Before I turn to a discussion of the ending, however, it is necessary to mention one more piece of Pushkiniana that Kataev contrives to import into his own self-narrative. This time the item in question is a story *about* Pushkin, namely Gogol's claim that

> [Pushkin] gave me his own subject, from which he has intended to make something in the nature of a narrative poem [*poèma*] and which, as he said, he would have given to no one else. This was the subject of *Dead Souls.*[29]

Kataev, who as a "Southerner" thinks of Gogol as a literary "relative" or "godfather,"[30] offers an updated version of this anecdote in which he himself (predictably) plays the Pushkin role:

> Back then, attracted by Gogol's Chichikov, I decided that the strength of *Dead Souls* consisted in the fact that Gogol had managed to find a mobile hero. . . . A search for jewels, hidden in one of twelve chairs scattered around the country by the Revolution, seemed to me to offer the possibility of sketching a satirical gallery of contemporary types of the NEP period.
> I laid all this before my friend and my brother [Ilf and Petrov], whom I

had resolved to turn into my literary Negroes, according to the example of Dumas *père:* I would propose the theme, the source, and they would work out this theme, clothe it in the flesh and blood of a satirical novel. (154)

Here we see Kataev emulating Pushkin by supplying the picaresque-satirical plot for a novel to be written by his literary protégés, a plot which (by emulating Gogol's *Dead Souls*) also allows Kataev to take credit for an authentically "Southern" work of literature, reconnecting him to the Southwestern discourse of his origins. The modus operandi across all these uses of Pushkin in *My Diamond Crown* is consistent: Kataev takes a Pushkin-related "story" and makes it come "true" by importing it into an autobiographical discourse authenticated by the narrator's lived experience.

Kataev's narrative is framed by two encounters, fifty years apart, with the "mad sculptor" mentioned in the passage about Marina's jewelry. Upon meeting Kataev in Paris, this sculptor, a man named Brunsvik, conceives a desire to sculpt Kataev and his Russian literary contemporaries. Brunsvik enthuses:

"I have found my theme! I will give you all eternity. I swear, I will do it. I just need to find a suitable material. If I find it . . . Oh, if only I can find it . . . then you will see what real sculpture is. Believe it, on one of the days of eternal spring in the Parc Monceau, among the pink and white flowering chestnuts, among the tulips and roses, you will finally see your likenesses, sculpted from an unheard-of material. . . . if, of course, I can find it . . ." (8, ellipses in original)

It is this same sculptor, Brunsvik—not noticeably mellowed by the passage of time—who excitedly summons Kataev to the park fifty years later:

"I finally found a suitable material. No! Not a material, but a substance! A suitable substance for your friends, of whom you told me so much!" he shouted from the threshold. "This substance was delivered to me from the area around Cassiopeia. The Universe is built from this substance. It's the best you can get on the global market. A substance from the depths of the galaxy. Hurry!" (207)

Fifty years, the amount of time that has passed between the publication of Kataev's *Embezzlers* and the publication of *My Diamond Crown*, has (it seems) been long enough to transform Brunsvik's language from a Buninesque idiom of "eternal spring" and "pink-and-white flowering chestnuts" into a kind of Space Age sentimentalism reminiscent of Kataev's "Mauvist" protégés Aksyonov and Bitov. This mirrors Kataev's own evolution from a disciple of Bunin in the 1910s and 1920s into a "literary godfather" to such writers as Aksyonov, Bitov, and Sokolov in the 1960s and 1970s.[31] Brunsvik, transparently a figure for Kataev himself (who is writing the novel that serves as a "garden of monuments" to his generation of Russian modernists) in much the same way that Shoyl was for Babel, "disappear[s], this time forever" after summoning Kataev's narrator to the Parc Monceau.

Arriving there alone, the narrator finds "white, shining statues without pedestals" of all his erstwhile colleagues dotted around the landscape. Like the ghostly Pushkin monument in Moscow, these statues are visible only to Kataev, whose special Mauvist vision allows him to transcend the limitations of time and space. Scarcely has he managed to take them all in when

> it suddenly seemed to me as if the starry frost of eternity, subtly at first, quite imperceptibly and unfrighteningly, touched the thinning gray hair around the tonsure of my uncovered head, making it sparkle, like a diamond crown. (214)

As he stands there, the narrator gradually loses the power of movement and is himself transformed into a sculpture "made of a cosmic substance by the mad fantasy of the Sculptor."[32]

In these closing paragraphs of Kataev's book, the narrator engages in a kind of literary arms race with Pushkin. At our last sight of him, he not only has become his own "monument not made by hands," but has also donned the crown that Pushkin himself was prepared to forgo. Where Pushkin erects his own monument, Kataev invents a fictional Sculptor to do it for him; the resulting monument is not only *nerukotvornyi,* not built by hands, but also *nezemnoi,* not of this earth. Where Pushkin presumes to assure only his own immortality, Kataev takes charge of the immortality of his entire literary generation. Finally, in his rewriting of *Boris Godunov,* Kataev plays all the parts—or at least all the crowned heads. He is Marina, putting on a diamond crown in the margins of Pushkin's text; he is the self-crowned Pretender (*samozvanets*), posing as king of the Russian writers of the 1920s; and, the "tonsure" allusion suggests, he is also Boris himself, trading his earthly kingdom for a heavenly one at the end of his reign. In short, every crown that Pushkin leaves lying around, Kataev picks up and puts on.

By importing Pushkin's fictional objects into a text about himself—one which, despite its author's strenuous efforts to defy generic categories, is probably best described by Borden's term, "solipsistic memoir"—Kataev, like Nabokov, legitimates himself as an heir to Russia's most canonical writer. And, like a true Odessan, he does so by manipulating the boundaries between "fiction" and "truth": Pushkin's *Boris Godunov,* a story taken (like Shklovsky's "South-West" or Shoyl's tall tales) from life, "comes true" as a part of Kataev's personal narrative.

Raoul Verlet's monument to Maupassant (1897) in the Parc Monceau, Paris

KATAEV AND BABEL

The adaptation of Pushkinian themes is not the only significant aspect of Kataev's sculpture garden, however. The location of the garden is also freighted with symbolism, leading back to another important "ghost" whose legacy Kataev could not avoid confronting: Isaac Babel. The Parc Monceau in Paris, fictional site of Kataev's "cosmic" monuments, is in real life famous for its statue of Guy de Maupassant (see above), the writer named by Babel in "Odessa" as a model for Odessan literature (and a kind of avatar of himself).[33] In a moment of uncharacteristic generosity, Kataev even places his fictional statue of Babel next to the real statue of Maupassant, thus creating what he himself might call an "associative connection" between the two. This is a significant gesture, since the definition of Mauvism set forth by Kataev two pages earlier—in a direct polemic with Babel—proclaims "the replace-ment of the chronological connection with the associative connection [*assot-siativnoi sviaz'iu*]" as the new structuring principle for artistic prose (212).

Like Paustovsky (see chapter 3), Kataev in *My Diamond Crown* uses Babel's own language when treating the topic of Babel, but where Paus-tovsky seems to do so in a spirit of discipleship, Kataev—who reportedly re-ferred to Paustovsky in one conversation as "that old liar Paustovsky with his idiotic stories"[34]—employs a frankly iconoclastic tone. Babel, as the prophet of literary Odessa and as its all-but-self-proclaimed literary Messiah, was an unavoidable topic both for a writer seeking to join the Odessa "school," like Paustovsky, and for a writer seeking to escape it, like Kataev. It is instructive to compare the two writers' methods of engagement with Babel's legacy.

As I have noted in earlier chapters, the commonplaces of Babel's per-sonal mythology are almost all drawn from his published stories, rather than from direct knowledge of his life. Kataev remarks disparagingly, "*konar-meets* led an enigmatic life; no one knew where he roamed, where he lived, whom he saw or what he was writing" (202). As the nickname suggests, what everyone did know was that Babel had traveled with Budyonny's Red Cav-alry, and what he had seen—or purportedly seen—there. They also knew that at the first Congress of Soviet Writers, he had half-jokingly bid farewell to "the right to write badly."[35] They knew that he wore "spectacles on his nose," and from that they could infer, following the logic of Arye-Leib in "How It Was Done in Odessa," that he also wore "autumn in his heart."[36] (Kataev's quest in *My Diamond Crown* is for a land of "eternal spring" [*vech-naia vesna*]—a contrast that may well be deliberate.) And, regarding Babel's poetics, they knew the famous aphorisms from his story "Guy de Maupas-sant": "No iron can enter the human heart as chillingly as a full stop placed at the right time," and "A phrase is born into the world good and bad at the same time. The secret lies in a barely perceptible turn. The lever must lie in one's hand and get warm. It must be turned once, and no more."[37] Paus-tovsky and Kataev both allude to these details of Babel's personal mythology in their memoiristic portraits of him, but in very different ways. Paustovsky, as we have seen in chapter 3, becomes a convert to Babel's philosophy of punctuation, marvels at the meticulousness that prompted Babel to draft a story twenty-two times before making it public, and perpetuates Babel's chosen self-metonyms: novelty, sunshine, jocularity, and the French influ-ence, specifically that of Maupassant. Kataev, on the other hand, ironizes the well-known features of Babel's reputation, for example by nicknaming him "*konarmeets*" when the major theme of *Red Cavalry* is, arguably, the narra-tor's ongoing *exclusion* from the ranks of the "real" cavalrymen—his failure to become a true member of the *konarmiia*. Similarly, Kataev turns Babel's famous reticence about himself upside down by interpreting it not as a form of self-concealment, but rather as "a special ploy to call additional attention to himself" (202). The spectacles on Babel's nose, the outward symptom of the perennial "autumn in his heart," are here caricatured as "the round spectacles of a small-town *intelligent,* wearing a Budyonny helmet with a red star but with a big automatic pen instead of a rifle" (201). In Kataev's portrait, Babel's insistence that the full stop is deadlier than a blade—or a bullet—is implicitly undermined by his narrators' inability to kill;[38] a bold pronouncement about the power of literature is transformed into a buffoonish admission of masculine inadequacy.

Elsewhere, Babel's celebrated perfectionism in matters of word choice and punctuation is invoked and ridiculed. Kataev reports:

> Our meetings were always accidental and brief. But [Babel] never let slip an opportunity to teach me a literary lesson:
> "Literature is an eternal battle. I spent the whole of last night battling with a word. If you don't defeat the word, the word will defeat you. Sometimes, for the sake of a single solitary adjective one is obliged to spend not just several nights, but even months of bloody labor. Remember that. In dialogue, there must not be a single inessential expression. One should resort to dialogue only in case of the most extreme need: the dialogue should be brief, in character, and should give off an astringent odor, so to speak . . ." (203, ellipsis in original)

The irony inherent in this interminable monologue about the need for parsimony and concision in dialogue is obvious. Kataev also takes this opportunity to parody Babel's famous equation of stylistic minutiae with lethal force (the "steel" that "enters the human heart"), as well as the gap between the "masculine [i.e., violent] language" on which Babel's autobiographical narrators dote, and the effete, intellectual sphere of action to which they tend to be confined.[39] In Kataev's exaggerated account, the ironically nicknamed "cavalryman" is hard pressed to win a battle with a single word, let alone an enemy soldier.

Kataev's most audacious rewriting of Babel's legacy comes when he sets up his own artistic doctrine of "Mauvism," in opposition to the "childish disease of Flaubertism" that paralyzes Babel with "horror before an insufficiently artistically placed adjective or even punctuation mark" (203). Congratulating himself on having "freed myself from these prejudices thought up for us by literary theorists and critics with no sense of beauty," Kataev goes on to offer his latest definition of Mauvism:[40]

> It is simply a new form, come to replace the old. The replacement of the chronological connection with the associative connection. The replacement of the search for beauty with the search for *authenticity,* no matter how

"bad" this authenticity might seem. *In French, "mauvais"—that is, "bad."* In a word, again—Mauvism. (204, my emphasis)

For all Kataev's bravado about "freedom" from the tyranny of careful word choice, the choice of words here (as elsewhere in *My Diamond Crown*) is highly significant. In the service of his supposed polemic with Babel, Kataev has calmly appropriated Babel's own signature vocabulary: "authenticity," the motto supposedly "inscribed on Babel's shield";[41] "bad" writing, which Babel had famously eulogized in 1934; even the little flourish of French. In fact, the choice of a French-derived name for Kataev's "school" of "bad writing" can only be intended as an affirmation of Mauvism's Babelian pedigree.[42]

This usurping of Babel's metonyms can be read as Kataev's de-Messianization of Babel, in preparation for his own self-coronation as Pushkin's heir at the end of *My Diamond Crown*. By 1977, Soviet literature had had plenty of occasion to reflect upon the canonical destiny of a literary (or any) "Messiah": namely, destruction at the hands of the temporal rulers. In appropriating Babel's quest for personal authenticity, his appeal on behalf of "bad" writing, and his Francophilism, Kataev arguably appropriates the very qualities that led to Babel's downfall—the equivalent of picking up the cross after the danger of crucifixion is over. At the same time, Kataev's overthrow of Babel and coronation of himself, like his topsy-turvy logic in interpreting Babel's reticence as ostentation and proclaiming "bad" writing to be good, is reminiscent of the "upside-down," "looking-glass" world of Odessan carnival. Perhaps Kataev is crowning himself, after all, not as Pushkin's successor, but as a Rabelaisian/Babelian Lord of Misrule. Most likely of all, in typically Odessan fashion, he is doing both at once.

MAUVISM AS ODESSANISM

Mauvism itself was conceived by Kataev precisely as a form of carnival— that is to say, as an inversion of "normal," everyday values, in this case those of official art. The establishment of Socialist Realism as the official method of Soviet art in 1934 was thematized, at the first Congress of Soviet Writers, as the death knell of "bad" writing.[43] The theme, introduced by Leonid Sobolev, was amplified by Gorky in his speech, and finally formed the peroration of Babel's address:

Following Gorky, I would like to say that on our standard should be written Sobolev's words, that everything is given to us by the Party and the government, and only one right has been taken away—to write badly.

Comrades, let us not conceal it. The right to write badly is a very important right indeed, and not a little is being taken away from us. It was a privilege which we used extensively.

So then, comrades, let's give up this privilege, and may God help us. Or rather, since there is no God, we'll help ourselves.[44]

Kataev, in turn, resurrects explicitly "bad" writing as an antidote to the "good" (i.e., officially acceptable) writing of Socialist Realism. That it is a resurrection rather than a true innovation is revealed not only by the Babel-derived name Kataev chooses for his method, but by the characteristics he associates with it in the definition quoted above: a new organizing principle (the supersession of chronolinearity by "associative" connections), and a new aesthetic criterion ("authenticity" rather than "beauty"). For Kataev, "beauty," as defined by the (presumably ideological) "prejudices thought up for us by literary theorists," has lost its value as a concept in opposition to "utility"—in fact, as the doctrine of Socialist Realism has collapsed together Horace's *dulce* and *utile,* beauty has become more or less a synonym for utility, a "scientific" and objective term rather than an artistic and subjective one.[45] Kataev, then, is calling for a subjective turn in literature: the "objective" structuring matrix of time is to be replaced with the subjective patterns supplied by the personal memories and perceptions of the narrator, and the official, corporate standard of beauty is to be abandoned in favor of the individual author's fidelity to the "authentic"—even if, in Kataev's paradoxical formulation, this authenticity takes the form of a "lie" (67).

Implicit in the rejection of conventional chronological structure is a further kind of "badness": a repudiation of the teleological perspective of Socialist Realism, in which chronological progression necessarily entails historical progress. In his proto–Socialist Realist production novel, *Time, Forward!,* Kataev had adhered to an exceptionally rigid chronological structure, confining the action to a single 24-hour period, the better to emphasize the novel's titular theme—the race to cram ever more production into the same unit of time. (To intensify the "rushed" effect and create a loophole later in the plot for a necessary chronological deviation—itself a "leap forward" in time to reveal the results of the stress tests performed on the concrete mixture devised by the novel's hero—Kataev "omitted" the first chapter, inserting the letter containing the results as an out-of-order "Chapter One" toward the end of the novel.) Moreover, the brisk forward motion and strict "tempo" exemplified by the novel's form and celebrated in its content were explicitly associated with Stalin, by means of his famous speech to the eighteenth Party Congress (1931), which Kataev's characters quote verbatim near the beginning and end of the novel:

The tempo must not be reduced! On the contrary, we must increase it as much as is within our powers and possibilities. This is dictated to us by our obligations to the workers and peasants of the USSR. This is dictated to us by our obligations to the working class of the whole world.

To slacken the tempo would mean falling behind. And those who fall behind get beaten. But we do not want to be beaten. No, we refuse to be beaten! One feature of the history of old Russia was the continual beatings she suffered because of her backwardness. . . . All beat her because of her backwardness, military backwardness, cultural backwardness, political backwardness, industrial backwardness, agricultural backwardness.

That is why we must no longer lag behind.[46]

As a Mauvist writer, Kataev not only dismantles strict chronological structure but embraces "backwardness": he frankly indulges in nostalgia, writing almost exclusively about events and personages from his youth, and confesses to his own inability to adjust, for example, to the new position of Pushkin's statue in Moscow. Kataev, in 1932 the champion of "tempos," makes it his business in *My Diamond Crown* to profess the opposite philosophy—to "lag behind."

Of the numerous ways in which writing, viewed from a Socialist Realist perspective, could be "bad," Kataev thus seems to emphasize two in particular: the privileging of the personal over the universal, and the privileging of the past over the future. The "right to write badly" that he exercises here is strongly reminiscent of the "right" claimed by Olesha in *his* speech to the first Congress of Soviet Writers, delivered the day before Babel's:

I have come to the conclusion that my greatest wish is the right to preserve the colors of my youth, the freshness of my vision, to defend that vision from assertions that it is not needed, from accusations that it is vulgar and worthless.[47]

Where Babel, albeit with reservations, acquiesces to the loss of the right to write badly, Olesha here seems to reassert his right to a kind of writing that others have called "vulgar and worthless," or in other words, "bad." Among these others was Kataev, who in a 1933 interview had applied a series of lethal adjectives—"decadent," "uncultured," "useless"—to Olesha's writing.[48] Olesha seems to enter into a polemic with Kataev when he goes on to say, with a faintly contemptuous inflection,

I could have gone out on a construction site, lived in a factory among the workers and described them in an article or even in a novel. But that was not my theme, the theme in my blood, in my breath. I couldn't handle that subject matter as a true artist. I would have been forced to contrive, to lie. (216)

While Kataev, alone among the Odessans, had done precisely that—"gone among the workers" to create a production novel that preempted the official adoption of Socialist Realism by the Writers' Union at that same 1934 meeting—Olesha was struggling to redeem his attraction to the past ("the colors of my youth") and the subjectivity of his vision. Even his speech to the Congress is an autobiographical narrative; after a single sentence of abstract generalization ("There is good and bad in every man") the personal pronoun "I" makes its appearance, and never disappears for very long thereafter. He reveals that *Envy*, too, was in some measure autobiographical:

> Six years ago, I wrote the novel *Envy*.
> The main character of my story was Nikolai Kavalerov. People told me that Kavalerov had many of my traits, that it was an autobiographical portrait; that, indeed, Kavalerov was me.
> Yes, Kavalerov did look at the world through my eyes. . . .
> But then, people declared that Kavalerov was a vulgar, worthless man. Knowing that Kavalerov embodied so much of myself, I took these accusations personally and was shocked. (215)

Earlier, Olesha has asserted that "a fictional character *can* kill an artist," suggesting a world in which fictional characters come to life and surpass their creators. Now, distraught by the world's rejection of him in the guise of Kavalerov, he undergoes the reverse process, turning himself, in stages, into a fictional beggar:

> I imagined myself as a beggar. . . . But then creative imagination came into play. . . . I decided to write a story about a beggar. . . . I became a beggar, actually a real beggar. (215)

Olesha's story about becoming a beggar having thus "come true" (if only metaphorically), he tells of wandering the countryside in his beggar's guise until one day he finds a ruined wall punctuated by a mysterious portal, passes through it, and finds his youth magically restored. This fictional return to the past, narrated in a story-within-a-speech, "comes true" in the writer's real life as a twofold epiphany: first, that his own past is not "vulgar and worthless" but valuable and usable; and, second, that as an artist he "can only write about things that are in him." He recommits himself to the past and to the personal.

The Kataev who is adumbrated in Olesha's speech is, for obvious reasons, the teleological Kataev of *Time, Forward!* However, the metaphor of the door in the wall—an image borrowed from an H. G. Wells story and associated with nostalgia for an innocent and inaccessible past—provided the later Kataev with a chance to write himself retroactively into Olesha's speech, by naming his first Mauvist work, *The Little Iron Door in the Wall*

119

(*Malen'kaia zheleznaia dver' v stene*, 1964), after the same Wellsian image.[49] By exploiting this opportunity for retroactive intertextuality, Kataev nails his colors to the mast of "bad" writing, Olesha-style, and reasserts his claim to the mantle of "Odessan" writing—to the bright, fresh colors of the youth that he shared with Olesha.

MY DIAMOND CROWN AND THE "SOUTH-WEST"

Asked point-blank about the "South-West school," Kataev is reported by one reviewer to have exclaimed:

> "What school! What South-West! That muddlehead [*putanik*] Shklovsky, for whom the most important thing on earth was to have a label, took the name from Bagritsky and stuck it on whomever he felt like, and now everyone repeats it after him like parrots: 'South-West!' But in actual fact, what South-West? two stories by Babel, three poems by Bagritsky! I created a school: Mauvism. Yes, that is a school; it has its principles, I have followers; whereas the South-West is just an invention of Shklovsky's, because he is a theorist, and a theorist isn't a theorist unless he thinks up some kind of school."[50]

Despite his disregard for Shklovsky's "theorizing," Kataev nonetheless grounds his own narrative of the 1920s in Shklovsky's vocabulary. In addition to claiming Gogol as a "godfather" (an ancestry invoked for the "South-West" by Shklovsky and, indirectly, by Babel), Kataev refers to himself and Bagritsky as "Levantines" (29)—the term Shklovsky used to explain the Odessans' orientation toward the West—and insists upon his own affinity for the Mediterranean, particularly Italy. Kataev's nickname for Bagritsky, *ptitselov* ("birdhunter," from Bagritsky's eponymous 1918 poem), also calls to mind Shklovsky's epithet for him, *ptitsevod* ("birdraiser").

My Diamond Crown's closest rival, the memoirs of "that old liar, Paustovsky," is also invoked, though Paustovsky himself is not admitted to Kataev's pseudonymous circle. In addition to satirizing Paustovsky's portrait of Babel, Kataev competes with Paustovsky over the figure of Bagritsky, who, however, represents in Kataev's text much the same principle that he stands for in Paustovsky's: the interweaving of "stories" with "real life." In *My Diamond Crown*, Kataev credits himself with "dragging the birdhunter to Moscow," away from the circle of

> young poets, his passionate and faithful disciples, for whom he was a deity. . . . Arriving from Moscow and seeing this picture, I realized that leaving the

birdhunter in Odessa was impossible. He would perish. He needed to move immediately to Moscow, where the whole flower of the young Russian Soviet literature had already gathered. (49–50)

Bagritsky, so naive and provincial that he doesn't believe Kataev's assurances that there will be a restaurant car on the train, brings provisions in his suitcase, including a block of *brynza* (sheep's-milk cheese) wrapped in a copy of *The Seaman,* the newspaper over which Paustovsky had presided during his tenure in Odessa and acquaintance with Bagritsky. The demotion of Paustovsky's periodical from reading material to food wrap is an appropriately scornful image with which to mark Bagritsky's transition from the provinces of Paustovsky to the capital lorded over by Kataev.

Kataev also seems to be in dialogue with Paustovsky when he presents his "where were you when you heard Blok was dead" story, a genre that plays a significant part in Paustovsky's memoir as well. In Paustovsky's *A Time of Great Expectations,* the writer I. Livshits brings the news from town and entreats Paustovsky, "Go to Isaac Emmanuilovich [Babel] and tell him about it. . . . I can't."[51] Paustovsky goes, but cannot bring himself to break the news. There follows a chapter dedicated to recording the ways in which Odessan writers commemorated Blok's death:

> In those days we spoke endlessly of Blok. Somehow toward evening, Bagritsky came from town. He stayed the night with us and practically all night recited Blok. Izya [Livshits] and I lay silently on the dark terrace. The night wind rustled in the dry leaves of the grapevine. . . .
>
> "Well, orphans," said Babel with warmth, "what on earth are we going to do now? We'll never live to see a second Blok, even if we wait two hundred years."
>
> "Did you ever see him?" I asked Babel.
>
> I expected Babel to answer "no," which would be a relief. I was generally free from the sentiment of envy. But all those who had seen and heard Blok in person, I envied long and hard.[52]

But Babel *has* met Blok, and proceeds to describe him—purposefully dismantling Paustovsky's expectations ("He was not at all a fallen angel, or an incarnation of rarefied thoughts and feelings")—and then, like Bagritsky, to quote Blok's verses from memory. Almost imperceptibly, the mood of Paustovsky's narrative shifts from a eulogy for Blok to admiration of Babel. (The sequel to this episode is the conversation with Bagritsky that I cited in chapter 3, in which Bagritsky, embodying his function as a symbol for "fabulism" in everyday life, parrots "an outlandish jumble" from Babel's speech about Blok, to the amusement of Paustovsky and Livshits.)

For Kataev, too, the moment when he learns of Blok's death is an experience shared with an Odessan colleague, in this case, Olesha:

> We went out onto the dry, littered square, heated to burning point by the midday Ukrainian sun, and suddenly saw, displayed behind the glass of a long-unwashed telegraph agency display window, a portrait of Alexander Blok. It was in a red and black calico frame.
>
> We froze, as if struck by lightning: our treasured dream had been someday to see Blok in the flesh, to hear his voice. We read the telegram displayed alongside the portrait, where the death of Blok was succinctly announced. . . .
>
> In one moment, all the musical and visual elements of his poetry, which had long since become a part of our souls, coursed through our imagination.
>
> "In an unmown ditch . . . beautiful and young . . . There is no name for you, my distant one . . . All valor I forgot and noble deeds . . . ." (83, last paragraph's ellipses in original)

In common with Paustovsky, Kataev remembers (or purports to remember) Blok's death as a shared experience, one that connects Kataev to his Odessan roots as well as to his sense of Blok as a "father" to all the writers of the Odessan (i.e., Revolutionary) generation, now become "orphans." The similarities between the two accounts—the dry heat, the supine mourning attitude, the spontaneous quotation of memorized verses—do not need to be deliberate to be striking. Whether Kataev intended his reminiscence to complement or to compete with Paustovsky's, the intertextuality works.

Bagritsky, the only writer of whom both Kataev and Paustovsky speak in warm personal terms, appears in *My Diamond Crown* in a role analogous to that of Babel and Kuprin in *A Time of Great Expectations:* that is, as the teller of stories that come true. Bearing out Paustovsky's claim in *The Golden Rose* that Bagritsky's stories "became woven into the texture of his life," making it "impossible to distinguish between fact and fiction,"[53] Bagritsky provides Kataev in *My Diamond Crown* with "memories" of things not yet seen:

> Having made our way through the subtropical garden with its pomegranate trees, fig trees, and strange never-before-seen flowers, we felt the damp warmth of the stagnant air and found ourselves before a natural stone wall of unusual height. One could imagine that this was a forever petrified smooth gray waterfall, motionlessly cascading from somewhere in the heights of the cloudless Sicilian sky. In that moment it seemed to me that I had seen that gray wall somewhere before, or at least heard about it.
>
> But where? When? (28)

It is only when the tour guide announces, "*Signori,* your attention. Before you is the *grotto Dioniso,* the grotto of Dionysus," that Kataev's narrator recalls hearing Bagritsky recite one of his own early poems ("Dionis," 1915), which described the scene exactly:

> I heard the gasping asthmatic voice of the young birdhunter—a schoolboy, apostrophizing from the farcical afternoon half-dark of the summer theater to the antique god:
> "Dionysus! Dionysus! Dionysus!"
> "There, where the cold gray projection throws itself down in the form of a waterfall, I shout in the silent cave: Dionysus! Dionysus! Dionysus!" (28–29)

The Italian tour guide goes on to explain that in this grotto, "the god Dionysus first pressed grapes and taught mankind to make wine." "Well, of course!" responds Kataev, slightly misquoting (as is his wont throughout *My Diamond Crown,* another of the ways in which "authentic" reality is made to conform to his subjectivity rather than the other way around): "You went off into the turquoise grottos to press the golden grape."[54] That is, he again recognizes a fact that he "already knows" from a long-ago poem by Bagritsky. "But," he marvels,

> how could that boy from Remeslennaya Street, who had never left his native city, who had spent the greater part of his life on a mezzanine to which one had to climb from the kitchen by means of a painted wooden ladder . . . how could he with such precision imagine the grotto of Dionysus? (29)

Trying to account for Bagritsky's mysterious foreknowledge of the grotto, Kataev posits both supernatural ("telepathy? clairvoyance?") and prosaic ("some merchant sailor from the Odessa-Syracuse route") sources for the information, but the mystery is insusceptible of solution, for Bagritsky is long dead—"the first of us Levantines to depart for that country whence there is no return" (29). Yet the word "Levantine" at this crucial juncture provides a clue; in Shklovsky's "South-West," this term had been used to indicate an affinity among the peoples of the Mediterranean and the Black Sea. Bagritsky might never have seen Dionysus's grotto in the flesh, but as a Levantine he was connected to the inhabitants of southern Italy who saw it every day. His "Dionysus" poem serves as another example of a theme "appropriated . . . via the West."[55]

In short, though Kataev overtly rejects Shklovsky's theory of a "South-West school," using Mauvism as a counterexample of a real "school," he makes use of several elements of the "South-West" theory, without apology or fanfare, in *My Diamond Crown.* The reference to "Levantines," the choice to title Bagritsky's character after one of his own poems (as Shklovsky had titled his article), the revelation of Bagritsky's absorption of a "Western" theme and image into his early poetry, and the Kataev-narrator's own search for the "land of eternal spring" in *western* Europe, are all ways in which *My Diamond Crown* pays homage to Shklovsky. While purporting to distinguish between "South-West"-ism and Mauvism, Kataev has instead connected them. Moreover, his "lying" Mauvist memoir exhibits all the classic features of Odessan modernism:

(1) The text connects to and rewrites other Odessan texts, specifically Babel's and Olesha's famous 1934 speeches at the All-Union Congress of Soviet Writers, into which speeches Kataev retrospectively writes himself as the reviver of "bad writing" in the 1960s.

(2) Kataev employs a quasi-autobiographical voice that, like Babel's, fosters an expectation (amply attested in the criticism) of "truth" in his readers, even as his text is explicitly and flamboyantly fictionalized.

(3) Like Babel and Olesha, Kataev engages in a carnivalesque reconciliation of seemingly disparate elements, concurrently playing two opposite roles: Pushkin's heir and Lord of Misrule.

(4) He further elaborates upon the quintessentially Odessan theme of "stories that come true," showcasing the transitions between fiction and fact (or, to borrow Paustovsky's words for Babel, between "improvisation" and "authenticity") that I have previously identified with Babel, Paustovsky, and (as represented in Paustovsky's and Kataev's memoirs) Bagritsky. In *My Diamond Crown*, these transitions operate in both directions, and in a number of different ways. Events from history, fictionalized by Pushkin in *Boris Godunov,* are de-fictionalized by Kataev's "autobiographical" narrator who adopts them into his "real life." Conversely, a "real" experience of the narrator's, his visit to the Dionysus grotto, is removed to the sphere of poetry as it is revealed to have its source in Bagritsky's poem "Dionysus."

KATAEV AND OLESHA

A much-discussed function of *My Diamond Crown* among readers and critics was the posthumous rehabilitation, not of Yury Olesha himself, but of Kataev's relationship to Olesha. For critics who counted Olesha among Stalin's (and, indeed, Kataev's) victims, this was one of the most difficult aspects of the book to swallow. The Kataev who in 1933 had denounced Olesha's use of metaphor as "decadent" now devotes several paragraphs to rhapsodizing about those same metaphors. Having shown himself rather a fair-weather friend to Olesha, he now refers to the latter as "my best friend." Where Olesha had ruminated in *No Day Without a Line* that he did not remember quite how he ended up writing satirical verse for *The Whistle*,[56] Kataev now steps in to take the credit. He even has the effrontery to criticize the title given to *No Day Without a Line* by its editors (who included Olesha's widow, Olga Suok, and his brother-in-law Viktor Shklovsky), claiming Olesha had expressed his true wishes—that the book be entitled *Proshchanie s zhizn'iu*, "A Farewell to Life"—to him, Kataev, in a private conversation. All this stands in vivid contrast to the self-effacing tones in which Olesha speaks of Kataev in *No Day Without a Line*: "Kataev writes better than I. He has written a lot; I, only fragments, a collection of metaphors" (161).

Despite the somewhat marginal literary status accorded to *No Day Without a Line* on account of its posthumous redaction, critics have identified numerous ways in which this text seems to have been crucial to the development of Kataev's Mauvism. At the very least, the parallels between *No Day* and subsequent Mauvist works such as *My Diamond Crown* are highly suggestive. First of all, *No Day* is a highly subjective autobiographical text (one almost cannot call it a "narrative"), in which the actual events and objects described are of subordinate importance to the consciousness of the person describing them. Second, Olesha's text is, so to speak, "shattered"—written entirely in "fragments" (*otryvki*, a word Olesha uses repeatedly to describe his project)—presaging the discontinuous narratives, held together by subjective "association," rather than chronolinearity, of Kataev's Mauvist works, and in particular the form of his *A Shattered Life* (*Razbitaia zhizn', ili volshebnyi rog oberona*, 1972), which presents a narrative of the author's Odessa childhood in the "fragmented" form of 120 short stories, related to but not dependent on each other. (Victor Peppard suggests, fruitfully, that this "fragmented" structure is continuous with Olesha's modernist commitment to the "principle of montage"—a technique also favored by the early Kataev.)[57] Third, Olesha deliberately blurs the line between autobiography and fiction (and, not incidentally, confounds genre) by referring to this fragmentary work as an "autobiographical novel" (10). Fourth, Olesha foregrounds the fallibility, spontaneity, and capriciousness of memory, letting misremembered facts and quotations stand in the text even when he acknowledges them, so that the structure of memory itself comes to serve as the basis for the structure (or lack thereof) of the book. Finally, in common with Babel and Paustovsky as well as Kataev, Olesha shows an explicit interest in "stories that come true" as well as in "truths" (lived experiences) that become stories.

The major difference between the style of *No Day* and that of Kataev's *My Diamond Crown* is one of tone. Where Kataev expresses pride in (and takes full credit for) the literary idiosyncrasies described in the foregoing paragraph, Olesha seems to apologize for them:

So what if I write fragments, not finishing them; I am still writing! It is still a
kind of literature—perhaps even the only kind in a certain sense: maybe such
a psychological type as I, in such a historical time as now, actually can't write
in any other way—and if he does write, and to some degree knows how to
write, then let him write, even in this way. (11)

This contrast in tone between the two authors—ebullient Kataev and apol-
ogetic Olesha—is nothing new; indeed, as Elizabeth Beaujour suggests
in "The Imagination of Failure," Olesha's first-person narratives (including *Envy, No Day,* and several of his short stories) "form a coherent image
that we are asked to contemplate: the self-portrait of the artist as failure,"[58]
whereas Kataev seems never to have doubted that he could succeed at the
genre of the moment: NEP satire (*The Embezzlers*), the production novel
(*Time, Forward!*), Socialist Realism (the *Black Sea Waves* tetralogy), and finally the "confessional prose" of the Thaw and post-Thaw periods. As Beaujour points out, Olesha's defeatism is as much of a literary pose as Kataev's
triumphalism is: "Not only does Olesha omit the successes that were in fact
his, but even among the failures he writes only about those, personal and
artistic, of which he could say, paraphrasing Kavalerov, 'It's not my fault; it's
their fault.' "[59] Even when Olesha and Kataev are doing virtually the same
thing—writing associative, fragmented, and subjective reminiscences about
the 1910s and 1920s—Olesha presents himself as a victim of the times, Kataev as their master. This contrast, between the "forward," self-aggrandizing
Kataev and the "backward," self-deprecating Olesha, not only informs the
two writers' personal (and mutual) mythologies, but to a large extent conditions their reception: where Kataev is criticized for "opportunism," Olesha is
held to exemplify "the indisputable absence of artistic compromise."[60]

THE OLESHA OF *NO DAY WITHOUT A LINE*

Despite its importance as a milestone in the post-Stalinist autobiographical
canon,[61] *No Day Without a Line* has suffered even more than Babel's "autobiographical" stories from being freely plundered as a source of "authentic" records concerning Olesha's thoughts on various subjects, even as it has
been neglected in the criticism because of its diffuse origins. Borden articu-
lates the conventional wisdom when he says, "Since the author himself was
not involved in the final structuring, *No Day Without a Line* cannot be analyzed for structural intent."[62] To say this, however, is to ignore two important
factors: the role played by the "canonical" structure of the book, imposed
by Viktor Shklovsky, Olga Suok-Olesha, Arkady Belinkov, and Mikhail Gromov, in its reception; and the very real possibility that Olesha himself in-

tended the book to be structured by chance, or by its readers, rather than by his own authorial intervention. While, certainly, Olesha's final intentions regarding the structure of the book cannot be divined, the structure imparted by Shklovsky and others to the 1965 version of the book undoubtedly organizes the reader's reception of its contents—and raises interesting questions about what alternative structures might be possible. It therefore should not be excluded from critical analysis.[63]

Before proceeding with such an analysis, it will be useful to give a brief account of the genesis and evolution of the book. According to Judson Rosengrant, it was not until 1954, twenty years after his passionate speech to the First Congress of Soviet Writers, that Olesha began to work on *No Day Without a Line* in a concentrated way.[64] In the intervening two decades, he had written and published a great deal of material in a wide variety of genres—articles, sketches, stories, screenplays, and radio commentaries—but the ephemerality of most of these works, and the resulting *critical* silence about them, has given the effect of a long hiatus between Olesha's stories of the early 1930s and the first publication of fragments from what would become *No Day*, in 1956.[65] Olesha himself, in *No Day*, seems to cultivate the suspense surrounding the prospect of his working on a substantial piece of fiction again, reporting a conversation at the Writer's Club in which the poet E. Tarakhovskaia asks him, "Is it true that you've written an autobiographical novel?" and expresses disappointment when Olesha denies the rumor. "From all sides I heard about my novel," continues Olesha:

> Well, obviously, they really want me to write it, if they believe in this rumor and even spread it around themselves. Maybe I have to write it, if that's what my contemporaries want? Moreover, they suggest the form—an autobiographical novel . . . That, incidentally, shows an understanding of the nature of my writings.
> Should I try it?
> Well, here's the beginning. (10, ellipsis in original)

In this fragment, Olesha establishes not only the readers' demand for his work, but also the genre to which the work is to belong, subverting that same genre all the while: if *No Day* is to be considered a novel, it is far from a conventional one. Consisting entirely of such "fragments" (*otryvki*), each more or less self-contained and tending to center on a single theme or incident, the book pursues no single narrative thread, although it is loosely held together by certain themes and motifs, and, of course, by Olesha's whimsical, wistful, perceptive narrating voice. Some of these fragments were published before Olesha's death, in *Literaturnaia Moskva* (1956; 2:721–51) and in a volume of selected works (*Izbrannye sochineniia*, 1956), but Olesha continued producing them until his death in 1960, leaving behind "piles of papers, filled with variants of the book *No Day Without a Line.*"[66]

Selections from the papers were again published, in *Oktiabr'* under the title "Ni dnia bez stroki," in 1961; but it was not until 1965 that *No Day* appeared in book form, having been collected, selected, sorted, and organized into a semblance of wholeness by Olesha's widow, Olga Suok-Olesha, and her brother-in-law, Viktor Shklovsky (with assistance, briefly, from Arkady Belinkov). Mikhail Gromov of Moscow University's Department of Journalism prepared the final copy, which included fragments that had not been previously published but also excluded some that had.[67] Violetta Gudkova has criticized the process of selection that determined the final contents of the book, a process she indicates was less deferential to the author's presumed intent than Shklovsky's tactful accounts imply:

> Apart from the state censorship, there operated the censorship of the editor, which was not so much high-minded as sanctimonious. . . . Everything that shocked the editor, "didn't appeal" to him, or where the editor "did not agree" with the author, was taken out. . . . On the archived pages one encounters annotations such as: "A complicated and strange entry that offers nothing to the reader." Both epithets are characteristic: they looked for the simple and the habitual.[68]

From Gudkova's account it is clear that, while the creators of the 1965 edition followed Olesha's stated intention in gathering his autobiographical fragments into a book, much of the material that Olesha would have preferred to include was omitted.

Completeness aside, how much of the book's structure can be said to be Olesha's? Shklovsky mentions "plans" left by Olesha, but he appears to be referring to passing comments in Olesha's personal correspondence (at least, this is all he quotes) rather than a comprehensive schema. In 1954, Olesha had written to his mother:

> By the way, I am now writing a book of reminiscences—really deeper than reminiscences, but the form of this book is closer to reminiscences than to anything else. Odessa appears in it, with the years of childhood and Gymnasium there. So that I find myself now in the sphere of childhood, and in proximity to you.[69]

The editors have converted this rather vague description into a structural blueprint, emphasizing the themes of "Childhood" and "Odessa" by naming the first two sections of the book after them and organizing the relevant fragments accordingly. (It is surely no coincidence that these two themes are also central ones for both Kataev and Babel.) Thus, fragments dealing with childhood themes and reminiscences appear in the first section, while the "Odessa" section centers on Olesha's time at the Rishelievsky Gymnasium, paralleling the progression of Babel's childhood stories, and emphasizing the importance of "time" and "place," respectively, to Olesha's sense of self. The third section, "Moscow," coincides in time and space with the action of Kataev's *My Diamond Crown*. The final two sections, organized along thematic rather than spatiotemporal lines, take place primarily in the present tense; these contain reflections that coincide with the time of writing, rather than harking back to the past. Part 4, "The Golden Shelf" ("Zolotaia polka"), contains Olesha's comments on works of literature and occasionally on the other arts, taking its title from the fragment placed first in the section, which explains, "The golden shelf is the one on which favorite books are placed" (187). Part 5, "The Wonderful Intersection" ("Udivitel'nyi perekrestok")— also named for a vivid image in its first-placed fragment—contains fragments that are valedictory in tone, focusing on old age, death, and the narrator's reflections on his physical surroundings.

The merits of the structure imposed by Shklovsky and others are several: it follows the few guiding remarks left by the author, it creates a more or less chronological narrative despite the impossibility of determining either the exact chronology of the fragments or the exact order in which they were composed;[70] and it *does* appear to arise organically from the thematics of the fragments themselves, which can by and large be said to fall into the five types represented by the five parts of the finished book, with a sixth type—Olesha's metaliterary reflections on *what* he is writing, and *how*—being scattered throughout the book, but heavily concentrated in the early pages of part 1. As Judson Rosengrant suggests, "the result is not necessarily what Olesha had in mind, and certainly not without its questionable and even careless decisions, [but] it remains a basically cogent alternative."[71] The question arises whether the book as we know it is not in fact rather *too* cogent. By compensating for the "disintegrated" nature of the text as well as it does, creating the illusion of something not entirely unlike a conventional autobiography, the "organic" structure preferred by Olesha's editors distracts the reader from the ways in which Olesha has manifestly suited form to content in *No Day*.

Although Olesha maintains his habitual pose of artistic failure by implying, in one above-quoted fragment, that he writes in *otryvki* because he has lost the ability to produce anything more sustained, another fragment placed on the same page claims a completely different motive:[72]

Contemporary prose items can have a value commensurate with the contemporary psyche only when they are written in one sitting. Reflections or reminiscences in twenty or thirty lines, maximum—that's the contemporary novel.

The epic seems to me neither necessary nor even possible.

Books are now read in short intervals—in the metro, even on its escalators—so why on earth should a book be long? I can't imagine a long-haul reader, one for the whole evening. In the first place there are millions of televisions; in the second, there are newspapers to be read. And so on. (11)

This opinion, perfectly orthodox for a modernist of the 1910s or 1920s but quite remarkably unorthodox by the time it was penned—Socialist Realism was nothing if not "epic" in its ambitions—exemplifies another of Olesha's favorite poses, a quasi-childish political naïveté.[73] No wonder Soviet critics thought Olesha had become somehow stuck in childhood, the victim of a kind of literary retardation brought on, perhaps, by the excessive consumption of fairy tales in extreme youth;[74] Olesha, with his twin poses of naïveté and helplessness, apparently adopted as a defense against the demands of Socialist Realism, invites such a diagnosis. But the diagnosis does not tell the whole story. Rather, Olesha is trying to tell us, the child coexists with the man: all the stages through which the self has passed are present in the memory simultaneously, and this jumble of impressions and attitudes, sometimes—perhaps inevitably—mutually contradictory, make up the substance of the self. Olesha's "autobiographical novel," seemingly devoid of novelistic plot and structure, aims to reproduce the author's concept of the self in textual form.

The Russian novel enjoys a noble tradition of defying generic expectations, beginning famously with Pushkin's "novel in verse," *Eugene Onegin,* and Olesha's "novel in fragments" can be fruitfully seen as a participant in this tradition. We can best understand *No Day Without a Line* not as Olesha's literal attempt "to proceed backwards through my life, as Marcel Proust managed to do in his time" (if judged solely on the success of such a Proustian project, the book manifestly fails, as Beaujour has pointed out),[75] but rather as a book *about a character who wishes to do so.* Indeed, much as *Envy*'s protagonist, Kavalerov, "had many of [Olesha's] traits" and "looked through [Olesha's] eyes," the autobiographical narrator of Olesha's fragmentary novel shares many traits with Kavalerov. Like Kavalerov, he is completely sincere, but also unremittingly subjective, so that his sincerity does not automatically translate into reliability—especially since he literally sees things differently from the people around him. He is especially conscious of the component bits of views: the play of light on a particular surface, the color of a person's hair, the pattern on a cup. (In this we might compare him not only to Kavalerov but to Babel's childhood narrator, whose "small and horrible" world is glimpsed through the slit of one entrail-besmirched eye as he lies with his face pressed into the ground.) Also like Kavalerov, Olesha's autobiographical narrator is a deeply nostalgic character (though not, perhaps, as unguardedly counterrevolutionary as critics eventually discovered Kavalerov to be); his chief concern is to bridge the fathomless gulf between the vividly remembered world of his childhood and the keenly observed world of his adult life as a writer. All these qualities make him both a particularly Oleshan and a particularly Odessan character.

The narrator's main project in *No Day Without a Line* is to capture and reassemble the floating fragments that make up the unitary self, or to put it another way, to solve the mystery of continuous identity. This means tackling the puzzle of memory: how does it work, what does it do, who (that is to say, which of his personae) is present when the writer of today recalls things that happened to the child of yesterday, and can his present-day self remember things of which his bygone self was not aware? In a passage highly reminiscent of the walks that open and close Babel's childhood cycle (see chapter 3), Olesha recalls being escorted by his grandmother to the Rishelievsky Gymnasium:

> My grandmother brought there not a writer, but also a little boy [*ne litera-tora, a tozhe malen'kogo mal'chika*: a nice example of "Odessan" grammar]. He did not see everything that the writer recalls now. Maybe all of that never happened! No, it all did happen! Unquestionably, it was autumn and the leaves were falling . . .
>
> Unquestionably, sailing past me, they creaked at the sides, like ships. And like ships, they described, as they sailed around me, a circle—two or three twists of a spiral—and quietly settled on the asphalt, on the edge where there was already a large quantity of them, a whole perished fleet. Occasionally the breeze would turn some of them to face a different direction . . . No, the boy did see all of this—the writer only recalls it now and draws it out from among other recollections, but it was seen by that very boy whose grandmother had brought him there. (61, ellipses in original)

Olesha thus tackles head-on the central problem of modern autobiography theory, the strained relations between "truth" and "design," *bios* and *gra-phein*, the accidental nature of experience versus the deliberate nature of literary craft. Whereas Babel, as we have seen, offers his readers several models of autobiographical storytelling and challenges us to unpick the paradoxes they generate, Olesha rather neatly solves the problem by offering this central paradox—the seeming contradiction between "truth" (experience) and "design" (story)—as a dialogue between two stages of the self, the "little boy" and the "writer." Both are authentically Olesha, and both are equally necessary to the creation of this fragment of memory. Olesha does not arrange them in a hierarchy with respect to each other, but allows both to emerge as necessary dimensions of the literary self-portrait.

It is precisely in the *moment of remembering* that the narrating subject becomes aware of the distance between these two selves—"little boy" and "writer"—yet, paradoxically, it is precisely the *act of remembering* that yokes them together. When the narrator says "No, it all did happen!" he acknowledges this link: yes, it was I who was present then, I who am present now. Memory, then, emerges as the mechanism by which these serial selves are linked into a single sense of self. But, as we already know, memory is elusive, a point Olesha brings into focus in another fragment:

> The work of memory is astonishing. We remember something for a reason completely unknown to us. Say to yourself, "Now I will remember something from my childhood." Close your eyes and say it. What gets remembered will be something completely unforeseen. The participation of the will is excluded here. A picture lights up, switched on by some kind of engineers behind your consciousness. The devil take it, my will is almost not in me! Rather, it is beside me! How little it influences the whole me! How little place I, the conscious one, I, possessed of desires and a name, occupy in the whole me, which does not possess desires and a name! (14)

Memory, Olesha suggests, rarely does one's bidding; it does not appear to organize its stored information into a logical sequence, and it preserves vivid impressions of things that no longer exist—even, sometimes, of things that never existed. Moreover, since the remembering self is inevitably different (removed in time and space) from the observing self who recorded the original impressions, at least two separate consciousnesses are at work whenever the self looks back on its own history. In fact, it is precisely these characteristics that Olesha takes as the structuring principles of his narrative. The reader of *No Day Without a Line* is forced to experience Olesha's sense of self as Olesha himself experiences it: that is, in a series of vivid, isolated miniatures that the memory produces by an unpredictable method and in an ungovernable order.

Seen from this perspective, the editorial structure imposed on the fragments, with its contemplative frame that announces the project at the beginning and reflects upon it at the end, and with its overall sense of chronological movement from evocations of childhood to end-of-life meditations, appears as something of a disadvantage. The spontaneity and ungovernability of memory would be better represented by a random assortment of fragments. However, while the given structure may impede our apperception of "the work of memory," it holds up a mirror to "the work of reading": that is, it replicates and makes visible the work performed in the mind of the reader, for whom such chronological sorting is an important strategy for penetrating the autobiographical text. Olesha's "autobiographical novel" represents a hybrid of several recognizable novelistic categories, including the *Bildungsroman,* the *Künstlerroman,* and the literary memoir. To navigate among these subgenres and among the shards of Olesha's memory, the reader must maintain an open-ended reading strategy. The editorial structure conflicts productively with this open-endedness as it performs preliminary organizational work on this hybrid text, sorting the fragments roughly into generic categories.

One pleasing result of this organization is the way it invites the reader to trace the narrator's shifting relationship to language and particularly to metaphor, a central feature of Olesha's literary technique.[76] Here, again, we are seeing at work simultaneously the mind of the writer and the mind of the reader—specifically, a reader who is also familiar with Olesha's 1928 story "Liompa," and who, consciously or unconsciously, makes sense of Olesha's autobiography through the lens of that story. As Andrew Barratt has shown, the three characters depicted in "Liompa" represent "three ages of man," each corresponding to a different stage in the human experience of the relationship between language and reality.[77] The youngest of these three symbolic characters, the "rubber boy," experiences *things* but not *words:* "Things rushed to meet him. He smiled at them, not knowing any of them by name."[78] The middle character, "young Alexander" (a "boy" who nevertheless acts "in a perfectly adult way," suggesting a kind of rapprochement between the "little boy" and the "writer" of Olesha's later fragment), is in full possession of both words and things, which are held in firm relationship to each other by means of "blueprints" and "laws" (143). The third figure, Ponomaryov—an old man on the verge of death—has only words, the *things* to which they correspond having abandoned him in the order in which they recede from the zone of his practical experience:

> Every day fewer of these things were left. A familiar object like a railroad ticket was already irretrievably remote. First, the number of things on the periphery, far away from him, decreased; then this depletion grew closer to the center, reaching deeper and deeper, toward the courtyard, the house, the corridor, the room, his heart. . . . Then the disappearances began to occur at a mad rate, right there, alongside him: already the corridor had slipped out of reach and, in his very room, his shoes had lost all meaning. . . . The vanishing things left the dying man only their names. (142–43)

Ponomaryov thus finds himself in the inverse position to that of Babel's narrator at the end of "Awakening," the end of the writer's trajectory rather than the beginning: instead of being tormented by things for which he doesn't know the names, he is tormented by names for which he can no longer access the things.

The process by which the things "disappear" is one of dematerialization, an atrophy of *res* that leaves *verba* intact but bereft of referent: "the flesh of a thing disappeared while the abstraction remained" (144). The world Olesha has depicted is one in which language gradually crowds out reality, as the "writer" supplants the "little boy." The word "Liompa" itself, meaningless to everyone but the old man who utters it (it is the name he bestows, in his morbid delirium, on a rat), and dying with him, comes to stand for this process. The title of the story, it can be understood only after the story is read—by which time it has again been evacuated of meaning, as the only person who knew what it meant is dead.

As Richard Borden has pointed out, the stage of childhood exemplified by the "rubber boy"—one in which he is constantly encountering *things,* but knows only a limited number of *words*—represents the "age of man" in which he is most prolifically producing metaphors: "Basically, children use metaphors to assimilate and describe unfamiliar experience because comparison with [that which] they already know and for which they already have a name is their lone option."[79] Although this seemingly poetic activity actually reflects "not the inventiveness of the child's imagination, but the poverty of his vocabulary,"[80] it represents, as Borden convincingly argues, a significant source of inspiration for Olesha, and the reason that, as critics have frequently noted, Olesha's style is particularly saturated with metaphors that invite the reader to "see the world anew, like a child."[81] The "three ages of man" portrayed in "Liompa," then, represent not only the three stages of the human relationship with language, but also the progress of the inverse relationship between verbal mastery and "poetic" perception. The child perceives metaphorical relationships all over the place, but lacks the verbal mastery to exploit them; as he gains in mastery, the words become more and more firmly attached to their accepted, conventional referents, until at last he is left with words that are useless, since they cannot be divorced from their corresponding objects, and the actual objects that fall within his purview grow fewer and fewer. Violetta Gudkova reports an intriguing remark supposedly made by Olesha to an acquaintance while riding in an elevator, again underscoring this inverse relationship between linguistic mastery and poetic production: "I didn't know how to write, and it got written; today I know how, and it doesn't get written!"[82]

No Day Without a Line, as organized by its 1965 editors, stages the same progression, from effortless metaphor in the early, "Childhood" fragments—"the barber waited all in white, like a wafer"(19)—to painstaking, literal description in the later, present-tense ones:

A duck tips its head forward into the water—do we notice how humorous and charming that motion is, do we laugh aloud, do we glance around to see what's going on with the duck?

She's not there! Where is she? She's swimming underwater. . . . wait, she'll surface presently! She has surfaced, flinging away with a motion of her head such a spray of sparkling drops that it's even hard to find a metaphor for them. (301–2)

These suggestive examples, moreover, reveal more than just the writer's shifting relationship to language; they also say something about the nature of memory. Olesha's narrator, though "old," accesses the childish ease of metaphor through the mechanism of memory; his project, in fact, is largely concerned with using memory as a means to unite the linguistic mastery (and independence from "things") of old age with the metaphorical perception of childhood.

ODESSAN COLOR IN *NO DAY WITHOUT A LINE*

Leonid Rzhevsky, writing of the "mutual influence, or rather, mutual belonging" among what he calls the Odessan "pleiad," singles out two salient characteristics of their writing:

(1) the generosity and emotionalism of the colors;
(2) the attitude of the author toward the object of his narration—irony, a half-smile, more rarely pathos—which so often determines the stylistic key.[83]

Although Rzhevsky abstracts these characteristics from a consideration of Babel's prose, they are equally—if not more—applicable to Olesha, whose most famous "autobiographical" narrator-character, Kavalerov, maintains what Party-line critics would come to consider a reprehensibly ironic attitude toward the New Soviet Men around him, and whose own depiction of that same Kavalerov could fairly be described as combining "a half-smile" with genuine pathos. Olesha's sensitivity to color, a subset of his general preoccupation with visual perception, is also striking—deliberately so, as his apologetics for "the colors of my youth" at the First Congress of Soviet Writers makes clear. In the same speech, it is colors that form the basis of his affinity with Kavalerov: "Kavalerov's colors . . . were mine. And they were the freshest, the brightest colors I have ever seen." Colors also provide the basis of Olesha's hoped-for relationship with the new Soviet reader, whom he imagines asking: "Who are you? What colors do you see?"

In naming "generosity and emotionalism of colors" as a feature of Odessan prose, Rzhevsky had in mind not only the brilliance of the literal colors described, but the vividness of the (generally metaphorical) language used to evoke them: among the examples he cites are Bagritsky's watermelons, Vera Inber's "sea the color of raging amethyst," Paustovsky's "knees like medium-sized yellow pumpkins," and Babel's "severed fingers, from [which] there dangled ribbons of black cheesecloth."[84] Rzhevsky does not mention Olesha, but as Victor Peppard observes, Olesha's texts are distinguished by a vivid color scheme explicitly associated with Odessa, but present also in his other works: "Even in the works such as *Envy,* whose setting is clearly not Odessa, there is an unmistakable Odessan subtext that manifests itself in their sunny landscapes of green and blue."[85] Likewise in *No Day,* particularly in fragments containing reminiscences about Odessa, the dominant colors are vegetal green, marine and empyrean blues, and solar yellow.

The one color conspicuously missing from Olesha's Odessa palette is the red that Babel associates with robust Russianness—the red also of triumphant Bolshevism and of the Soviet flag. If "the colors of [Olesha's] youth" were to be considered "vulgar and worthless," even suspect, by Soviet readers, it is hard to avoid the conclusion that this was because there was no proper Socialist red among them. In the section of *No Day Without a Line* entitled "Odessa," only one fragment dwells on the color red with anything like the attention lavished on the yellow, green, and blue areas of the spectrum:

> Of all colors, the most beautiful is carmine. Both its name and its color are lovely. Why is it called "carmine"? Aren't they some sort of mollusc? What could be more pleasant than holding in your hand a brush that had just been dipped in carmine! And now it begins to lie down on the Alexandrine paper, giving birth to the petal of a poppy—a little tongue, almost swaying on the paper, as if in the breeze . . .
>
> Right now only one thing interests me—learning to write much and freely. Let it be about carmine or about poppies, let it be about . . .
>
> Let it be a story about the drawing class at the Gymnasium, when, sitting in the assembly hall, we drew a stuffed hawk from life. (85, ellipses in original)

The fragment goes on for four more paragraphs, but, despite Olesha's exhortations in the second paragraph, neither carmine nor poppies, nor anything remotely red, ever actually materializes. The event Olesha gets around to describing, concerning the art teacher's approbation of one Kolya Danchov, bears no apparent relation to the rhapsody about carmine that precedes it, leaving the latter to appear sterile, its potential never realized. A later fragment about scarlet fever hints at downright sinister associations: Olesha writes, "The very sound 'scarla' made me tremble" (93).

Like Babel's childhood, Olesha's is frequently tinted with yellow, but whereas Babel associates yellow with the stifling, cultured, restricted indoor sphere of his grandmother and her ambitions for him, Olesha associates it exuberantly with nature and spontaneity. The golden yellow of the sun suffuses Olesha's happier childhood memories; yellow light gilds solid objects, creating a tangible link between the everyday world and the sun itself:

> By the entrance to the cellar, whither the sun still reached, worked a carpenter. It's very important that it was precisely the sun: the shavings turned gold in it. And how strong always is the bond between them and the sun! How lovingly it treats the shavings! Sometimes, when you're not looking at them, but distracted by the conversation, it will suddenly seem that a nymph has appeared, right there next to the workbench!
>
> I don't remember what the carpenter was working on. . . . His rule flew up from time to time, also yellow, yellow like matches, like a soldier, like the sun . . .
>
> While working in the basement, the carpenter made for me something like a model of an army rifle—or rather, its outline cut from white, slightly yellowish, pine wood. It's difficult for me to describe the delight that seized me when I took that object in my hands for the first time. (37–38, second ellipsis in original)

Another fragment establishes a similar fusion of light with its environment, this time taking the form of a synesthetic relationship between sight and smell:

> The yard smelled of rosin. . . . That smell was yellow, as the sun lying on the stones of the yard and the bricks of the wall was yellow—yes, yes, a yellow sunny smell. Around the yard walked languid Vitya Koyfman with plump lips, with untanned, pleasantly pale face.
>
> Later we scrambled up a ladder at the risk of falling and saw, through doors temporarily cut in the wall of the outbuilding that was going up, the interior of an already finished room, also bathed in the yellow of the sun (40).

The sun is a particularly important image in *No Day Without a Line*, uniting the halcyon atmosphere of the narrator's remembered childhood, the warmth of the spring-summer landscapes in which most of his fictions are set, and the metaphorical radiance of poetic inspiration.[86] This all-integrating radiance may be seen as the source of the metaphorical light "switched on by some kind of engineers behind your consciousness," in the earlier fragment on "the work of memory." Shklovsky's edition of the text ends with a triumphant vision of it:

> Obviously, at my every step since entering the world, I have been governed by an external medium; obviously, the sun, which holds me on a wire, on a string, and moves me, and serves as my eternal charging station.
>
> It emerges in the form of a dimly shining circle visible through a diffuse but nearly impenetrable barrier of cloud—just barely emerges, and look, shadows are visible on the stone. Scarcely distinguishable, but all the same I see on the pavement my shadow, the shadow of the gate, and most important, even the shadow of some spring catkins hanging from a tree.
>
> What is it then, the sun? Nothing in my human life would have taken place without the participation of the sun, be it concrete or hidden, real or metaphoric. Whatever I have done, wherever I have gone, whether dreaming, waking, in darkness, young, or old, I have always been at the tip of a sunbeam. (303)

This passage, enormously rich in poetic significance, seems to transform Olesha himself into one of the irridescent light-reflecting objects that have drawn critical attention in his fiction. It also presents, as Beaujour remarks, "a typically romantic image . . . of poetic election," even as it makes "an admission of dependence on some external force,"[87] thus capturing simultaneously Olesha's claim to a specialized and important poetic vision and his pose of childish helplessness.

But the sun Olesha invokes is not only abstract and metaphoric, it is also a "concrete" and "real" sun—the warm, yellow (or as Bagritsky would have it, "thick, big") sun of Odessa. Borden notes that "the sun is one of Olesha's most significant, recurrent images and symbols," "nearly always . . . associated with moments of happiness, of grace, of the sensation of life's richness, of beauty, of fulfillment."[88] He argues that the source of the sun, as well as "all of the perspectives and central images of Olesha's work," is childhood itself, and *No Day Without a Line* certainly provides plenty of support for this claim.[89] But Olesha's childhood was spent in Odessa, and in reading the paragraph that concludes the 1965 edition of *No Day*, one cannot help but think of Babel's "Odessa" essay and the "joyful, clear description of the sun" he promises will come from "the sun-washed steppes, lapped by the sea"— the "fruitful bright sun of Gogol," resurrected and restored by his South-Western inheritors. Kataev would respond to Olesha's paean to the sun by concluding his own "fragmented life" with a solar eclipse, symbolizing the death of his childhood, of the pre-Revolutionary Russian state, and of the "golden age" chronicled over the course of the book.[90] Kataev—who also used the word "eclipse" (*zatmenie*) to describe the decline of Olesha's career after the 1920s—seems to suggest that the "joyful, bright depiction of the sun" promised by the Odessan invasion of Russian literature was destined to fall dark in the post-Revolutionary literary landscape, an attitude echoed by Babel in the title and action of his 1927 play *Sunset*. But Olesha, committed to "the colors of my youth [and] the freshness of my vision," stubbornly continues to uphold that yellow sun.

STORIES THAT COME TRUE

Olesha is in some ways the one of the Odessa writers who is most visibly fascinated with the borderland between truth, particularly autobiographical truth, and fiction. Part 2 of *Envy* opens with a selection of Ivan Babichev's autobiographical reminiscences, centering on his wonderful inventions—inventions whose reality or otherwise is left deliberately ambiguous. The first of these is a machine designed to induce dreams to order:

> "Fine," said [Ivan's] father, who was a school principal and a classicist. "I believe you. I want a dream about the history of Rome."
>
> "What specifically?" the boy asked, businesslike.
>
> "Anything—the Battle of Pharsalus. But if it doesn't work, you will be spanked."[91]

As it turns out, the machine indeed "doesn't work," and the boy Ivan is duly spanked. But then the plot thickens. Later that same day, the housemaid Frosia confides to Ivan's mother: "All night I kept seeing horses. Galloping. Horrible horses, wearing masks. Horses in a dream mean lies" (59). It seems that Frosia has intercepted the dream meant for Ivan's father. Even more intriguingly, she interprets the dream as "true" (that is, having a direct bearing on real life); it reveals to her the "truth" that someone has been telling lies. But whose are the lies? Frosia's fiancé's, as she surmises? Ivan's, in pretending to be able to control dreams? Or his father's, in pretending that the machine didn't work? Perhaps, as the adult Ivan later suggests, *history itself* turns out to be a lie, exposed by his dream machine:

> "I believe," [Ivan] went on, "that the night after that humiliating day, my papa *did* dream of the Battle of Pharsalus. In the morning he didn't leave for school. Mother took a glass of mineral water to his study. Possibly he was shocked by some of the details of the battle. Perhaps the dream made a farce of his idea of history and he couldn't get over it. Possible the battle was de-

cided, in his dream, by Balearic slingshot men who landed from balloons . . ."
(61, ellipsis in original)

Balloons provide the connection to young Ivan's second invention, "a special soapy solution and a special little tube with which to blow an amazing soap bubble," which bubble the young inventor brags will attain the proportions of a hot-air balloon before exploding and "fall[ing] in a golden rain on the city" (60). Again, the boy's father is convinced that this is a tall tale; his astonishment therefore knows no bounds when, shortly before dusk, he observes a "large orange sphere" floating slowly across the sky, apparently at Ivan's behest. Taking pity on his father, who is now completely spooked, Ivan reveals his prior knowledge of the fact that "Ernesto Vitollo was scheduled to fly over the city in a balloon that day." In other words, his bubble invention was a hoax. But here the third-person narrator chimes in, in confidential parentheses:

(It is a fact that, at the time Ivan was a twelve-year-old schoolboy, manned flight was not very common and it was rather unlikely that a flight be staged over a provincial city. Whether this story was true or not does not matter. Fantasy is the beloved of reason.) (61)

This leaves the reader to work out the following chain of reasoning: (1) Ivan told a story about a magnificent-bubble-blowing invention; (2) he falsely substantiated his story by appropriating a manned balloon flight as his "bubble"; but (3) according to history, the story of the manned balloon flight is equally false. What then did Ivan's father see? Is it possible that, like the dream machine, the bubble contraption is not a hoax after all? Ivan's inventions work like Shoyl's lies, Babel's "improvisations," and Bagritsky's Dionysus poem: positing themselves at first as fanciful fictions, a metaphorical parallel to the inventive fictions of Olesha himself, they proceed to "substantiate" themselves in subsequent plot events. The interventions of the third-person narrator, offered as if in clarification, serve only to increase the confusion, adding further layers of (potential) truth and (potential) mendacity: it is possible (4) that not just the inventions but the entire story is a lie, just a yarn the grown-up Ivan is spinning to his friends in a bar; but (5) it ultimately "doesn't matter" whether or not the story is true.

Ivan, of course, is a fictional character, and his games with truth and lying can extend only as far as the boundaries of the text that contains him. In *No Day Without a Line*, however, Olesha becomes fascinated with a "real-life" Ivan Babichev: Dante Alighieri, whose "autobiography" includes fantastic adventures in Hell, Purgatory, and Heaven, as well as encounters with a variety of celebrated persons living, dead, and fictional. "Let us remember," writes Olesha, almost seeming to believe in the journey,

> Dante descends to Hell while living, not in the capacity of a ghost but specifically living, as the same person he was at the threshold of Hell, on Earth. All the rest are shades; Dante is a human being. (190)

Olesha is particularly taken by a passage in canto 21 in which Dante and Virgil are stymied by the absence of a bridge Virgil had expected to use:

> It ought to be right here, this bridge. The bridge, however, is not there. Maybe the wrong direction had been taken from the very beginning? The picket of demons—simply a dastardly, drunken band—turns up again and again.
> "Is there a bridge somewhere around here?" asks Virgil.
> "There is!" answers one of the demons. . . . "There is a bridge! There is! It's over there! Go that way!"
> The bridge is not over there either (it has been destroyed altogether), but the demons want to instill a panic in both travelers, to turn them aside from their path once and for all. (190–91)

The episode that so beguiles Olesha is one in which three different kinds of story are united: Dante's rich fantasy, of which Olesha justly stands in awe; Dante's autobiographical narrative, which on the face of it purports to be a record of real, if rather extraordinary, experiences that Dante has had (it is worth bearing in mind here Dante's appeal to the Muses to aid his verses "that my tale not be divergent from the fact");[92] and Christian doctrine, a different kind of "true" story. It is the latter—specifically, the story of Christ's descent to and "Harrowing" of Hell, on the Saturday in between the Crucifixion and the Resurrection—that turns out to be responsible for the missing bridge. In Olesha's summation:

> I don't have the book handy, and I can't recall how the adventure ends . . . I'll only mention the extraordinary reason invented by the author to explain why there turned out to be no bridge. It fell down during the earthquake that took place in hell when Christ descended there!
> What power of authenticity!
> It's not surprising that, meeting Dante on the streets of Florence, passersby would recoil in holy terror:
> "Oh, my God, he was in hell!" (191)

141

What impresses Olesha is not (as Rosengrant's translation would have it) Dante's "power of invention,"[93] but precisely his power of *authenticity*, the same word that Babel takes as his motto in *A Time of Great Expectations*.[94] Dante may, like Babel, be "improvising," but he creates something so "authentic" that, like Babel's childhood stories and Kataev's Mauvist works, it breaks the bounds of its fiction and obtrudes upon real life: Dante's readers, represented here by the nervous Florentines, emerge with the conviction that he has really been to Hell—that his tale is indeed "not divergent from the fact." (Of course, the encounter between Dante and his Florentine readers is itself a fiction, since as far as is known, Dante never returned to Florence after his exile in 1302! Like the "rational explanation"—a manned balloon flight—for the wondrous bubble seen by Ivan's father in *Envy*, this supposedly authenticating image of the credulous contemporary readers proves to be itself incredible, thus completing the Cretan paradox and confounding the reader's efforts to distinguish "truth" and "fiction" once again.) Thus, in the pages of Olesha's "autobiographical novel," Dante becomes the very model of an Odessan modernist; his marriage of the autobiographical pact with virtuosic flights of imagination may be seen as a blueprint for the literary discourse practiced by Olesha and his fellow Odessans.

The Odessan Self

IN THE PRECEDING pages, I have posited that the literary projection of a specifically Odessan self-consciousness is characterized by several interrelated discursive features: paradox, multivocality, and carnivalesque inversion; a sense of exile in both time and space, often manifested in the narrator's positioning of himself as an outsider in the world he depicts; a roguish manipulation of the distinctions between autobiographical and fictional narrative; and a preoccupation with stories (often, "lies") that come true, and their inverse, "truths that become stories."

I refer above to a "blurring of distinctions" between autobiography and fiction—or as Shklovsky would have it, "literature" and "memoirs"—but it is perhaps more accurate to say that the already vague boundaries separating those two narrative modes are cannily exploited by the Odessa writers, often on several levels at once. When Babel's "autobiographical" narrator pits his own credibility against that of an autobiographical narrator he has invented—Great-Uncle Shoyl—the immediate effect is to place the main narrator above Shoyl in the epistemological hierarchy, as someone whose story is "more true" than the ones Shoyl tells. When, however, Shoyl's allegedly mendacious stories are independently verified by another character, they become more "true" within the world of the narrative, while the narrator's claims become more suspect. Meanwhile, outside the world of the narrative, Babel's adoption of the autobiographical mode to tell stories in which he blandly breaches the autobiographical pact creates an additional contradiction; his quasi-autobiographical stories become "true" in the sense that they invite credence from the reader, taking a place (albeit under false pretenses) in the popular perception of Babel's "real life."

Similar translations between the world of fiction and the world of memoir take place when Paustovsky's "real life" is invaded by a story, in the guise of Sashka the fiddler from Kuprin's "Gambrinus"; when Kataev, standing before the grotto of Dionysus, sees a Bagritsky poem come to life before his eyes, creating the effect of an experience that *postdates* his "memory" of it; or when Olesha cites an apocryphal Florentine reader's response to

Dante's "autobiographical" account of Hell. In each of these examples, and the many others cited in the foregoing chapters, what is at stake is the difference between "authenticity" and "invention"; the two categories almost never emerge intact, instead metamorphosing into each other when the reader least expects it. The borderlands between autobiography and fiction prove, for the Odessan writers, a particularly fruitful playground in which to explore, and subvert, this dichotomy.

If the most striking feature of Odessan self-narrative is its love of paradox, its second most striking feature is its collaborative effect. As Arkady Lvov puts it, Paustovsky served as Babel's "apostle and author of an apocrypha" about him, a role which not incidentally increased Paustovsky's own standing, since "that apocrypha, *A Time of Great Expectations,* the fourth book, proved the most widely read portion of his *Story of a Life.*"[1] This apostolizing on Paustovsky's part helped cement a canonical conception of "Odessa" or "South-West" literature that had been put in place by Babel and Shklovsky, forcing a resentful Kataev (at least in Lvov's account) to choose between conforming to the canonical lore about the Odessa school, or deviating from it and being accused of "lying," "heresy," and even "vampirism." *Plus ça change, plus c'est la même chose:* freed from the more extreme constraints of Socialist Realism, Kataev found himself battling a separate orthodoxy. At the same time, it is his deviation from that orthodoxy that accounts for much of the pungency of *My Diamond Crown;* paradoxically, it is in violating the boundaries of received truths about the "Odessa school" that Kataev shows himself most Odessan. The paradox of the narrative that is at once fictional and mendacious is a central interest of all four authors I have examined in this study.

These two essential qualities in the narratives I have examined—their play with fiction and truth, and their mutually interactive character—can be seen as related: what is at stake is a narrative breaking of bounds. Whether or not they would have conceded it, these authors share an interest in stories that break free of their generic and epistemological territory and invade other spaces: other narratives, other people's books, the "real world." For each of the authors analyzed in this study—Babel, Paustovsky, Olesha, and Kataev—my main goal has been to describe the strategies they use to negotiate (and breach) the nebulous boundaries dividing fiction and autobiography, "literature" and "memoirs," "invention" and "authenticity," and in so doing, to arrive at a conception of what it means, in literary terms, to be an "Odessan self." Finally, as I have sought to show, the "self" served as the canvas on which Odessan writers created the colorful, inventive, sunny, and ironic literature that, by virtue of its entwinement with their collective identity, came to be identified with Odessa in the minds of the reading public.

The invention of themselves as a literary school and, more importantly, as an emblem of Odessan identity, encompassing the roguery, playfulness, and resistance to the laws of logic, physics, and official aesthetics alike that characterized that identity, is the lasting accomplishment of the Odessa writers—the ultimate "story that came true." Through a combination of "lying," "bad writing," and literary sleight of hand, these literary rogues succeeded in creating a looking-glass image of themselves and their milieu that allows the reader both "to see them where they are not" and to "discover their absence from the place where they are." Their literary heterotopia stands as one of the most puzzling, and most pleasing, virtual monuments of Soviet-era literature.

Notes

INTRODUCTION

1. Vladimir Toporov writes: "The text enters along with other facts into the plural quantity [*mnozhestvo*] understood as space, and the space together with other kinds of texts forms the plural quantity understood as the text." V. N. Toporov, "Prostranstvo i tekst," in *Tekst: Semantika i struktura,* ed. T. V. Tsiv'ian (Moscow: Nauka, 1983), 227.

2. Iu. M. Lotman, "Simvolika Peterburga i problemy semiotiki goroda," in *Semiotika goroda i gorodskoi kul'tury: Peterburg* (Tartu: Uchenye zapiski tartuskogo gorodskogo universiteta, 1984), 35.

3. Julie A. Buckler, *Mapping St. Petersburg: Imperial Text and Cityshape* (Princeton: Princeton University Press, 2004), 1, 5, my italics. I follow Buckler's lead in expanding Toporov's notion of the "city text" to comprehend not only an agreed-upon canon of works belonging to "high" literature but also "cultural and literary history, social and political thought, biography, autobiography, memoir, and oral lore" (Buckler, 25).

4. I. E. Babel, *Sochineniia* (Moscow: Khudozhestvennaia literatura, 1990), 1:64. I will analyze this text in detail in chapter 1.

5. V. N. Toporov, "Peterburg i 'peterburgskii tekst' russkoi literatury," in *Semiotika goroda i gorodskoi kul'tury,* 11.

6. Vladimir Jabotinsky, "Memoirs by My Typewriter," in *The Golden Tradition: Jewish Life and Thought in Eastern Europe,* ed. Lucy S. Dawidowicz (Syracuse, N.Y.: Syracuse University Press, 1996), 397.

7. Michael Riffaterre, *Fictional Truth* (Washington: Johns Hopkins University Press, 1990), 1.

8. Philippe Lejeune, "Qu'est-ce que le Pacte Autobiographique?," 2006, published online at http://www.autopacte.org/pacte_autobiographique.html. In this essay, Lejeune concisely summarizes the arguments advanced in his seminal work on autobiography, *Le Pacte autobiographique* (Paris: Seuil, 1975).

9. Quoted in J. D. Clayton, *Ice and Flame: Aleksandr Pushkin's "Eugene Onegin"* (Toronto: University of Toronto Press, 1985), 18.

10. Elizabeth Klosty Beaujour, *The Invisible Land: A Study of the Artistic Imagination of Iurii Olesha* (New York: Columbia University Press, 1970), 4.

11. V. B. Shklovskii, "Iugo-zapad," *Literaturnaia gazeta*, no. 1 (Jan. 5, 1933); reprinted in *Gamburgskii schet: Stat'i—vospominaniia—esse (1914–1933)* (Moscow: Sovetskii pisatel', 1990), 470–75 (this quotation, p. 475). The article takes its name from Bagritskii's 1928 collection of verses.

12. More detailed attention will be paid to the interrelationship of "autobiographicity" and the critical reception of the Odessa school in chapter 2.

13. E. Karakina, *Po sledam "Iugo-Zapada"* (Novosibirsk: Svinin i synovia, 2006), 53, my italics.

14. See Petr Ershov, "Odesskaia literaturnaia kolybel'," *Opyty* 8 (New York, 1957): 93–106.

15. As later chapters will show, it is a dangerous business to take Babel at his word; I remain skeptical about these alleged French juvenilia, which as far as I know have never surfaced (he claims them in "Avtobiografiia," in *Sochineniia* 1:31–32). His Hebrew and Yiddish credentials are confirmed by Efraim Sicher in *Jews in Russian Literature After the Revolution* (Cambridge, Eng.: Cambridge University Press, 1995):

> Babel's grandparents spoke Yiddish, and his parents also knew Yiddish, but they talked with their children in Russian. This is a familiar pattern of acculturation in a fairly assimilated middle-class Jewish family that was urbanized and aspired to social mobility. Isaak Babel was nevertheless and quite naturally tutored at home in Hebrew, Yiddish, the Bible and Talmud. . . . Babel, though brought up speaking Russian, had a command of Yiddish as well as some knowledge of Hebrew. (74)

Regarding Olesha, it seems clear from his autobiographical writings (discussed in detail in chapter 4) that Polish was his first language, though his competence in it may not have progressed past childhood. In *No Day Without a Line,* Olesha recalls that the first book he ever read was "probably one in Polish called *Baśnie ludowe* (Folk Tales)," and consoles himself for his difficulty completing a sentence "with the fact that I'm a Pole and that Russian is, after all, alien to me and not my native tongue." While the latter pronouncement must be at least partly tongue-in-cheek, Judson Rosengrant concurs with my conclusion that Olesha's Russian "seems to have [been] learned on a substratum of childhood Polish." Olesha, *No Day Without a Line,* trans., ed., and intro. Judson Rosengrant (Ann Arbor, Mich.: Ardis, 1979), 28–29, vii.

16. Maxim Shrayer asserts that "by writing in Russian, a Jew becomes a Russian," in *Russian Poet/Soviet Jew: The Legacy of Eduard Bagritskii* (Lanham, Md.: Rowman and Littlefield, 2000), 1. For a parallel discussion of the motives that led S. Y. Abramovitsh and others to select Yiddish as their language of composition, see Dan Miron, *A Traveller Disguised* (reprint; Syracuse, N.Y.: Syracuse University Press, 1996), chaps. 1 and 2.

17. See, e.g., L. I. Skorino, *Pisatel' i ego vremia: Zhizn i tvorchestvo V. P. Kataeva* (Moscow: Sovetskii pisatel', 1965), chap. 1. Skorino goes into some detail regarding the reading materials supplied to Kataev by his parents during his formative years. They included works by Ivan Bunin (a frequent visitor to Odessa and mentor to the young Kataev, although Kataev would later distance himself from certain aspects of Bunin's work), Lermontov, and Tolstoy; more ideologically suspect writers of the tsarist era, such as Dostoevsky, are not mentioned.

18. Richard Borden, *The Art of Writing Badly: Valentin Kataev's Mauvism and the Rebirth of Russian Modernism* (Evanston, Ill.: Northwestern University Press, 2000) 10.

19. These early episodes in the collective life of the Odessans are sketched in Rita Feld, "The Southwestern School of Writers" (Ph.D. dissertation, Georgetown University, 1987), 17–27. Partial accounts are also given in monographs on individual Odessan writers, including Elizabeth Klosty Beaujour's *The Invisible Land: A Study of the Artistic Imagination of Iurii Olesha,* and Maxim Shrayer's *Russian Poet/Soviet Jew: The Legacy of Eduard Bagritskii* (see bibliography).

20. See below, chapters 2 and 3.

21. Shklovskii, "Iugo-zapad," *Gamburgskii schet,* 470. Subsequent page references for this work will be given in parentheses in the text.

22. On the general significance of this geopolitical terminology, see Alexei Miller, "A Testament of the All-Russian Idea," in *Extending the Borders of Russian History: Essays in Honor of Alfred J. Rieber,* ed. Marsha Siefert (Budapest: Central European University Press, 2003), 233–44, esp. 233–34. For its literary application, see Taras Kosnarsky, "Three Novels, Three Cities," in *Modernism in Kyiv: Jubilant Experimentation,* ed. Irena R. Makaryk and Virlana Tkacz (Toronto: University of Toronto Press, 2010), 98–137, esp. 107–8. I am indebted to Taras Kosnarsky as well for providing invaluable comments on this section of the manuscript, and prodding me to consider in more detail the implications of the term "South-West."

23. For further discussion of Odessa's "demotic" character, see my article "From 'Underground' to 'In the Basement': How Odessa Replaced St. Petersburg as Capital of the Russian Literary Imagination," in *American Contributions to the 14th International Congress of Slavists, Ohrid, September 2008,* vol. 2, ed. David M. Bethea (Bloomington, Ind.: Slavica), 203–16, esp. 204.

24. Politically speaking, Shklovsky's project in "South-West" was doomed from the start. As Gregory Freidin puts it, in an essay explaining why Babel eventually turned away from the "Odessa" theme: "In 1918, the road to Russia's future [had] swung to the east and from then on ran through the new capital, Moscow." Freidin, "Two Babels—Two Aphrodites: Autobiography in *Maria* and Babel's Petersburg Myth," in *The Enigma of Isaac Babel,* ed. Gregory Freidin (Stanford, Calif.: Stanford University Press, 2009), 19.

25. M. L. Slonimskii, letter to Lev Lunts, Nov. 2, 1923; cited in Shklovskii, *Gamburgskii schet,* 538 (*Primechaniia*).

26. I. Makar'ev, "O 'zapadnikakh' i 'pochvennikakh,'" *Izvestiia,* Feb. 8, 1933, quoted in Shklovskii, *Gamburgskii schet,* 538–39 (*Primechaniia*).

27. Shklovskii, *Gamburgskii schet,* 540 (*Primechaniia*).

28. See, e.g., Cukierman, "The Odessa School of Writers," and Feld, "The Southwestern School of Writers." A distinct Odessophilia is also a feature of these two foundational studies in English.

CHAPTER ONE

1. Quoted in Roshanna P. Sylvester, *Tales of Old Odessa: Crime and Civility in a City of Thieves* (De Kalb: Northern Illinois University Press, 2005), 48.

2. Ibid., 49.

3. Ibid., 49.

4. Michel Foucault, "Of Other Spaces," *Diacritics* 16 (Spring 1986): 24. My emphasis.

5. Ibid., 24–25.

6. Tanya Richardson, *Kaleidoscopic Odessa: History and Place in Contemporary Ukraine* (Toronto: University of Toronto Press, 2008), 171–72, 187–88. Richardson's title takes its inspiration from a metaphor I employ later in this chapter; in appropriately "looking-glass"-ish fashion, this chapter now takes some of its inspiration from Richardson's book.

7. Robert Weinberg, *The Revolution of 1905 in Odessa: Blood on the Steps* (Bloomington: Indiana University Press, 1993), 13.

8. Leonard Prager, "Er lebt vi got in frankraych," *The Mendele Review: Yiddish Literature & Language,* Vol. 04.016 (Dec. 12, 2000), accessed April 20, 2010, http://yiddish.haifa.ac.il/tmr/tmr04/tmr04016.htm.

9. Sholem Aleichem, *The Letters of Menachem-Mendl & Sheyne-Sheyndl,* trans. Hillel Halkin (New Haven, Conn.: Yale University Press, 2002), 11. The "voice" in this excerpt belongs not to Aleichem himself but to Menachem-Mendl, whose letters to and from his wife make up the content of this epistolary novel.

10. Jarrod Tanny, "The Many Ends of Old Odessa: Memories of the Gilded Age in Russia's City of Sin," transcript of talk delivered at the Berkeley Program in Soviet and Post-Soviet Studies, 2007, accessed April 20, 2010, http://www.escholarship.org/uc/item/2p3674pw, 18–19.

11. Feld, "The Southwestern School," 7; Weinberg, *The Revolution of 1905 in Odessa,* 7. Simon Sebag Montefiore describes the capture of the Turkish fortress Hadjibey and the subsequent establishment of Odessa on that site in *Prince of Princes: The Life of Potemkin* (London: Weidenfeld and Nicholson, 2000), 278, 426.

12. Richardson notes, "Russia's borders with Poland, the Ottoman Empire, and the Crimean Khanate changed a total of six times in the period 1772–1795

as a result of wars and annexations," and points out that "Odessa's founding was nearly contemporaneous with" these shifts (*Kaleidoscopic Odessa*, 173).

13. A detailed exploration of the role of Italian architects in building the city of Odessa appears in Anna Malkolkin, *The Nineteenth Century in Odessa: One Hundred Years of Italian Culture on the Shores of the Black Sea* (Lewiston: Edwin Mellen, 2007), chap. 1. See also Patricia Herlihy, *Odessa: A History 1794–1914* (Cambridge, Mass.: Harvard University Press, 1987), 133ff., and *Odessa Memories* (Seattle: University of Washington Press, 2003), 12, 94–95.

14. Armand Emmanuel Sophie Septimanie de Vignerot du Plessis, 5th Duc de Richelieu (*gradonachal'nik* of Odessa from 1803 and governor-general of Novorossiia from 1805; resigned both posts to return to France in 1814); succeeded by Count Louis Alexandre Andrault de Langeron (military governor of Kherson and Odessa, commander in chief of the Bug and Black Sea Cossacks, and governor of Yekaterinoslav, Kherson, and Crimea from 1815 until his retirement due to failing health in 1823). See Alexander Mikaberidze, *The Russian Officer Corps of the Revolutionary and Napoleonic Wars: 1792–1815* (New York: Savas Beatie, 2005), 328–29, 218–20.

15. Herlihy, *Odessa: A History,* 317n1. The Odessa Pushkin Museum at No. 13, vul. Pushkinska, houses, among other things, manuscript pages from Pushkin's writings of this period. The Richelieu who appears in *The Queen of Spades* (1833) is Louis François Armand de Vignerot du Plessis, the third Duc de Richelieu (1696–1788) and a famous womanizer. The influence of Byron, and in particular *Don Juan,* on *Eugene Onegin* and Pushkin's works of the "Southern exile" period has been extensively documented by Pushkin scholars including Nabokov, Zhirmunskii, Greenleaf, Bethea, Hoisington, and others.

16. Like Richelieu and Langeron, de Ribas (who joined the Russian Imperial Army as a captain in the Infantry Cadet Corps in 1774) had fought at the siege of Ismail and been awarded a golden sword for his distinguished service in that battle. Mikaberidze, *Russian Officer Corps,* 327–28; Montefiore, *Prince of Princes,* 278.

17. Weinberg, *The Revolution of 1905 in Odessa,* 13. Anna Makolkin, in *A History of Odessa, the Last Italian Black Sea Colony* (Lewiston, N.Y.: Edwin Mellen, 2004), explores in extensive detail the influence of Italian immigrants on the establishment and early history of Odessa.

18. Sarah Johnstone, *Lonely Planet: Ukraine* (Oakland, Calif.: Lonely Planet, 2005), 119. I was able to confirm this charming, though sometimes inconvenient, detail during a research trip to Odessa in 2007.

19. Weinberg, *The Revolution of 1905 in Odessa,* 3–4; see also Herlihy, *Odessa: A History,* 113.

20. Sydney Adamson, "Odessa—The Portal of an Empire," *Harper's Monthly Magazine,* November 1912, 907–13.

21. Walter Vickery, "Odessa—Watershed Year: Patterns in Puškin's Love

Lyrics," in *Puškin Today,* ed. David M. Bethea (Bloomington: Indiana University Press, 1993), 136.

22. See Skorino, *Pisatel' i ego vremia,* chap. 1.

23. Herlihy, *Odessa: A History,* 283; Neil Ascherson, *Black Sea* (New York: Hill and Wang, 1996), 156–57.

24. Weinberg, *The Revolution of 1905 in Odessa,* 63–64.

25. See, e.g., Lionel Trilling's introduction to the 1955 translation of Babel's collected stories, reprinted in Babel, *Collected Stories,* trans. and ed. David McDuff (London: Penguin Books, 1994), 339–64.

26. Isaak Babel', *Detstvo i drugie rasskazy* (Jerusalem: Aliya, 1979), 306.

27. Weinberg, *The Revolution of 1905 in Odessa,* 8.

28. Ibid., 7, 11, 13.

29. Ibid., 11–13.

30. An interesting side question is why the city produced such famous authors in these *three* traditions, and not in the obvious fourth—Ukrainian literature. Partly the problem is just that Ukrainian literature has been neglected relative to Russian literature, for reasons both political and practical (more scholars receive Ph.D.s in Russian than in Ukrainian, which has had to fight for its very status as a language). There *are* Odessa texts in Ukrainian, and part of the permanent exhibition at the Odessa Literary Museum is devoted to the role played by the city in the life and work of selected Ukrainian writers (including Ivan Franko, Lesia Ukrainka, and Mykhailo Kotsiubynskyi). However, as Tanya Richardson documents, "when the exhibits were constructed a certain percentage of Ukrainian material had to be included where available. This illustrates the Soviet cultural policy through which the 'national culture' of a given republic could be represented in the literary narrative of the Soviet Union albeit in a subordinate position. Yet, the most prominent Odessan writers wrote in Russian, and as a result the most evocative and enduring representations of Odessa have been inscribed in Russian rather than Ukrainian texts. Thus, in framing either a Soviet or local narrative of literary history, the Ukrainian material appears deficient and marginal" (Richardson, "Odessa, Ukraine: History, Place and Nation-Building in a Post-Soviet City," Ph.D. dissertation, University of Cambridge, 2004, pp. 124–25).

Moreover, Ukrainian culture has had difficulty claiming the "Russian," "cosmopolitan" Odessa as its own at all; twenty years after the collapse of the Soviet Union, and following a government-imposed Ukrainianization of the whole country, Russian remains the language of everyday life in Odessa. A local joke recounted by Richardson encapsulates Ukrainians' difficulty at gaining cultural purchase on the Russian and Jewish "El Dorado": "Two villagers, Petro and Pavlo, go to Odesa [the Ukrainian spelling of "Odessa"] for a day. When they return, a fellow villager asks Petro: 'Why do you look so happy and Pavlo so dejected?' Petro responds: 'Because he was cheated at the beginning of the day and I only at the end!'" Richardson concludes, "Ukrainians, in other words, are naïve country folk unwise to the cosmopolitan ways of the city. Although by population, ethnic Ukrainians make up a majority of the city's residents, they are often perceived as being foreign to the city" (Richardson, *Kaleidoscopic Odessa*, 197–98).

31. Richard Hallett, *Isaac Babel* (New York: Bradda Letchworth, 1972), 7. Hallett states as an unequivocal fact that between the census of 1892 and the Revolution of 1917, "the number of Jews in Odessa increased from 32.9% to 50% of the total population." This figure deviates from the ones generally cited by historians, however; Herlihy (1986) gives the proportion in 1912 as 32.25 percent (slightly down from the 1897 high of 34.41 percent). While Hallett's claim appears exaggerated, it underlines the general point that Jews in Odessa constituted a numerically consequential, though politically marginalized, group.

32. "Autobiography," in Isaac Babel, *Collected Stories*, trans. and ed. David McDuff (London: Penguin Books, 1994), xi. Where possible, I quote Babel in McDuff's excellently faithful translation; any exceptions are noted. This collection of stories has now been republished by Penguin Classics under the title *Red Cavalry and Other Stories;* the content and pagination of the volume are unchanged.

33. Quoted in Herlihy, *Odessa: A History*, 274.

34. Tanny, "The Many Ends," 8–9; Feld, "The Southwestern School of Writers," 18.

35. S. Rubinshtein, *Odes'ka periodichna presa (1917–1921)* (Odessa, 1929), quoted in Feld, "The Southwestern School of Writers," 22–23; these numbers reflect, more or less, the prevalence of various native languages reported in the 1897 census, of which Herlihy gives a table in *Odessa: A History* (242). Russian was the most widely reported "first language" of Odessans in 1897, with 193,254 speakers (50.78 percent of the population); next came Yiddish (32.50 percent), Ukrainian (5.66 percent), Polish (4.48 percent), German (2.61 percent), and Greek (1.32 percent).

36. See Konstantin Paustovsky, *Years of Hope*, trans. Manya Harari and Andrew Thomson (New York: Pantheon, 1968), 122; and Robert A. Rothstein, "How It Was Sung in Odessa: At the Intersection of Russian and Yiddish Folk Culture," *Slavic Review* 60, no. 4 (2001): 782–85. A substantial local literature exists devoted to the specifics of Odessa Russian; its leading figure is the writer and local historian Valerii Smirnov, whose work is available in numerous formats in the "Kraevedenie" section of most Odessa bookstores and includes *Bol'shoi polutolkovyi slovar' odesskogo iazyka* (2003). Jarrod Tanny's Ph.D. dissertation includes a substantial, and very amusing, discussion of the idiosyncrasies of Odessa Russian (Tanny, "City of Rogues and Schnorrers: The Myth of Old Odessa in Russian and Jewish Culture," Ph.D. dissertation, University of California at Berkeley, 2008, pp. 292–97).

37. Judah Waten, *From Odessa to Odessa: The Journey of an Australian Writer* (Melbourne: Cheshire, 1969), 179.

38. Mark Twain, *The Innocents Abroad; Roughing It* (New York: Library of America, 1984), 306–7.

39. Adamson, "Odessa," 907.

40. Ibid.

41. Adamson, "Odessa," 912. Of course, the "Gogolian" tenor of the official encounter, while quintessentially "Russian" to Adamson, does encode a very oblique reference to an earlier source of Ukrainian exotica in Russian literature. Both Babel (in "Odessa") and Shklovsky (in "South-West") would explicitly reference Gogol as a literary forerunner of the Odessan writers.

42. Boris Briker, "The Underworld of Benia Krik and I. Babel's *Odessa Stories*," *Canadian Slavonic Papers* 36, nos. 1–2 (1994): 115. For an outline of the "city text" theory elaborated by semioticians of the Tartu school, see my "Introduction."

43. Briker, "The Underworld of Benia Krik," 115.

44. David Shneer, "The Path of a Russian Jewish Writer," book review of Maxim Shrayer's *Russian Poet/Soviet Jew,* on "H-Russia," February 2002, archived at http://www2.h-net.msu.edu/reviews/showrev.cgi?path=227510153 44845.

45. Aleksandr Pushkin, *Eugene Onegin,* trans. Vladimir Nabokov, revised ed., vol. 1 (Princeton, N.J.: Princeton University Press, 1965), 331. Ellipsis in original.

46. For a detailed history of the status of "Onegin's Journey" relative to the novel from which it was eventually excluded, see Pushkin, *Eugene Onegin,* trans. Nabokov, vol. 3 (*Commentary*), 254ff.

47. Tanny, "The Many Ends," 5.

48. Eduard Bagritskii, "Vstrecha," reprinted in *Retsepty odesskoi kukhni,* ed. Boris Eidelman (Odessa: Optimum, 2006). For a detailed reading of the sensory world Bagritsky constructs in his poems of this period, see Wendy Rosslyn, "The Path to Paradise: Recurrent Images in the Poetry of Eduard Bagritsky," *Modern Language Review* 71, no. 1 (January 1976): 97–105.

49. A statue on Odessa's Bulvar' Isskustv commemorates this apparently successful gambit.

50. Eidelman, *Retsepty odesskoi kukhni,* 248–49; the quotation beginning the next sentence is from the same volume, p. 227.

51. I. E. Babel', *Sochineniia,* ed. A. Pirozhkova (Moscow: Khudozhestvennaia literatura, 1990), 1:134. Hereafter this edition will be referred to simply as *Sochineniia.*

The writers examined here are not the only Odessans to have left a record of their hunger for local delicacies: Odessa's "Mother-in-Law's Bridge" (*Teshchin most,* erected in 1969) was purportedly built to facilitate the then mayor's access to his mother-in-law's delicious cooking. A modern guidebook notes: "Of course, the mayor, or as he was then called, the First Secretary of the Odessa City Executive Committee, had an official car. But the epithet was witty and has 'stuck' for thirty years to the bridge" (Elena Karakina et al., *Touring Odessa* [Odessa: Baltija Dryk, 2004], 39).

52. Buckler, *Mapping St. Petersburg*, 5–8.

53. Amelia Glaser, "The Marketplace and the Church: Jews, Slavs and the Literature of Exchange, 1829–1929" (Ph.D. dissertation, Stanford University, 2004),

54. Ascherson, *Black Sea*, 156.

55. Pushkin, *Eugene Onegin*, trans. Nabokov, vol. 1 (*Translation*), 331–33.

56. Alexander Pushkin, *Eugene Onegin*, trans. James Falen (Oxford University Press, 1995), 226.

57. K. G. Paustovskii, *Chernoe more: Povest', rasskazy, ocherki, stat'i* (Simferopol': Tavriia, 1973), 101.

58. See Chapters 2 and 3.

59. I. E. Babel', "Odessa," in *Sochineniia*, 1:62.

60. Ibid., 62.

61. Babel', "Odessa," 64. Gabriella Safran, in "Isaak Babel''s El'ia Isaakovich as a New Jewish Type" (*Slavic Review* 61, no. 2 [2002]: 253–72), undertakes a nuanced and persuasive reading of Babel's "Odessa" alongside one of his early stories in order to argue that the "clear description of the sun" for which Babel calls can be read on one level as a metaphor for a more uplifting depiction of the Jews—a depiction Maksim Gorky, who in 1916 had published a philo-Semitic anthology called *The Shield* (*Shchit*) to benefit Jewish causes, is cited as having striven for but failed to attain: his version comes off, according to Babel, as "not quite genuine" (Babel, "Odessa," 65). I tend to think that the sun Babel talks about in this essay is first and foremost a literal one, but it can of course be metaphorical at the same time.

62. Barry Scherr, "Synagogues, Synchrony, and the Sea: Babel''s Odessa," in *And Meaning for a Life Entire: Festschrift for Charles A. Moser on the Occasion of His Sixtieth Birthday*, ed. Peter Rollberg (Columbus: Slavica, 1997), 337–350; this discussion, 340–41.

63. Emma Lieber, "'Woe Unto Us': Gogol, Babel, and the Human Predicament," M.A. thesis, Columbia University, 2005, 4.

64. As Gregory Freidin points out in his essay "Two Babels—Two Aphrodites: Autobiography in *Maria* and Babel's Petersburg Myth," Babel would end up following much the same trajectory he ascribes to Gogol here, abandoning the "sunshine" of Odessa for a newly somber tone in three stories based in Petersburg/Petrograd and published in 1932: "The Road," "The Ivan-and-Maria," and—most ironically of all—"Guy de Maupassant." Freidin writes: "Wearied of his association with Odessa, it seems, Babel wished to appear as

the author of several new *Petersburg* stories." In *The Enigma of Isaac Babel,* ed. Freidin, 28–29.

65. The French tags may also serve as an allusion to the French-sprinkled Russian spoken in Odessa (see above).

66. Babel', "Moi pervyi gus'," in *Sochineniia,* 2:32; translation by David MacDuff in Babel, *Collected Stories* (London: Penguin, 1995), 119. Safran ("Isaak Babel''s El'ia Isaakovich," 264n) connects this androgyny in Babel to Rozanov's theories regarding Jewish male sexuality, specifically its "fecundity and femininity"—which, of course, are traits also associated with the city of Odessa (see above, under "The Odessa Text"). In this context, it is interesting to note that many of the more flamboyantly androgynous passages in Babel's "autobiographical" stories (see chapters 2 and 3) were excised from published versions during the Soviet period.

67. Scherr, "Babel''s Odessa," 341.

68. To clarify, this is my point, not Scherr's. I return to Scherr's argument in the following sentence.

69. Viktor Shklovsky, "Isaac Babel: A Critical Romance," in *Modern Critical Views: Isaac Babel,* ed. Harold Bloom (New York: Chelsea House, 1987), 12. Of Olesha, Shklovsky made a similarly influential pronouncement: "His world is the world of sport and the circus," quoted in Victor Peppard, *The Poetics of Yury Olesha* (Gainesville: University of Florida Press, 1989), 15.

70. Peppard, *The Poetics of Yury Olesha,* especially 76ff.

71. Briker, "Underworld of Benia Krik," 119–22; Sylvester, *Tales of Old Odessa,* 49, 60.

72. See M. B. Iampol'skii, *Babel'/Babel,* written with A. K. Zholkovskii (Moscow: Carte Blanche, 1994), 174.

73. I. Toporkova, ed., *Tsyplenok zharneyi: Blatnye pesni* (Moscow: EKSMO, 2004), 22. In case Odessa's claim to criminal fame was in any doubt, this volume contains numerous songs set in Odessa: see, e.g., 21–22, 35–36, 40, 41–43, 58–59, 101–3, 126–29.

74. Lewis Hyde, *Trickster Makes This World: Mischief, Myth, and Art* (New York: North Point, 1999), 65. Hyde goes on to collapse the distinction between stealing and lying, observing that "a lie is a kind of mental imitation of a theft."

75. Catharine Theimer Nepomnyashchy, *Abram Tertz and the Poetics of Crime* (New Haven, Conn.: Yale University Press, 1995), 1.

76. Mark Lipovetsky, *Charms of the Cynical Reason: The Trickster's Transformations in Soviet and Post-Soviet Culture* (Boston: Academic Studies Press, 2011), 13–14, 42–43, 60. Lipovetsky offers an exhaustive and useful analysis of the significance, and the evolution, of the "trickster" archetype over the course of the Soviet period; while he does not dwell on the Odessa connection, several of the examples he mentions (Olesha's Ivan Babichev, Babel's Benya Krik, and especially Ilf and Petrov's Ostap Bender, the subject of Lipovetsky's third chapter) boast an Odessan pedigree.

77. Nepomnyashchy, *Abram Tertz*, 263 (this is her own translation). Italics in the original. Sinyavsky-Tertz—who continued to use his "Odessan" pseudonym even after emigration—also discusses the thief-writer connection, and the importance of the *blatnaia pesnia* (criminal song) genre closely associated with Odessa as a metaphor for the "criminal" brotherhood of Soviet dissidents, in a 1979 article entitled simply "Fatherland, criminal song . . ." (Abram Tertz, "Otechestvo, blatnaia pesnia . . ." *Sintaksis* 4 [1979]: 72–118).

78. Babel, *Sochineniia*, 2:217.

79. Nepomnyashchy, *Abram Tertz*, 264, my emphasis.

80. These characters appear, respectively, in Babel's *Odessa Tales;* Ilf and Petrov's two novels, *The Twelve Chairs* and *The Golden Calf;* and Olesha's *Envy.*

81. See Safran, "Isaak Babel"s El'ia Isaakovich."

82. I. E. Babel', "Kak eto delalos' v Odesse," in *Sochineniia,* 1:127; translation by McDuff, *Collected Stories,* 244.

83. See Rachel Rubin, *Jewish Gangsters of Modern Literature* (Urbana: University of Illinois Press, 2000). Rubin argues that the authors who wrote of Jewish gangsters, including Babel, can be compared to their protagonists as "rebels 'kneebreaking' their way into the literary canon while continuing to 'do business' with the system." She also sees in the character of the Jewish gangster a fertile terrain for exploring numerous other concerns of early twentieth-century—especially Soviet—literature: sexuality, the role of the vernacular in literature, the place of art within a political economy, and (for Babel and the American Jewish writers she analyzes) the fate of Jewish community in the "new worlds" of the United States and the Soviet Union.

84. David G. Roskies, *The Jewish Search for a Usable Past* (Bloomington: Indiana University Press, 1999), 29, 34; quoted in Rothstein, "How It Was Sung," 795.

85. A. I. Kuprin, "Gambrinus," in *Izbrannoe* (Moscow: Moskovskii rabochii, 1956), 456. My translation.

86. Gorky is quoted in Safran, "Isaak Babel's El'ia Isaakovich," 255.

87. The division, in the works of the Odessans, between "men of action" (to whom revelry and enjoyment are available) and "men of contemplation" (to whom they are not) deserves, and in later chapters will receive, further attention. Kuprin, like his contemporary Chekhov, assigns the role of irretrievably sad outsider to a Jewish protagonist, the fiddler Sashka (whose violin may indeed be a literary descendant of Rothschild's).

88. Rosemary Marangoly George argues, in *The Politics of Home: Post-Colonial Relocations and Twentieth-Century Literature* (Cambridge, U.K.: Cambridge University Press, 1996), that the discursive re-creation of home is a fundamental literary drive.

89. Aleksandr Deribas, *Staraia Odessa: Zabytye stranitsy, istoricheskie ocherki i vospominaniia* (Kiev: Mistetstvo, 2004), 178.

90. Tanny, "The Many Ends"; the quoted sentence is from page 5.

91. Carol J. Avins, *Border Crossings: The West and Russian Identity in Soviet Literature, 1917–1934* (Berkeley and Los Angeles: University of California Press, 1983), 79.

92. Svetlana Boym, *The Future of Nostalgia* (New York: Basic Books, 2001), 264.

93. Carol J. Avins, introduction to Isaac Babel, *1920 Diary*, ed. and trans. Carol Avins (New Haven, Conn.: Yale University Press, 1995), xx.

94. Here I am using, but contextually reinterpreting, the terminology of Claude Lévi-Strauss; see his *The Raw and the Cooked* (New York: Harper and Row, 1975).

95. Another example: in book 4 of the *Iliad*, several lines are devoted to an extended ("Homeric") simile comparing the death of a young soldier, Simoeisios, to the fall of a tree which is subsequently used by a chariot maker as raw material for a wheel. This image also serves as a metaphor for the "wheel" Homer makes from Simoeisios's death, namely the minutely crafted example of ring composition represented by the Simoeisios passage itself (*Iliad* 4:473–89). That Simoeisios is never mentioned again underscores the lesson that it is the "cooking" of the raw material—the carving of a wheel or composition of a lyric passage—that creates meaning and thereby fixes the object in human historical memory. Simoeisios owes his permanence to Homer; being owes its permanence to making.

96. Boym, *The Future of Nostalgia*, 264.

97. Daniel Mendelsohn, "Epic Endeavors," review of three novels by John Banville, David Malouf, and Zachary Mason, *The New Yorker*, April 15, 2010, 78.

98. Homer, *Odyssey*, trans. Richmond Lattimore (New York: Harper and Row, 1967), 177 (11:363–66).

99. On *polutropos*, see Hyde, *Trickster Makes This World*, 52–54.

100. A more detailed analysis of the uses and reception of autobiography by Soviet writers and readers follows in chapter 2.

101. I do not intend here to suggest that creative tinkering with the details of one's personal past is politically or ethically comparable to Socialist Realism. Rather, I wish to propose that the period in which the Odessan writers rose to prominence was one in which formal experimentation coincided with conscious efforts both to remake language (whether from a Formalist, Futurist, proletarian, or some other perspective) and to remake reality through language.

102. See chapters 2 and 4 for more detailed descriptions of these rebuttals.

CHAPTER TWO

1. I. E. Babel', *Sochineniia*, ed. A. Pirozhkova (Moscow: Khudozhestvennaia literatura, 1990), 2:179. Translation by David McDuff, in Isaac Babel, *Collected Stories*, ed. Efraim Sicher, trans. and intro. David McDuff (London:

Penguin, 1995), 49. Here as elsewhere, I have found it difficult to improve on McDuff's translations, which I shall use throughout this chapter except where specifically noted otherwise. Henceforth, page references for these two editions will be given in parentheses in the text, as follows: (2:179/49), where the first reference is to the page number in the 1990 *Sochineniia*, the second to the Penguin translation by McDuff.

2. Lionel Trilling, "Introduction" to Isaac Babel, *Collected Stories*, trans. and ed. Walter Morison (New York: Criterion Books, 1955); reprinted in Babel, *Collected Stories*, ed. Efraim Sicher, trans. David McDuff (London: Penguin, 1995), 351.

3. Philippe Lejeune, "Qu'est-ce que le Pacte Autobiographique?," 2006, published online at http://www.autopacte.org/pacte_autobiographique.html.

4. Michael Riffaterre, *Fictional Truth* (Baltimore: Johns Hopkins University Press, 1990), 1.

5. Ibid., *Fictional Truth*, 1. Riffaterre provides a list of typical "signs" or fictionality markers on 29–30.

6. Renato Poggioli, in his essay "Isaac Babel in Retrospect" in *The Phoenix and the Spider* (Cambridge, Mass.: Harvard University Press, 1957), makes a similar error to Trilling's. Others whom Nathalie Babel chides for their credulousness include Bernard G. Guerney, Marc Slonim, and Olga Andreyev Carlisle (Isaac Babel, *The Lonely Years: 1925–1939*, ed. and intro. Nathalie Babel, trans. Andrew R. MacAndrew and Max Hayward [New York: Farrar, Straus, 1964], x–xi).

7. In order, these quotations are drawn from "In the Basement" (the fourth childhood story), "First Love" (the third), and "Awakening" (the fifth).

8. Nathalie Babel, "Introduction" to Babel, *The Lonely Years*, xiv. See also Cynthia Ozick, "The Year of Writing Dangerously," *New Republic*, May 8, 1995, 31–38. The best biography of Babel in English to date remains Gregory Frei-din's entry on him in *European Writers: The Twentieth Century*, vol. 11, ed. G. Stade (New York: Charles Scribner's Sons, 1990), 1885–1914. A book-length critical biography by Freidin has been in the works for many years and is anxiously awaited. In German, Reinhard Krumm's *Isaak Babel: Eine Biographie* (Norderstedt: Books on Demand GmbH, 2004) is available, but even Krumm (the only one of Babel's many would-be biographers to have finished his book, as far as I am aware) complains of the many lacunae his research proved unable to supply. Reinhard Krumm, "Writing a Biography of Isaac Babel: A Detective's Task" (unpublished conference paper), "The Enigma of Isaac Babel" International Conference, Stanford, Calif., 2004.

9. Patricia Blake, "Researching Babel's Biography: Adventures and Misadventures," in *The Enigma of Isaac Babel*, ed. Freidin, 15.

10. Robert Rosenstone, *King of Odessa* (Evanston, Ill.: Northwestern University Press, 2003); Travis Holland, *The Archivist's Story* (New York: Dial,

2007); Jerome Charyn, *Savage Shorthand: The Life and Death of Isaac Babel* (New York: Random House, 2005).

11. Elif Batuman, *The Possessed: Adventures with Russian Books and the People Who Read Them* (New York: Farrar, Straus, and Giroux 2010), 79.

12. Charyn, *Savage Shorthand*, 39.

13. Ozick, "The Year of Writing Dangerously," 32–35.

14. This quotation and the next one are from Ozick, "The Year of Writing Dangerously," 35.

15. Nathalie Babel, "Introduction" to *The Lonely Years*, xiv–xvi.

16. Frank O'Connor, "The Lonely Voice: A Study of the Short Story," 1962, quoted in Harold Bloom, "A Jew Among the Cossacks," *New York Times Book Review*, June 4, 1995, 13.

17. Babel', *Sochineniia*, 2:456n.

18. First Cavalry Commander Semen Budennyi, "Open Letter to Maxim Gorky," trans. Andrew R. MacAndrew in Babel, *The Lonely Years*, 384–87. The original appeared in *Krasnaia gazeta*, October 26, 1928.

19. Paul de Man, "Autobiography as De-Facement," *Modern Language Notes* 94 (1979): 920.

20. See my "Introduction."

21. Alice Stone Nakhimovsky, *Russian-Jewish Literature and Identity* (Baltimore: Johns Hopkins University Press, 1992), 106. My emphasis.

22. Quoted in Freidin, "Isaac Babel," in *European Writers: The Twentieth Century*, vol. 11, p. 1892. My emphasis.

23. Elizabeth Houston Jones, *Spaces of Belonging: Home, Culture, and Identity in 20th-Century French Autobiography* (Amsterdam: Rodopi, 2007), 96. For a detailed discussion of autofiction, see chapter 2 of Jones's book, "Contemporary Life Writing," especially pages 90–99; and Marie Darrieussecq, "L'autofiction, un genre pas sérieux," *Poétique* 107 (September 1996): 369–80.

24. The division of autobiography theory into "waves" is a useful structuring device employed by Sidonie Smith and Julia Watson in their admirable primer, *Reading Autobiography: A Guide for Interpreting Life Narratives* (Minneapolis: University of Minnesota Press, 2001).

25. De Man, "Autobiography as De-Facement," 920.

26. The presence of a capricious first-person narrator who appears to have a great deal in common with the author—a technique also used by Pushkin's successors, Lermontov and Gogol—also invites the reader to bring an autobiographical lens to bear on the text, although since the main plot deals with clearly fictional third-party characters, the problem is less pronounced than with the other texts I cite in this chapter.

27. For example: M. H. Abrams calls *The Prelude* "a fully developed poetic equivalent of . . . the *Bildungsroman* . . . and the *Künstlerroman*," more or less sidestepping the question of its reflexivity—that is, the identification between

the speaker/narrator and the author. Conversely, W. B. Gallie declares baldly, "[*The Prelude*] is an autobiography; it contains profound reflections on psychology, education and politics; and there are passages of an almost purely lyrical character" (Abrams, "The Design of *The Prelude*," and Gallie, "Is *The Prelude* a Philosophical Poem?" in *The Prelude: 1799, 1805, 1850: A Norton Critical Edition* (New York: W. W. Norton, 1979), 585–98 and 663–78, respectively.

28. See chapter 4.

29. An excellent survey of the Western and Soviet literature on autobiography, 1960–1990, may be found in Jane Gary Harris, "Diversity of Discourse: Autobiographical Statements in Theory and Praxis," introduction to *Autobiographical Statements in Twentieth-Century Russian Literature* (Princeton, N.J.: Princeton University Press, 1990), 3–35. Harris goes into the details of the theory at greater length than I will do here, but manages to compress thirty years of history into as many pages, and to make some thoughtful comparisons.

30. M. M. Bahktin, "Forms of Time and of the Chronotope in the Novel," in *The Dialogic Imagination,* ed. and trans. J. M. Holquist (Austin: University of Texas Press, 1981), 84–258; section on ancient autobiography, 130–40.

31. O. Mandelstam, *Mandelstam: The Complete Critical Prose and Letters,* trans. and ed. Jane Gary Harris (Ann Arbor, Mich.: Ardis, 1979), 200.

32. Cristina Vatulescu, *Police Aesthetics: Literature, Film, and the Secret Police in Soviet Times* (Stanford, Calif.: Stanford University Press, 2010), 40.

33. Ibid., 45, 46.

34. M. Kuznetsov, "Memuarnaia proza," in *Zhanrovo-stilevye iskaniia sovremennoi sovetskoi prozy* (Moscow: Nauka, 1971), 127.

35. Jane Gary Harris offers a number of formulations of this basic duality informing autobiographical discourse: "We . . . must recognize the writer-narrator as a kind of mediator in the continuing dialogue between objective and subjective principles of art, between aesthetic interpretation and authenticity . . . expression and experience, invention and memory." Harris, "Diversity of Discourse," 24.

36. These two responses have been voiced by critics working on a fairly diverse range of texts. For a sampling of the arguments underlying them, see de Man, "De-Facement"; William Spengemann, *The Forms of Autobiography: Episodes in the History of a Literary Genre* (New Haven, Conn.: Yale University Press, 1980); Avrom Fleishman, *Figures of Autobiography: The Language of Self-Writing* (Berkeley: University of California Press, 1983); and Mutlu Konuk Blasing, *The Art of Life: Studies in American Autobiographical Literature* (Austin: University of Texas Press, 1977).

37. Barrett John Mandel, "Full of Life Now," in *Autobiography: Essays Theoretical and Critical,* ed. James Olney (Princeton, N.J.: Princeton University Press, 1980), 58.

38. Lejeune, "Le Pacte Autobiographique"; Elizabeth Bruss, *Autobiographi-*

cal Acts: The Changing Situation of a Literary Genre (Baltimore: Johns Hopkins University Press, 1976).

39. Timothy Dow Adams, *Telling Lies in Modern American Autobiography* (Chapel Hill: University of North Carolina Press, 1990), 8.

40. Babel, *Sochineniia*, 1:31–32. Translated in Nathalie Babel's "Introduction" to *The Lonely Years* (xii–xiii).

41. Nathalie Babel, "Introduction" to *The Lonely Years*, xiii–xiv.

42. Ozick, "The Year of Writing Dangerously," 34.

43. Nathalie Babel, "Introduction" to *The Lonely Years*, xviii.

44. Ibid., xvi.

45. Charyn, *Savage Shorthand*, 39.

46. Harris, "Diversity of Discourse," 24.

47. Not that it is ever safe to make such an assumption with Babel. Nathalie Babel posits, plausibly, that Babel's goal in "Avtobiografiia" was "to present an appropriate past for a young writer who was not a member of the Communist Party" (*The Lonely Years*, xiv). Whether this project would have seemed to him a primarily political or a primarily artistic one depends upon one's opinion of Babel.

48. Nathalie Babel, "Introduction" to *The Lonely Years*, xiii.

49. Detailed publication information for "Childhood. At Grandmother's" is given in Isaac Babel, *You Must Know Everything: Stories 1915–1937*, ed. Nathalie Babel, trans. Max Hayward (New York: Farrar, Straus, 1966), 3–4. In this volume, the story is given the title "You Must Know Everything," which derives from a line spoken by the grandmother.

50. Patricia Carden, *The Art of Isaac Babel* (Ithaca, N.Y.: Cornell University Press, 1972), 157.

51. For a further discussion of Babel's symbolic use of color, see Danuta Mendelson, *The Function of Metaphor in Babel's Short Stories* (Ann Arbor, Mich.: Ardis, 1982), 76; and Ephraim Sicher, *Style and Structure in the Prose of Isaac Babel'* (Columbus: Slavica, 1985), 46–61.

52. The violin teacher is "Sorokin" here, "Zagursky" in "Awakening"; Sorokin makes house calls, whereas Zagursky expects children to visit him in his "Wunderkind factory" (2:171/59), but both are viewed by the narrator as purveyors of confinement and "misery."

53. Throughout, where I refer to members of the Babel family portrayed in the stories, I of course mean the fictional family of "Babel," the narrator, and not the historical Babel family from whom the real Babel, the author, took his descent. I drop the quotation marks around "Babel" beginning in this paragraph because they are untidy to look at, and—presuming ordinary discernment on the part of the reader—unnecessary.

54. "The Story of My Dovecote," "In the Basement."

55. See Babel's letter to his mother of Oct. 14, 1931 (*Sochineniia*, 1:319), translated in *The Lonely Years*: "Before leaving I asked Katya to send you and

Zhenya each a copy of the magazine *Molodaya Gvardia*. In it, I make my debut, after several years of silence, with a small extract from a book which will have the general title [*budet ob"edinena obshchnim zaglaviem*] of *The Story of My Dovecote" (The Lonely Years,* 189).

56. Carden, *Art of Isaac Babel,* 169.

57. Blasphemy in "The Story of My Dovecote," forgery in "In the Basement"—although the two accusations are by no means incompatible.

58. The date of 1861 does not in fact correspond to either of the major nineteenth-century Polish uprisings against Russian imperial rule, which occurred in 1830–31 (the November Uprising) and 1863–64 (the January Uprising) respectively. 1861, however, saw considerable unrest in Poland partly relating to the imperial decree abolishing serfdom, issued on March 3, which simultaneously offered a promise of reform and fell short of the demands of many of the dissenting political groups then organizing in Warsaw. A large demonstration on Warsaw's Castle Square on April 8 was fired upon by Russian troops, and "conspiracies and demonstrations" continued through the summer. Finally, in October, "a state of emergency was declared. Cossacks broke into the churches to disperse the worshippers. Patriotic hymns were banned. Catholic and Jewish clergymen were deported. The Citadel was packed with thousands of arrested persons" (Norman Davies, *God's Playground: A History of Poland, Volume 2: 1795 to the Present* [New York: Columbia University Press, 1982], 350–51). It seems to me that Babel is up to one of two things here: either he intends the date of 1861 to be read as further evidence of Shoyl's unreliability (or of the narrator's efforts to discredit Shoyl), or he is deliberately focusing on a moment that is comparatively marginal in Polish history but central to Shoyl's personal narrative. The latter choice could be prompted either by the author's awareness that he would have greater poetic license in dealing with less well-known events, or by certain echoes and correspondences between the Polish situation in 1861 and the situation in Odessa and Nikolayev in 1905: a proclamation by the tsar (the emancipation decree in 1861, the October Manifesto in 1905) is accompanied by widespread demonstrations and violence, in some cases touching on religious identity. The pattern of unrest beginning in spring, simmering through the summer, and coming to a head in October is also reminiscent of 1905 in Odessa (see Weinberg, *The Revolution of 1905 in Odessa*).

59. Although the term *bobe-mayse* (meaning a fanciful story) has become associated with grandmothers (Yidd. *bobe*), this conventional translation is etymologically incorrect. Originally spelled *bove-mayse,* the word properly referred to the sixteenth-century Yiddish romance the *Bove-Bukh;* a process of folk etymology converted the term to *bobe-mayse,* or grandmother's tale. Nonetheless, the association with grandmothers is strong enough that for readers familiar with Yiddish, this would have been the likely first association to come to mind in connection with the grandmother's stories.

60. See chapter 3.

61. A. I. Kuprin, *Granatovyi braslet: Povesti i rasskazy (na angliiskom ya-zyke)*, trans. Stepan Apresyan (Moscow: Progress, 1982), 275.

62. Gabriella Safran, "Isaak Babel''s El'ia Isaakovich," 254.

63. K. Paustovskii, *Vremia bol'shikh ozhidanii* (Odessa: Maiak, 1977), 149. All translations from this text are my own.

64. See, e.g., Feld, "The Odessa School of Writers," 30.

65. Paustovskii, *Vremia bol'shikh ozhidanii*, 191. My ellipsis.

CHAPTER THREE

1. Nakhimovsky, *Russian-Jewish Literature and Identity*, 102.

2. I. S. Turgenev, *First Love and Other Stories*, trans. Richard Freeborn (Oxford: Oxford University Press, 1989), 145. My ellipsis is in square brackets to distinguish it from Turgenev's ellipses (which are copious).

3. Ibid., 170.

4. There are, of course, other dimensions to this rivalry, not directly related to my thesis; for example, the dueling biographies could be seen in the light of conflicting views among early *twentieth*-century European Jewry about how to make the history of Jewish thought "useful" for contemporary ideological ends.

5. I. E. Babel', *Sochineniia*, ed. A. Pirozhkova (Moscow: Khudozhestven-naia literatura, 1990), 2:174–75; translation in Babel, *Collected Stories*, trans. David McDuff (London: Penguin, 1995), 63. As in the previous chapter, further references to these two editions will be given in parentheses in the text, as follows: (2:174–75/63).

6. Isaak Babel', *Detstvo i drugie rasskazy* (Jerusalem: Aliya, 1979), 37. Like other excised portions of Babel's stories, this sentence is present in the original published version of the story, but is omitted from most Soviet editions of Babel's works, including the two-volume 1990 *Sochineniia*.

7. Nakhimovsky, *Russian-Jewish Literature and Identity*, 104.

8. The Jewish Museum New York, wall text from exhibition "Marc Chagall 1907–1917," March 31–August 4, 1996.

9. The Royal Academy of Arts, catalogue text from exhibition "Paris: Capital of the Arts 1900–1968," formerly available at http://www.royalacademy.org.uk/?lid=262; retrieved January 3, 2003. Robert Alter, in an essay entitled "Babel, Flaubert, and the Rapture of Perception," also compares Babel to Chagall: "[Babel's] extruded simile of the sun as the pink tongue of a thirsty dog. . . . might suggest a painter more like Chagall than the sort of nineteenth-century French realist that Flaubert often had in mind" (Friedin, ed., *The Enigma of Isaac Babel*, 143).

10. Nathalie Babel, "Introduction" to *The Lonely Years*, xv.

11. See Efraim Sicher, *Style and Structure in the Prose of Isaac Babel'* (Columbia: Slavica, 1985), 47.

12. Donald Fanger, "Nikolai Gogol," in *Handbook of Russian Literature,* ed. Victor Terras (New Haven, Conn.: Yale University Press, 1985), 177.

13. Gary Rosenshield discusses the stereotype of the red-headed Jew in his *The Ridiculous Jew,* noting that medieval plays instituted a tradition of depicting both the devil and Judas Iscariot as red-headed. These portrayals, with their strongly negative connotation, subsequently made their way into "the stock of modern Jewish stereotypical physical features." See Rosenshield, *The Ridiculous Jew: The Exploitation and Transformation of a Stereotype in Gogol, Turgenev, and Dostoevsky* (Stanford, Calif.: Stanford University Press, 2008), 9, 207n16.

14. It is interesting, though perhaps not directly relevant, to note the similarity between the symptoms portrayed here by Babel and those of demonic possession, as depicted in William Friedkin's 1973 horror film, *The Exorcist.* The sense that Babel's narrator-protagonist has been somehow taken over by a force beyond his control—be it History, anti-Semitism, or sexual maturity—does hover over the narrative of "First Love."

15. The "triumph" associated with these "ultimate exertions of love" that make Galina writhe with fear recalls, in a twisted way, Reb Arye-Leib's description of Benya Krik in "How It Was Done in Odessa" ("You can spend the night with a Russian woman, and the Russian woman will be satisfied"). Can a Jewish man only hope to "satisfy" a Russian woman through violence? In Babel's fiction, for a Jewish man to exert power over a Russian woman seems to be both the ultimate triumph and, for his autumn-souled autobiographical narrator, profoundly unnatural and disturbing.

16. Charyn, *Savage Shorthand,* 48–49.

17. Babel', *Detstvo i drugie rasskazy,* 56; translated by McDuff in Babel, *Collected Stories,* 49; this passage does not appear in the 1990 *Sochineniia,* but may be found in early editions of the story, including I. Babel', *Istoriia moei golubiatni* (Paris: Imprimerie scientifique et commerciale, 1927), 40.

18. Vatulescu, *Police Aesthetics,* 44.

19. Paustovskii, *Vremia bol'shikh ozhidanii,* 146.

20. Ibid., 139. My translation.

21. Plato, *The Republic,* trans. Desmond Lee (London: Penguin, 1987), 436.

22. Plato, *The Republic,* 435; Babel, *Sochineniia* 2:183–85/*Collected Stories* 55–57.

23. Plato, *The Republic,* 437.

24. Simon Sebag Montefiore, *Stalin: The Court of the Red Tsar* (New York: Vintage, 2005), 96. On the contention that Stalin, in this speech, was quoting Olesha (a plausible one, since Olesha himself was of an engineering turn of mind, liked mechanical things, and was the author of a story called "Human Material"), see Iu. B. Borev, *Staliniada: Memuary po chuzhim vospominaniiam s istoricheskimi anekdotami i razmyshleniiami avtora* (Moscow: Olimp, 2003), 95. Note that the source of the anecdote is none other than Victor Shklovsky.

25. Riffaterre, *Fictional Truth,* 5. The phrase "inchoate or future text" appears in the same paragraph. For a different, but compatible, analysis of Babel's concern with the relationship of his art to "reality," see Elif Batuman, *"Pan* Pisar': Clerkship in Babel's First-Person Narration," in *The Enigma of Isaac Babel,* ed. Gregory Freidin (Stanford, Calif.: Stanford University Press, 2009), 157–74.

26. Gregory Freidin, "Fat Tuesday in Odessa: Isaac Babel's 'Di Grasso' as Testament and Manifesto," *Russian Review* 40, no. 2 (April 1981); reprinted in Harold Bloom, ed., *Modern Critical Views: Isaac Babel* (New York: Chelsea House, 1987), 200.

27. See chapter 1.

28. Scherr, "Synagogues, Synchrony, and the Sea," 337–50; this discussion, 343ff.

29. Ibid., 346.

30. As Freidin points out, however, "The End of the Almshouse" represents Babel's forcible superannuation of the Odessa theme and the characters that peopled it. See Freidin, "Two Babels—Two Aphrodites," 36.

31. See Trilling (following the 1955 Walter Morison translation): "We can only wonder at the vagary of the military mind by which Isaac Babel came to be assigned as a supply officer to a Cossack regiment. . . . He was an intellectual, a writer—a man, as he puts it in striking phrase, with spectacles on his nose and autumn in his heart." Lionel Trilling, "Introduction" to Babel, *Collected Stories* (1955); reprinted in McDuff, 348.

32. Freidin, "Isaac Babel," in *European Writers: The Twentieth Century,* vol. 11, p. 1894.

33. I do not speak here of Babel's *style;* much has already been written about Babel's use of Odessan *skaz* in the *Odessa Tales* (see, e.g., James Falen, *Isaac Babel: Russian Master of the Short Story* [Knoxville: University of Tennessee Press, 1974], chap. 5; Walenty Cukierman, "The Odessa Myth and Idiom in Some Early Works of Odessa Writers," *Canadian-American Slavic Studies* 14, no. 1 [Spring 1980]: 36–51), and this adoption of his heroes' native idiom does not, to me, constitute an erasure of Babel's narrative *voice.*

34. Scherr, "Synagogues, Synchrony, and the Sea," 348.

35. V. B. Shklovskii, "Pis'mo redaktoru," *Literaturnaia gazeta,* April 29, 1933; translated and quoted in Feld, "The Southwestern School of Writers," 2.

36. For a fascinating treatment of this topic, and a comprehensive list of examples, see Freidin, "Fat Tuesday in Odessa."

37. Charles Rougle, "Isaak Emmanuilovich Babel," in *Russian Prose Writers Between the World Wars,* ed. Christine Rydel (*Dictionary of Literary Biography* vol. 272; Detroit: Gale, 2003), 4.

38. Elif Batuman, *The Possessed: Adventures with Russian Books and the People Who Read Them* (New York: Farrar, Straus and Giroux, 2010), 79 (my

emphasis). Batuman relies here on the research of Alexander Zholkovsky, presented in his article "Isaac Babel, Author of Guy de Maupassant," *Canadian Slavonic Papers/Revue canadienne des slavistes,* 36:1/2 (1994: Mar/June): 89–105.

39. K. G. Paustovskii, *The Golden Rose,* trans. Susanna Rosenberg, ed. Dennis Ogden (Moscow: Foreign Languages Publishing House, 1957), 119.

40. Ibid. (my emphasis).

41. For a detailed exploration of the influence of Babel on Paustovsky (and vice versa), as well as on other Soviet writers of his own generation and later, see Marietta Chudakova, "Thinned and Diluted: Babel in Published Russian Literature of the Soviet Period," in *Enigma of Isaac Babel,* ed. Freidin, 125–35.

42. Paustovskii, *The Golden Rose,* 123–24; my emphasis.

43. Riffaterre, *Fictional Truth,* 29.

44. Ibid., 124–25.

45. Paustovskii, *Vremia bol'shikh ozhidanii,* 155.

46. Paustovskii, *The Golden Rose,* 209.

47. Paustovskii, *Vremia bol'shikh ozhidanii,* 141.

48. Ibid., 145.

49. Ibid., 128.

50. Nathalie Babel, "Introduction" to *The Lonely Years,* xiv.

CHAPTER FOUR

1. Elizabeth Klosty Beaujour, *The Invisible Land: A Study of the Artistic Imagination of Iurii Olesha* (New York: Columbia University Press, 1970), 1.

2. Judson Rosengrant, "Translator's Introduction" to Yury Olesha, *No Day Without a Line* (Ann Arbor, Mich.: Ardis, 1979), 11.

3. Skorino, *Pisatel' i ego vremia,* 9–10.

4. Critics have generally taken at face value Kataev's hero worship of Bunin, whose "conscientious pupil" he claimed to be (Gleb Struve, *Soviet Russian Literature, 1917–50* [Norman: University of Oklahoma Press, 1951], 147). Richard Borden, however, shows how the relationship was, as usual with Kataev, not straightforward: see Borden, *The Art of Writing Badly,* 31–32.

5. Robert Russell, *Valentin Kataev* (Boston: Twayne, 1981), 147. The quotation in the next sentence is from the same book, p. 14. The *Waves of the Black Sea* tetralogy (*Volny Chernogo Moria,* 1936–61) comprises the four novels *A White Sail Gleams* (*Beleet parus odinokii,* 1936); *The Farm in the Steppe* (*Khutorok v stepi,* 1956); *Winter Wind* (*Zimnii veter,* 1960); and *Catacombs* (*Katakomby,* 1961).

6. Alexandra Smith, "Valentin Petrovich Kataev," in *Russian Prose Writers Between the World Wars,* ed. Christine Rydel (*Dictionary of Literary Biography,* vol. 272; Detroit: Gale, 2003), 176.

7. Ibid.

8. Rosengrant, "Introduction" to *No Day Without a Line,* 17. Despite his fading from the literary scene, Olesha did continue working, mostly as a journalist, publishing over a hundred articles between 1934 and 1954 (by Olesha's own estimate; cited in Rosengrant, *No Day,* 18). Like many other writers who had fallen from official favor, he also translated works by non-Russian (Ukrainian and Turkmen) writers into Russian, and worked on film scenarios. By these means, Olesha and his wife managed to survive (albeit sometimes precariously) until 1954, when he was assigned "a rather modest apartment in the writers' building on Lavrushinsky Lane across from the Tretyakov Gallery in Moscow" (Rosengrant, *No Day,* 18). By then Olesha was drinking heavily, spending most of his days "sitting at a table in central Moscow restaurants, including a Georgian restaurant on Tver' Boulevard and the restaurant at the Hotel National," where he "took notes, drank, and generally held court with other diners" (Victor Peppard, "Iurii Karlovich Olesha," in *Russian Prose Writers Between the World Wars,* ed. Christine Rydel. [*Dictionary of Literary Biography,* vol. 272; Detroit: Gale, 2003], 273). This method of working naturally also impeded Olesha's literary production, and played a role in the fragmentary form of *No Day Without a Line,* the autobiographical work I discuss in detail later in this chapter.

9. I. E. Babel', "Rech' na pervom vsesoiuznom s"ezde sovietskikh pisatelei," *Sochineniia,* 2:381.

10. The denunciation and execution of Benya Krik was part of a broader "retirement" of the Odessa theme in Babel's work of the later 1920s and 1930s. See Gregory Freidin, "Two Babels—Two Aphrodites," 20, 27, 35–37.

11. See the ending of the second Ostap Bender novel, *The Little Golden Calf* (*Zolotoi Telenok,* 1931).

12. Simon Morrison, *The People's Artist: Prokofiev's Soviet Years* (Oxford: Oxford University Press, 2009), 88, 102–3.

13. Borden, *The Art of Writing Badly,* 10–11. As Borden notes, Kataev's only serious brush with official opprobrium, which occurred during the Zhdanovite era of artistic repressions, was occasioned by the second volume of the tetralogy, *For the Power of the Soviets* (*Za vlast' sovetov,* 1948; reissued with alterations as *The Catacombs* [*Katakomby*] in 1951). Kataev's sin was one of omission: he had forgotten to adhere to the second principle of Socialist Realism, *partiinost'* or Party-mindedness. However, as Borden points out, Kataev's punishment— being "well-scolded in public" and "forced to rewrite his book on someone else's terms"—was "nothing of consequence" in comparison to the career- and sometimes life-ending repercussions suffered by other artists in the same period. Borden, *Writing Badly,* 12, 353n.

14. Iurii Olesha, "Speech to the First Congress of Soviet Writers" (August 22, 1934), in *Envy and Other Works,* trans. Andrew R. MacAndrew (New York: Doubleday Anchor, 1967), 216.

15. Elizabeth Klosty Beaujour, "The Imagination of Failure: Fiction and Autobiography in the Work of Yury Olesha," in *Autobiographical Statements in Twentieth-Century Russian Literature.*, ed. Jane Gary Harris (Princeton, N.J.: Princeton University Press, 1990), 123–32.

16. Valentin Kataev, *Almaznyi moi venets* (Moscow: DEM, 1990), 66. Henceforth, the page numbers for quotations from this volume will be given in parentheses in the text.

17. "The thought that is expressed is a lie" (*Mysl' izrechennaia est' lozh'*), a famous line from Tiutchev's poem "Silentium" (1830). Kataev refers to this line immediately following the passage just quoted. He is also, probably unbeknownst to himself, echoing Babel's words to his mother about the *Dovecote* stories (see chapter 2).

18. Turgenev, *First Love and Other Stories*, 67. My emphasis.

19. *Kliuchik* might mean "little key," "little clue," or "little spring"—or all of the above at once. I have chosen "little key" because the initial letter of Olesha's given name, Yury (the Russian letter Ю, pronounced "Yu") somewhat resembles a key, which I imagine to have influenced Kataev's choice of nickname—but he may also have had in mind the metaphorical sense of "(well)spring" as "inspiration," as well as a possible gesture toward the importance of Olesha as a "key" figure in his text.

20. Arkadii L'vov, "Prostota neslykhannoi eresi," *Vremia i my* 40 (April 1979): 161–76. This conversation will be discussed in more detail below.

21. Obviously, I am writing from the point of view of hindsight. While the Party, of course, did what it could to destroy the reputation of any writer who was purged, in most cases literary merit has proved more durable than the Soviet regime itself. "Posterity" in this case should be taken to refer to post-Soviet opinion.

22. Vladimir Nabokov, "An Evening of Russian Poetry" (1945), in *Poems* (Garden City: Doubleday, 1959), 20.

23. Though my focus here is on the use of Pushkin as a literary "ancestor," and not on a full-blown comparison of Kataev's autobiographical (or quasi-autobiographical) method to Nabokov's, the two writers certainly invite such a comparison. A concise list of similarities between Nabokov's approach and Kataev's is provided by Borden in *The Art of Writing Badly* (115–16). The most important of these is the two writers' rejection of chronolinearity, which gave increased importance to the subjectivity of the narrator as the source of the principles (subjective patterns or associations) by which the plot is organized.

24. Vladimir Nabokov, *The Gift* (New York: Vintage, 1991), 382.

25. The omitted scene, which appears in Pushkin's manuscript but not in the published version of *Boris Godunov*, preceded the ball scene headed "The Castle of the Governor Mnishek in Sambor" ("Zamok voevody Mnishka v Sambore"). See A. S. Pushkin, *Sobranie sochinenii v desiati tomakh* (Moscow: Gos-

udarstvennoe izdatel'stvo Khudozhestvennoi Literatury, 1959–62), vol. 4. The scene can also be accessed in the electronic version of the above edition, online at http://www.rvb.ru/pushkin/01text/05theatre/03edit/0854.htm#exclsc2. The verses Kataev quotes here are (like Nabokov's Onegin stanza in *The Gift*) "disguised" in his text as prose, and I have translated them as such.

26. Borden, *The Art of Writing Badly*, 121.

27. See Kataev, *Almaznyi moi venets*, 9–10; and Borden, *The Art of Writing Badly*, 119.

28. A. S. Pushkin, *Izbrannye sochineniia* (Moscow: Academia, 1992), 66. My emphasis.

29. N. V. Gogol, "An Author's Confession" ("Avtorskaia ispoved'," 1847), quoted in Donald Fanger, *The Creation of Nikolai Gogol* (Cambridge, Mass.: Harvard University Press, 1979), 152.

30. Kataev, *Almaznyi moi venets*, 65. See also the "Introduction" to this study.

31. Borden, *The Art of Writing Badly*, 9. Borden points out that "as one of the last surviving players from the glory days of Russian modernism and the raucous and vibrant first years of Soviet literature, Kataev acted for a whole generation—for writers from Aksenov to Zinik—as a conduit to an age in which literary experimentation seemed to know no bounds" (*The Art of Writing Badly*, 8).

32. Like the "door in the wall" image and the solar imagery in *A Shattered Life* (see below), Kataev's use of statuary here can also be seen in terms of a dialogue with Olesha's autobiographical writings. In *No Day Without a Line*, Olesha writes: "A broken statue moves inside me in its accidental casing, expressing together with it the effects of some strange and terrible enchantment, some detail of a myth from which I will be able to apprehend only one thing: my own death" (Yurii Olesha, *Ni dnia bez strochki* [Moscow: Sovetskaia Rossiia, 1965], 170). Characteristically, Kataev converts this imagery of enchanted statuary and death into something positive and affirming—another "crown."

33. Though the Parc Monceau also boasts other famous statues, Maupassant's—which happens to have been erected in the year Kataev was born, 1897—is the only one of these "real" monuments mentioned in Kataev's narrative.

34. L'vov, "Prostota neslykhannoi eresi," 165.

35. See Babel, "Rech' na pervom vsesoiuznom s"ezde sovetskikh pisatelei," *Sochineniia* 2:382.

36. Babel, "Kak eto delalos' v Odesse," *Sochineniia*, 1:127.

37. Babel, *Sochineniia*, 2:217; translation by McDuff, *Collected Stories*, 74.

38. See "How It Was Done in Odessa," where the narrator is accused of "brawling at your writing-desk [but] stuttering in the presence of others" (Babel, *Sochineniia*, 1:127; trans. McDuff, 244); "The Death of Dolgushov," where the narrator cannot bring himself to deliver the coup de grâce (*Sochineniia*, 2:44–46; trans. McDuff, 132–35); and "After the Battle," which ends with the narra-

tor "begging fate for the simplest of abilities—the ability to kill a man" (*Sochineniia*, 2:124; trans. McDuff, 222).

39. For a discussion of the autobiographicity of Babel's narrators, see chapter 3, above. For an insightful discussion of Liutov's attempts to master the "masculine language" of *Red Cavalry*, see Eliot Borenstein, *Men Without Women: Masculinity and Revolution in Russian Fiction, 1917–1929* (Durham, N.C.: Duke University Press, 2000), 73–124.

40. Kataev offered numerous definitions, descriptions, and diagnoses of "Mauvism" in his works between 1965 and 1986. A cogent history of these is supplied by Borden in chapter 1 of *The Art of Writing Badly*. Since I am only concerned with Mauvism insofar as it relates to the Odessa theme, I will limit myself to commenting on this particular, intriguingly worded, description.

41. See chapter 3.

42. Borden (*The Art of Writing Badly*, 25) traces the roots of Mauvism to Babel's "writing badly" speech. I will not repeat his conclusions here but expand upon them.

43. John Garrard and Carol Garrard, *Inside The Soviet Writers' Union* (New York: Free, 1990), 40–41.

44. Babel, *Sochineniia*, 2:382 (my translation).

45. As I will discuss in the next section, Kataev also includes Shklovsky among the "theorists" guilty of thinking up "prejudice," and Shklovsky's designation of a "South-West" movement in Soviet literature is among the "prejudices" Kataev is keen to reject.

46. J. V. Stalin, "Speech Delivered at the First All-Union Conference of Leading Personnel of Socialist Industry" (February 1931), in *Works*, vol. 13 (Moscow: Foreign Languages Publishing House, 1955), 39.

47. Yury Olesha, "Speech to the First Congress of Soviet Writers" (August 22, 1934), in *Envy and Other Works*, trans. Andrew R. MacAndrew (New York: Doubleday Anchor, 1967), 216.

48. Vladimir Sobolev, "Izgnanie metafory: Beseda s V. Kataevym," *Literaturnaia gazeta*, May 17, 1933.

49. For a detailed discussion of the uses to which this motif was put in Russian literature, see Richard Borden, "H.G. Wells' 'The Door in the Wall' in Russian Literature," *Slavic and East European Journal* 36, no. 3 (Fall 1992).

50. L'vov, "Prostota neslykhannoi eresi," 166.

51. Paustovskii, *Vremia bol'shikh ozhidanii*, 149. Ellipsis in original.

52. Ibid., 150–52.

53. Paustovskii, *The Golden Rose*, 209.

54. The full text of Bagritsky's poem is reproduced below as it appears in Eduard Bagritskii, Nikolai Zabolotskii, and Igor' Volgin, *Stikotvoreniia i poemy* (Moscow: Pravda, 1984), 23. The first two stanzas, which Kataev is quoting (slightly inaccurately, and ostensibly from memory) here, run as follows:

Там, где выступ холодный и серый
Водопадом свергается вниз,
Я кричу у безмолвной пещеры:
"Дионис! Дионис! Дионис!"

Утомясь после долгой охоты,
Запылив свой пурпурный наряд,
Он ушел в бирюзовые гроты
Выжимать золотой виноград . . .

(There, where the cold and gray projection
throws itself down like a waterfall,
I shout to the silent cave:
"Dionysus! Dionysus! Dionysus!"

Exhausted after the long hunt,
His purple livery dustied,
He went off into the turquoise grottos
To press the golden grape . . .)

55. Shklovskii, "Iugo-zapad," 472. See my "Introduction."

56. Yurii Olesha, *Ni dnia bez strochki* (Moscow: Sovetskaia Rossiia, 1965), 140. Henceforth, page references to this edition will be given in parentheses in the text.

57. Peppard, *Poetics of Yury Olesha*, 48.

58. Beaujour, "The Imagination of Failure," 124. Compare Gregory Freidin's observation regarding Babel's various works: "Babel's *major* fiction is all of a piece. The three cycles share the same narrator, though they emphasize his different facets, and we continue to encounter him in the later stories which, accordingly, borrow their settings, or sets, from *Red Cavalry, The Story of My Dovecote* and *The Tales of Odessa.*" Freidin, "Isaac Babel," in *European Writers: The Twentieth Century*, vol. 11, p. 1887.

59. Beaujour, "The Imagination of Failure," 124.

60. E. Kazakevich, reminiscence in O. Suok-Olesha and E. Pel'son, eds., *Vospominaniia o Iurii Oleshe* (Moscow: Sovetskii pisatel', 1975), 294. Arkadii Belinkov, in his *Sdacha i gibel' sovetskogo intelligenta: Iurii Olesha* (Madrid, 1976; reprint Moscow: RIK "Kul'tura," 1997), is at pains to correct this view of Olesha, pointing out that he was not above toeing the Party line on occasion and attributing his loss of stature after 1934 to Olesha's own weakness, rather than a heroic refusal to write insincerely. However, the fact that Belinkov felt so strongly that it should be dispelled (and devoted 500 pages to doing so) indicates the power of the myth.

61. Violetta Gudkova writes, "Today it seems that the 'confessional prose' of the new generation of writers, which made a lot of noise at the end of the 'fif-

ties, counts Olesha's books among its direct literary predecessors. They [Olesha's books] even became the catalyst for the later works of V. Kataev—*The Grass of Oblivion* and *Holy Well* with their 'Mauvism' that did not catch on." V. Gudkova, "O Iurii Karloviche Oleshe e ego knige, vyshedshei bez vedoma avtora," introductory article to Iu. Olesha, *Kniga proshchaniia* [Moscow: Vagrius, 1999], 19. See also Beaujour, *The Invisible Land*, 174.

62. Borden, *The Art of Writing Badly*, 143.

63. The edition produced by Shklovsky, Suok-Olesha, and others in 1965 is no longer definitive, having been superseded by the more comprehensive edition, entitled *Book of Farewell* (*Kniga proshchaniia*), produced by Violetta Gudkova in 1999 (see bibliography). However, as the only stand-alone edition of the text in book form before 1999, and the one chosen for publication in English translation by Ardis in 1979, it is arguably the most widely read version of Olesha's reminiscences, as well as the one Kataev and other Soviet authors knew and responded to in their works. For the purposes of this study, therefore, I treat the 1965 edition as canonical.

64. Rosengrant, "Introduction" to *No Day Without a Line*, 18. It should be noted that in the 1999 edition of Olesha's "diary," which includes the material published in *No Day Without a Line*, and retains dates where the author saw fit to note them, the earliest fragment is dated January 20, 1930.

65. The question of Olesha's ersatz "silence" is addressed forcefully by Arkadii Belinkov in *Sdacha i gibel'*, where it forms part of the author's argument against the received mythology of Olesha as (in Belinkov's words) "a great martyr." See *Sdacha i gibel'*, 482–91; also Peppard, *Poetics of Yury Olesha*, 12–14; and Rosengrant, "Introduction" to *No Day Without a Line*, 17–18.

66. Viktor Shklovskii, preface to Olesha, *Ni dnia bez strochki*, 7.

67. The foregoing account of the evolution of the book is based on information given in Shklovskii's preface to the 1965 edition of *Ni dnia bez strochki;* in Rosengrant's "Introduction" to the 1979 translation of *No Day;* in Belinkov, *Sdacha i gibel';* and in Beaujour, "The Imagination of Failure" and *The Invisible Land.*

68. Gudkova, "O Iurii Karloviche Oleshe e ego knige," 20.

69. As quoted by Shklovskii in his preface to *Ni dnia bez strochki*, 5.

70. According to Violetta Gudkova, the papers in the "pile" left by Olesha were more often than not dated, but frequently only by day and month, without the year (Gudkova, "O Iurii Karloviche Oleshe e ego knige," 21).

71. Rosengrant, "Introduction" to *No Day Without a Line*, 19.

72. Critics have generally followed one or other of Olesha's leads in accounting for the fragmentary form of *No Day:* Chudakova (*Masterstvo Iuriia Oleshi*, 94) and Belinkov (*Sdacha i gibel'*, 478) are of the opinion that it constituted a deliberate artistic choice on Olesha's part; Beaujour (*Invisible Land*, 175–76) and Peppard (*Poetics of Yury Olesha*, 49–50), that it signaled Olesha's

failure to manage anything more sustained. Rosengrant ("Introduction" to *No Day Without a Line*, 21–22), embraces both theories simultaneously.

73. For a compelling description of the "epic" ambitions cherished for Soviet literature in official quarters, and pressure on writers to comply with those ambitions, see Cathy Popkin, *The Pragmatics of Insignificance: Chekhov, Zoshchenko, Gogol* (Stanford, Calif.: Stanford University Press, 1993), 55ff.; and Freidin, "Isaac Babel," in *European Writers: The Twentieth Century*, vol. 11, p. 1892.

74. This argument is made in an article summarized by Richard Borden in "The Magic and the Politics of Childhood: The Childhood Theme in the Works of Iurii Olesha, Valentin Kataev and Vladimir Nabokov" (Ph.D. dissertation, Columbia University, 1987), 49–50. The article in question, "Vospominaniia o detstve V. Kataeva i Iu. Oleshi" by I. S. Cherniavskaia, published in *Problemy detskoi literatury*, ed. L. P. Sokolova (Petrozavodsk, 1976), is typical of Soviet literary biography in pointing to the dangers of an "incorrect" literary upbringing and the concomitant benefits of a "correct" one. Kataev, in contrast to Olesha, is credited with a healthy aesthetic outlook on childhood, the result of being raised on a wholesome diet of Russian "critical realists," notably Nekrasov and Tolstoy. L. I. Skorino, in *Pisatel' i ego vremia*, makes a similar point about Kataev (9–10). Borden himself implies that Olesha fled back into his childhood as an escape from a post-Revolutionary era whose values he could not assimilate, and calls *No Day* a "somewhat futile literary exercise," evidence that Olesha "had, in a sense, been transformed into a literary 'child'" (28). While this seems to be, in part, what Olesha wants his readers (or at least some of them) to think, I do not believe it is the whole story.

75. Beaujour, "Proust-Envy: Fiction and Autobiography in the Works of Iurii Olesha," *Studies in Twentieth-Century Literature* 1, no. 2 (Spring 1977): 123–34.

76. For discussion of Olesha's use of metaphor, see Beaujour, *The Invisible Land;* Chudakova, *Masterstvo Iuriia Oleshi;* Shklovskii, "Mir bez glubiny" and "Struna zvenit v tumane," and of course Kataev's remarks in Sobolev, "Ignanie metafory: Beseda s V. Kataevym," and in *My Diamond Crown,* discussed above.

77. Andrew Barratt, "Olesha's Three Ages of Man: A Close Reading of 'Liompa,'" *Modern Language Review* 75 (1980): 597–614.

78. Yurii Olesha, "Liompa," in *Izbrannoe* (Moscow: Khudozhestvennaia literatura, 1974), 193; trans. Andrew R. MacAndrew, in Olesha, *Envy and Other Works* (New York: Doubleday Anchor, 1967), 144. For quotations from Olesha's fiction, I have preferred the translations by MacAndrew in the above-listed edition. Page references to this edition will hereafter be given in parentheses in the text.

79. Richard Borden, "Iurii Olesha: The Child Behind the Metaphor," *Modern Language Review* 93, no. 2 (April 1998): 441–54; this quotation, 446.

80. Barbara Leondar, "Metaphor and Infant Cognition," *Poetics* 4 (1975), 285; quoted in Borden, "Child Behind the Metaphor," 446.

81. Viktor Shklovskii, "Struna zvenit v tumane," *Znamia* 12 (1973): 194–205. Kataev and Shklovsky both commented on this aspect of Olesha's work: disparagingly in 1933, admiringly in later years after the publication of *No Day*. See bibliography.

82. Gudkova, "O Iurii Karloviche Oleshe e ego knige," 17.

83. L. D. Rzhevskii, *Prochtenie tvorcheskogo slova* (New York: New York University Press, 1970), 76.

84. Ibid., 77–80.

85. Peppard, *Poetics of Yury Olesha*, 6.

86. Victor Peppard notes, "Virtually all of Olesha's important works take place either in summer or spring" (Peppard, *Poetics of Yury Olesha*, 59). For more in-depth discussions of sun imagery in Olesha's works, see Beaujour, *The Invisible Land*, 61–64 and 191–93. For a discussion of the way this image resurfaces in Kataev, see Borden, *The Art of Writing Badly*, 153–54.

87. Beaujour, *The Invisible Land*, 193.

88. Borden, "The Magic and the Politics of Childhood," 36.

89. Ibid., 37.

90. The final story of *A Shattered Life* (*Razbitaia zhizn', ili volshebnyi rog oberona*, 1972) is entitled "Eclipse of the Sun" ("Zatmenia solntsa"). For interpretation, see Borden, "The Magic and the Politics of Childhood," 34–35, 304–5.

91. Yury Olesha, *Envy and Other Works*, trans. Andrew R. MacAndrew (New York: Anchor Books, 1967), 58.

92. Dante, *Inferno*, 32:12: in the original Italian, "sì che dal fatto il dir non sia diverso."

93. Olesha, *No Day Without a Line*, trans. Rosengrant, 203.

94. See chapter 3, above; and Paustovskii, *Vremia bol'shikh ozhidanii*, 145.

CONCLUSION

1. L'vov, "Prostota neslykhannoi eresi," 165.

Bibliography

WORKS BY ODESSA AUTHORS

Babel', Isaak Emanuilovich (Isaac Babel). *Collected Stories*. Edited by Efraim Sicher. Translated and with an introduction by David McDuff. London: Penguin Books, 1994.

———— (Isaac Babel). *Collected Stories*. Translated and edited by Walter Morison. Introduction by Lionel Trilling. New York: Criterion Books, 1955.

————. *Detstvo i drugie rasskazy*. Jerusalem: Aliya, 1979.

————. *Istoriia moei golubiatni*. Paris: Imprimerie scientifique et commerciale, 1927.

———— (Isaac Babel). *The Lonely Years 1925–1939: Unpublished Stories and Correspondence*. Edited and with an introduction by Nathalie Babel, translated by Andrew R. MacAndrew and Max Hayward. New York: Farrar, Straus, 1964.

————. *1920 Diary*. Introduced and edited by Carol Avins. Translated by H. T. Willetts. New Haven, Conn.: Yale University Press, 1995.

————. *Sobranie sochinenii v 4 tomakh*. Edited by I. N. Sukhkih. Moscow: Vremia, 2005–6.

————. *Sochineniia*. 2 vols. Edited by A. Pirozhkova. Moscow: Khudozhestvennaia literatura, 1990.

Kataev, Valentin Petrovich. *Almaznyi moi venets*. Moscow: DEM, 1990.

Olesha, Iurii Karlovich (Yury Olesha). *Envy and Other Works*. Translated by Andrew R. MacAndrew. New York: Doubleday Anchor, 1967.

————. *Izbrannoe*. Moscow: Pravda, 1983.

————. *Ni dnia bez strochki*. Moscow: Sovetskaia Rossiia, 1965.

———— (Yury Olesha). *No Day Without a Line*. Translated, edited, and with an introduction by Judson Rosengrant. Ann Arbor, Mich.: Ardis, 1979.

Paustovskii, Konstantin Georgievich. *Chernoe more: Povest', rasskazy, ocherki, stat'i*. Simferopol': Tavriia, 1973.

————. *The Golden Rose*. Translated by Susanna Rosenberg. Edited by Dennis Ogden. Moscow: Foreign Languages Publishing House, 1957.

————. *Sobranie sochinenii v deviati tomakh.* Moscow: Khudozhestvennaia literatura, 1980–86.

————. *Vremia bol'shikh ozhidanii.* Odessa: Maiak, 1977.

———— (Konstantin Paustovsky). *Years of Hope.* Translated by Manya Harari and Andrew Thomson. New York: Pantheon, 1968.

SECONDARY AND RELATED WORKS

Abrams, M. H. "The Design of *The Prelude.*" In *The Prelude: 1799, 1805, 1850: A Norton Critical Edition.* New York: W. W. Norton, 1979. 585–98.

Adams, Timothy Dow. *Telling Lies in Modern American Autobiography.* Chapel Hill: University of North Carolina Press, 1990.

Adamson, Sydney. "Odessa—The Portal of an Empire." *Harper's Monthly Magazine* 125 (November 1912): 902–13.

Aleichem, Sholem (pseudonym of Sholem Rabinowitz). *The Letters of Menachem-Mendl & Sheyne-Sheyndl.* Translated by Hillel Halkin. New Haven, Conn.: Yale University Press, 2002.

Alter, Robert. "Babel, Flaubert, and the Rapture of Perception." In *The Enigma of Isaac Babel,* edited by Gregory Freidin. Stanford, Calif.: Stanford University Press, 2009. 139–48.

Armstrong, J. M. "Babel's 'First Love.'" *Essays in Poetics* (Keele) 14, no. 1 (1989): 99–106.

Ascherson, Neil. *Black Sea.* New York: Hill and Wang, 1996.

Avins, Carol J. *Border Crossings: The West and Russian Identity in Soviet Literature, 1917–1934.* Berkeley: University of California Press, 1983.

Babel, Nathalie, ed. and intro. *The Lonely Years: 1925–1939* (stories and correspondence of Isaac Babel.) New York: Farrar, Straus, 1964.

Badikov, V. V. "Pod luchom istorii: Iz publitsistiki Iuriia Oleshi." *Literaturnoe Obozrenie* 11 (1979): 102–6.

Bagritskii, Eduard, Nikolai Zabolotskii, and Igor' Volgin. *Stikotvoreniia i poemy.* Moscow: Pravda, 1984.

Bakhtin, M. M. *The Dialogic Imagination.* Edited by Michael Holquist. Translated by Michael Holquist and Caryl Emerson. Austin: University of Texas Press, 1981.

Balburov, E. A. *Poetika liricheskoi prozy: 1960s–1970s.* Novosibirsk: Nauka, 1985.

Bar-Josef, H. "On Isaac Babel's 'The Story of My Dovecot.'" *Prooftexts* 6 (1986): 264–71.

Barratt, Andrew. *Yury Olesha's "Envy."* Birmingham Slavonic Monographs 12, 1981.

————. "Yury Olesha's Three Ages of Man: A Close Reading of 'Liompa.'" *Modern Language Review* 75 (1980): 597–614.

Barthes, Roland. "The Death of the Author." In *Image, Music Text*, translated by Stephen Heath. New York: Hill and Wang, 1977.

Batuman, Elif. *The Possessed: Adventures with Russian Books and the People Who Read Them.* New York: Farrar, Straus and Giroux, 2010.

———. "Pan Pisar': Clerkship in Babel's First-Person Narration." In *The Enigma of Isaac Babel*, edited by Gregory Freidin. Stanford, Calif.: Stanford University Press, 2009. 157–74.

Beaujour, Elizabeth Klosty. "The Imagination of Failure: Fiction and Autobiography in the Work of Yury Olesha." In *Autobiographical Statements in Twentieth-Century Russian Literature*. Edited by Jane Gary Harris. Princeton, N.J.: Princeton University Press, 1990. 123–32.

———. *The Invisible Land: A Study of the Artistic Imagination of Iurii Olesha.* New York: Columbia University Press, 1970.

———. "Proust-Envy: Fiction and Autobiography in the Works of Iurii Olesha." *Studies in Twentieth-Century Literature* 1, no. 2 (Spring 1977): 123–34.

Belinkov, Arkadii. *Sdacha i gibel' sovetskogo intelligenta: Iurii Olesha.* Madrid, 1976; reprint Moscow: RIK "Kul'tura," 1997.

——— (Arkady V. Belinkov). "The Soviet Intelligentsia and the Socialist Revolution: On Yury Olesha's *Envy*." *Russian Review: An American Quarterly Devoted to Russia Past and Present* 30 (1971): 356–68.

Bhabha, Homi K. "Interrogating Identity." In *The Location of Culture*. London: Routledge, 1994.

Blake, Patricia. "Researching Babel's Biography: Adventures and Misadventures." In *The Enigma of Isaac Babel*, edited by Gregory Freidin. Stanford, Calif.: Stanford University Press, 2009. 3–15.

Blasing, Mutlu Konuk. *The Art of Life: Studies in American Autobiographical Literature.* Austin: University of Texas Press, 1977.

Bloom, Harold, ed. *Isaac Babel.* New York: Chelsea House, 1987.

———. "A Jew Among the Cossacks." *New York Times Book Review*, June 4, 1995.

Booth, Wayne. *The Rhetoric of Fiction.* Chicago: University of Chicago Press, 1961.

Borden, Richard Chandler. *The Art of Writing Badly. Valentin Kataev's Mauvism and the Rebirth of Russian Modernism.* Evanston, Ill.: Northwestern University Press, 2000.

———. "H.G. Wells' 'The Door in the Wall' in Russian Literature." *Slavic and East European Journal* 36, no. 3 (Fall 1992).

———. "Iurii Olesha: The Child Behind the Metaphor." *Modern Language Review* 93, no. 2 (April 1998): 441–54.

———. "The Magic and the Politics of Childhood: The Childhood Theme in Works of Iurii Olesha, Valentin Kataev and Vladimir Nabokov." Ph.D. dissertation, Columbia University, 1987.

Borenstein, Eliot. *Men Without Women: Masculinity and Revolution in Russian Fiction, 1917–1929.* Durham, N.C.: Duke University Press, 2000.

Borev, Iu. B. *Staliniada: Memuary po chuzhim vospominaniiam s istoricheskimi anekdotami i razmyshleniiami avtora.* Moscow: Olimp, 2003.

Boym, Svetlana. *The Future of Nostalgia.* New York: Basic Books, 2001.

Brainina, Berta. *Valentin Kataev: Ocherk tvorchestva.* Moscow: Gospolitizdat, 1960.

Briker, Boris. "The Underworld of Benia Krik and I. Babel's *Odessa Stories.*" *Canadian Slavonic Papers* 36, nos. 1–2 (March-June 1994): 115–34.

Brown, Edward J. *Russian Literature Since the Revolution.* Cambridge, Mass.: Harvard University Press, 1982.

Bruss, Elizabeth. *Autobiographical Acts: The Changing Situation of a Literary Genre.* Baltimore: Johns Hopkins University Press, 1976.

Buckler, Julie A. *Mapping St. Petersburg: Imperial Text and Cityshape.* Princeton, N.J.: Princeton University Press, 2004.

Budennyi, S. Open letter to Gorky. *Krasnaia gazeta,* October 26, 1928. Translated in Isaac Babel, *The Lonely Years,* 384–87.

Canadian Slavonic Papers 36, nos. 1–2 (March-June 1994). A special volume commemorating the centenary of Babel's birth, with articles on his life and works.

Carden, Patricia. *The Art of Isaac Babel.* Ithaca, N.Y.: Cornell University Press, 1972.

Caws, Mary Ann, ed. *City Images: Perspectives from Literature, Philosophy, and Film.* New York: Gordon and Breach, 1991.

Charyn, Jerome. *Savage Shorthand: The Life and Death of Isaac Babel.* New York: Random House, 2005.

Choseed, Bernard. "Jews in Soviet Literature." In *Through the Glass of Soviet Literature,* edited by Ernest Simmons. New York: Columbia University Press, 1953.

Chudakova, M. *Masterstvo Iuriia Oleshi.* Moscow: Nauka, 1972.

———. "Thinned and Diluted: Babel in Published Russian Literature of the Soviet Period." In *The Enigma of Isaac Babel,* edited by Gregory Freidin. Stanford, Calif.: Stanford University Press, 2009. 116–35.

Clayton, John Douglas. *Ice and Flame: Aleksandr Pushkin's "Eugene Onegin."* Toronto: University of Toronto Press, 1985.

Coe, Richard N. *When the Grass Was Taller: Autobiography and the Experience of Childhood.* New Haven, Conn.: Yale University Press, 1984.

Cornwell, Neil. "At the Circus with Olesha and Siniavskii." *Slavonic and East European Review* 71, no. 1 (January 1993): 1–13.

Cukierman, Walenty. "Isaac Babel's Jewish Heroes and Their Yiddish Background." *Yiddish: A Quarterly Journal* 2, no. 4 (1977): 15–27.

———. "The Odessa Myth and Idiom in Some Early Works of Odessa Writers." *Canadian-American Slavic Studies* 14, no. 1 (Spring 1980): 36–51.

———. "The Odessa School of Writers, 1918–1923." Ph.D. dissertation, University of Michigan, 1976.

Cunningham, Marina. "Isaac Babel: The Identity Conflict." Ph.D. dissertation. Northwestern University, 1976.

Dalglish, Robert. "Katayev and His Critics." Introduction to V. P. Kataev, *The Grass Of Oblivion*, trans. Dalglish. London: Macmillan, 1969.

Dante Alighieri. *Inferno*. Translated by Allen Mandelbaum (parallel texts in Italian and English). New York: Bantam, 1980.

Darrieussecq, Marie. "L'autofiction, un genre pas sérieux." *Poétique* 107 (September 1996): 369–80.

Davies, Norman. *God's Playground: A History of Poland, Volume 2: 1795 to the Present*. New York: Columbia University Press, 1982.

Day, Geoffrey. *From Fiction to the Novel*. London: Routledge and Kegan Paul, 1987.

de Man, Paul. "Autobiography as De-Facement." *Modern Language Notes* 94 (1979): 919–30.

Debreczeny, Paul. "The Reception of Pushkin's Poetic Works in the 1820s: A Study of the Critic's Role." *Slavic Review* 28, no. 3 (September 1969): 394–415.

Deribas, Aleksandr. *Staraia Odessa: Zabytye stranitsy, istoricheskie ocherki i vospominaniia*. Kiev: Mistetstvo, 2004.

Eakin, Paul John. *Fictions in Autobiography: Studies in the Art of Self-Invention*. Princeton, N.J.: Princeton University Press, 1985.

Ehre, Milton. *Isaac Babel*. Boston: Twayne, 1986.

Eidelman, Boris, ed. *Retsepty odesskoi kukhni*. Odessa: Optimum, 2006.

Erenburg, Ilya. *Memoirs: 1921–41*. Translated by Tatiana Shebunina, with Yvonne Ka. New York: Universal Library, 1966.

Erlich, Victor. *Russian Formalism: History—Doctrine*. 3rd edition. New Haven, Conn.: Yale University Press, 1981.

Falen, James. *Isaac Babel: Russian Master of the Short Story*. Knoxville: University of Tennessee Press, 1974.

Fanger, Donald. *The Creation of Nikolai Gogol*. Cambridge, Mass.: Harvard University Press, 1979.

———. "Nikolai Gogol." In *Handbook of Russian Literature*, edited by Victor Terras. New Haven, Conn.: Yale University Press, 1985. 174–77.

Feld, Rita. "The Southwestern School of Writers." Ph.D. dissertation, Georgetown University, 1987.

Fleishman, Avrom. *Figures of Autobiography: The Language of Self-Writing*. Berkeley: University of California Press, 1983.

Folkenflik, Robert, ed. *The Culture of Autobiography: Constructions of Self-Representation.* Stanford, Calif.: Stanford University Press, 1993.

Foucault, Michel. "Of Other Spaces," *Diacritics* 16 (Spring 1986): 22–27.

Freidin, Gregory, ed. *The Enigma of Isaac Babel.* Stanford, Calif.: Stanford University Press, 2009.

———. "Fat Tuesday in Odessa: Isaac Babel's 'Di Grasso' as Testament and Manifesto." *Russian Review* 40, no. 2 (April 1981): 101–21. Reprinted in *Modern Critical Views: Isaac Babel,* edited by Harold Bloom. New York: Chelsea House, 1987.

———. "Isaac Babel." In *European Writers: The Twentieth Century.* Vol. 11. Edited by G. Stade. New York: Charles Scribner's Sons, 1990. 1885–1914.

———. "Two Babels—Two Aphrodites: Autobiography in *Maria* and Babel's Petersburg Myth." In *The Enigma of Isaac Babel,* edited by Gregory Freidin. Stanford, Calif.: Stanford University Press, 2009. 16–56.

Friedberg, Maurice. *How Things Were Done In Odessa.* Boulder, Colo.: Westview, 1991.

———. "Yiddish Folklore Motifs in Isaac Babel's *Konarmija.*" In *American Contributions to the Eighth International Congress of Slavists,* edited by Victor Terras. Columbus, Ohio: Slavica, 1978.

Fukson, L. Iu. "Mir rasskaza Iu. Olesha 'Liompa' kak sistema tsennostei." *Filologicheskie Nauki* 1 (1992): 38–44.

Galanov, B. E. *Valentin Kataev: Ocherk tvorchestva.* Moscow: Detskaia literatura, 1982.

———. *Valentin Kataev: Razmyshleniia o mastere i dialogi s nim.* Moscow: Khudozhestvennaia literatura, 1989.

Gallie, W. B. "Is *The Prelude* a Philosophical Poem?" In *The Prelude: 1799, 1805, 1850: A Norton Critical Edition.* New York: W. W. Norton, 1979. 663–78.

Garrard, John, and Carol Garrard. *Inside The Soviet Writers' Union.* New York: Free, 1990.

George, Rosemary Marangoly. *The Politics of Home: Post-Colonial Relocations and Twentieth-Century Literature.* Cambridge, U.K.: Cambridge University Press, 1996.

Gillis, John R., ed. *Commemorations: The Politics of National Identity.* Princeton, N.J.: Princeton University Press, 1994.

———. "Memory and Identity: The History of a Relationship." In *Commemorations: The Politics of National Identity,* edited by John R. Gillis. Princeton, N.J.: Princeton University Press, 1994. 3–24.

Glaser, Amelia. "The Marketplace and the Church: Jews, Slavs and the Literature of Exchange, 1829–1929." Ph.D. dissertation. Stanford University, 2004.

Goodwin, James. *Autobiography: The Self Made Text.* New York: Twayne, 1993.

Grayson, Jane. "Double Bill: Nabokov and Olesha." In *From Pushkin to Palisan-*

driia: Essays on the Russian Novel in Honor of Richard Freeborn, edited by Arnold McMillin. New York: St. Martin's, 1990.

Grinberg, I. "Vdoxnovennoe masterstvo: K 80–letiju V. Kataeva." *Moskva* 1 (1977): 206–8.

Gudkova, V. "O Iurii Karloviche Oleshe e ego knige, vyshedshei bez vedoma avtora." Introductory article to Iu. Olesha, *Kniga proshchaniia.* Moscow: Vagrius, 1999.

Gusdorf, George. "De l'autobiographie initiatique à l'autobiographie littéraire." *Revue d'histoire littéraire de la France* 75 (1975): 957–94.

Hall, Stuart. "Cultural Identity and Diaspora." In *Colonial Discourse and Post-Colonial Theory: A Reader*, edited by Patrick Williams and Laura Chrisman. New York: Columbia University Press, 1994. 392–403.

Hallett, Richard. *Isaac Babel.* New York: Bradda Letchworth, 1972.

Handler, Richard. "Is Identity a Useful Concept?" In *Commemorations: The Politics of National Identity*, edited by John R. Gillis. Princeton, N.J.: Princeton University Press, 1994. 27–40.

Harkins, William E. "No Day Without a Line: The World of Iurii Olesha." In *Russian Literature and American Critics: In Honor of Deming B. Brown*, edited by Kenneth N. Brostrom. Ann Arbor: University of Michigan Press, 1984.

———. "The Theme of Sterility in Olesha's *Envy.*" In *Major Soviet Writers: Essays in Criticism*, edited by Edward J. Brown. Oxford: Oxford University Press, 1973. 280–94.

Harris, Jane Gary, ed. *Autobiographical Statements in Twentieth-Century Russian Literature.* Princeton, N.J.: Princeton University Press, 1990.

———. "Diversity of Discourse: Autobiographical Statements in Theory and Praxis." Introduction to *Autobiographical Statements in Twentieth-Century Russian Literature.* Princeton, N.J.: Princeton University Press, 1990. 3–35.

Hayward, Max. *Writers in Russia, 1917–1928.* San Diego: Harcourt Brace Jovanovich, 1983.

Herlihy, Patricia. *Odessa: A History 1794–1914.* Cambridge, Mass.: Harvard University Press, 1986.

———, contrib. *Odessa Memories.* See Iljine, Nicholas V.

Holland, Travis. *The Archivist's Story.* New York: Dial, 2007.

Homer. *Iliad.* Translated by Richmond Lattimore. Chicago: University of Chicago Press, 1951.

———. *Odyssey.* Translated by Richmond Lattimore. New York: Harper and Row, 1967.

Iljine, Nicholas V., ed. *Odessa Memories.* With essays by Bel Kaufman, Oleg Gubar, Alexander Rozenboim, and Patricia Herlihy. Seattle: University of Washington Press, 2004.

Ivanova, N. "Schastlivyi dar Valentina Kataeva." *Znamia* 11 (November 1999): 194–206.

Jones, Elizabeth Houston. *Spaces of Belonging: Home, Culture, and Identity in 20th-Century French Autobiography.* Amsterdam: Rodopi, 2007.

Karakina, E. *Po sledam "Iugo-Zapada."* Novosibirsk: Svinin i synovia, 2006.

Karakina, E., Tatyana Samoilova, and Anna Ishchenko. *Touring Odessa.* Odessa: Baltija Dryk, 2004.

Karpenko, Iu. A. "Onomasticheskie zagadki V. P. Kataeva." *Russkaia Rech'* 4 (July-August 1984): 9–14.

Kazakevich, E. *Vospominaniia o Iurii Oleshe.* Edited by O. Suok-Olesha and E. Pel'son. Moscow: Sovetskii pisatel', 1975.

Kholmogorov, M. "'Ia vygliadyvaiu iz vechnosti . . .': Perechityvaia Iuriia Oleshu." *Voprosy Literatury* 4 (July-August 2000): 98–119.

Kiziria, Dodona. "Four Demons of Valentin Kataev." *Slavic Review* 44, no. 4 (Winter 1985): 647–66.

Kosnarsky, Taras. "Three Novels, Three Cities." In *Modernism in Kyiv: Jubilant Experimentation,* edited by Irena R. Makaryk and Virlana Tkacz. Toronto: University of Toronto Press, 2010. 98–137.

Kotova, M, and O. Lekmanov. *V labirintakh romana-zagadki: Kommentarii k romanu V. P. Kataeva "Almaznyi moi venets."* Moscow: Agraf, 2004.

Krumm, Reinhard. *Isaak Babel: Eine Biographie.* Norderstedt: Books on Demand GmbH, 2004.

Krymova, N., and E. Knipovich. "Diskussion um Katajews Meine diamantene Krone." *Kunst und Literatur: Zeitschrift für Fragen der Aesthetik und Kunsttheorie* 28, no. 8 (1980): 825–50.

Kunitz, Joshua. *Russian Literature and the Jew.* New York: Columbia University Press, 1929.

Kuprin, A. I. "Gambrinus." In *Izbrannoe.* Moscow: Moskovskii rabochii, 1956.

———. *Granatovyi braslet: Povesti i rasskazy (na angliiskom yazyke).* Translated by Stepan Apresyan. Moscow: Progress, 1982.

Kuznetsov, M. "Memuarnaia proza." In *Zhanrovo-stilevye iskaniia sovremennoi sovetskoi prozy.* Moscow: Nauka, 1971.

LeBlanc, Ronald D. "The Soccer Match in *Envy.*" *Slavic and East European Journal* 32, no. 1 (Spring 1988): 55–71.

Lehan, Richard D. *The City in Literature: An Intellectual and Cultural History.* Berkeley: University of California Press, 1998.

Lejeune, Philippe. *Le Pacte Autobiographique.* Paris: Seuil, 1975.

Lévi-Strauss, Claude. *The Raw and the Cooked.* New York: Harper and Row, 1975.

Lieber, Emma Kusnetz. "'Woe Unto Us': Gogol, Babel, and the Human Predicament." Unpublished M.A. thesis. Columbia University, 2005.

Lipovetsky, Mark. *Charms of the Cynical Reason: The Trickster's Transformations in Soviet and Post-Soviet Culture*. Boston: Academic Studies Press, 2011.

Logvin, G. P. "O masterstve Iu. Oleshi v proizvedeniiakh vtoroi poloviny 20–x godov." *Voprosy Russkoi Literatury* 1, no. 37 (1981): 80–86.

Lotman, Iu. M. "Simvolika Peterburga i problemy semiotiki goroda." In *Semiotika goroda i gorodskoi kul'tury: Peterburg*. Tartu: Uchenye zapiski tartuskogo gorodskogo universiteta, 1984.

Lukács, Georg. *Theory of the Novel*. Translated by Anna Bostock. Cambridge, Mass.: MIT Press, 1971.

Luplow, Carol. *Isaac Babel's Red Cavalry*. Ann Arbor, Mich.: Ardis, 1982.

L'vov, Arkadii. "Prostota neslykhannoi eresi," *Vremia i my* 40 (April 1979): 161–76.

Maguire, Robert A. "Literary Conflicts in the 1920s." *Survey* 18 (Winter 1972): 98–128.

———. *Red Virgin Soil: Soviet Literature in the 1920s*. Ithaca, N.Y.: Cornell University Press, 1987.

Makolkin, Anna. *A History of Odessa, the Last Italian Black Sea Colony*. Lewiston, N.Y.: Edwin Mellen, 2004.

———. *The Nineteenth Century in Odessa: One Hundred Years of Italian Culture on the Shores of the Black Sea (1794–1894)*. Foreword by Terence J. Fay. Lewiston, N.Y.: Edwin Mellen, 2007.

Mandel, Barrett John. "Full of Life Now." In *Autobiography: Essays Theoretical and Critical*, edited by James Olney. Princeton, N.J.: Princeton University Press, 1980.

Mandelstam, Osip. *Mandelstam: The Complete Critical Prose and Letters*. Translated and edited by Jane Gary Harris. Ann Arbor, Mich.: Ardis, 1979.

———. *The Noise of Time: The Prose of Osip Mandelstam*. Translated and edited by Clarence Brown. San Francisco: North Point, 1986.

"Marc Chagall 1907–1917." Exhibition at the Jewish Museum New York. March 31–August 4, 1996.

Maxwell, William. *So Long, See You Tomorrow*. New York: Knopf, 1980.

Mendelsohn, Daniel. "Epic Endeavors." Review of three novels by John Banville, David Malouf, and Zachary Mason. *The New Yorker*, April 15, 2010. 74–79.

Mendelson, Danuta. *The Function of Metaphor in Babel's Short Stories*. Ann Arbor, Mich.: Ardis, 1982.

Mikaberidze, Alexander. *The Russian Officer Corps of the Revolutionary and Napoleonic Wars: 1792–1815*. New York: Savas Beatie, 2005.

Miller, Alexei. "A Testament of the All-Russian Idea." In *Extending the Borders of Russian History: Essays in Honor of Alfred J. Rieber*, edited by Marsha Siefert. Budapest: Central European University Press, 2003. 233–44.

Mints, Z. G., et al. "'Peterburgskii tekst' i russkii simvolizm." In *Semiotika goroda i gorodskoi kul'tury: Peterburg.* Tartu, Estonia: Uchenye zapiski tartuskogo gorodskogo universiteta, 1984.

Miron, Dan. *A Traveler Disguised.* 2nd edition. Syracuse, N.Y.: Syracuse University Press, 1996.

Montefiore, Simon Sebag. *Prince of Princes: The Life of Potemkin.* London: Weidenfeld and Nicholson, 2000.

———. *Stalin: The Court of the Red Tsar.* New York: Vintage, 2005.

Morrison, Simon. *The People's Artist: Prokofiev's Soviet Years.* Oxford: Oxford University Press, 2009.

Moser, Charles A., ed. *The Russian Short Story.* Boston: Twayne, 1986.

Muratov, A. B., and L. A. Iesuitova, eds. *Avtointerpretatsiia: Sbornik statei.*

Nabokov, Vladimir, trans. and ed. *Eugene Onegin: Translation and Commentary.* By A. S. Pushkin. 4 vols. Princeton, N.J.: Princeton University Press, 1965.

———. *The Gift.* New York: Vintage, 1991.

———. *Poems.* Garden City, N.Y.: Doubleday, 1959.

Nakhimovsky, Alice Stone. *Russian-Jewish Literature and Identity.* Baltimore: Johns Hopkins University Press, 1992.

Nepomnyashchy, Catharine Theimer. *Abram Tertz and the Poetics of Crime.* New Haven, Conn.: Yale University Press, 1995.

Nilsson, Nils Ake. "A Hall of Mirrors: Nabokov and Olesha." *Scando-Slavica* 15 (1969): 5–12.

———. "Through the Wrong End of Binoculars: An Introduction to Jurij Oleša." In *Major Soviet Writers: Essays in Criticism,* edited by Edward J. Brown. Oxford: Oxford University Press, 1973. 254–79.

Notkina, Aleksandra. "Avtor i ego vremia." *Voprosy Literatury* 3 (May-June 2000): 107–26.

Novikova, O., and V. Novikov. "Zavist': Perechityvaia Valentina Kataeva." *Novyi Mir* 1, no. 861 (January 1997): 219–23.

Olney, James, ed. *Autobiography: Essays Theoretical and Critical.* Princeton, N.J.: Princeton University Press, 1980.

———, ed. *Studies in Autobiography.* Oxford: Oxford University Press, 1988.

Ozick, Cynthia. "The Year of Writing Dangerously." *New Republic,* May 8, 1995, 31–38.

"Paris: Capital of the Arts 1900–1968." Exhibition catalogue. Royal Academy of Arts, UK. http://www.royalacademy.org.uk/?lid=262.

Pascal, Roy. *Design and Truth in Autobiography.* New York: Garland, 1985.

Pashin, D. "Chelovek pered zerkalom: Neskol'ko fragmentov o zhizni i o siuzhete." *Oktiabr'* 3 (March 1994): 179–86.

Peppard, Victor. "Iurii Karlovich Olesha." In *Russian Prose Writers Between the World Wars,* edited by Christine Rydel. *Dictionary of Literary Biography,* vol. 272. Detroit: Gale, 2003. 260–77.

———. "Olesha's *Envy* and the Carnival." In *Russian Literature and American Critics: In Honor of Deming B. Brown,* edited by Kenneth N. Brostrom. Ann Arbor: University of Michigan Press, 1984.

———. *The Poetics of Yury Olesha.* Gainesville: University of Florida Press, 1989.

"Philologos." *Forward* (English edition). New York, October 18, 2002.

Plato. *The Republic.* Translated by Desmond Lee. London: Penguin, 1987.

Plutnik, Albert. "We Must Look Life Straight in the Face: Interview with Valentin Katayev." *Soviet Literature* 6, no. 435 (1984): 96–102.

Poggioli, R. "Isaac Babel in Retrospect." In *The Phoenix and the Spider.* Cambridge, Mass.: Harvard University Press, 1957.

Popkin, Cathy. *The Pragmatics of Insignificance: Chekhov, Zoshchenko, Gogol.* Stanford, Calif.: Stanford University Press, 1993.

Prager, Leonard. "Er lebt vi got in frankraych." *Mendele Review: Yiddish Literature & Language,* Vol. 04.016 (Dec. 12, 2000). http://yiddish.haifa.ac.il/tmr/tmr04/tmr04016.htm.

Pushkin, A. S. *Eugene Onegin.* Translated by Vladimir Nabokov. 4 vols. Princeton University Press, 1965.

———. *Eugene Onegin.* Translated by James Falen. Oxford: Oxford University Press, 1995.

———. *Sobranie sochinenii v desiati tomakh.* Moscow: Gosudarstvennoe izdatel'stvo Khudozhestvennoi Literatury, 1959–62. Also available electronically at Russkaia Virtual'naia Biblioteka (RBV), http://www.rvb.ru/pushkin/.

Richardson, Tanya. *Kaleidoscopic Odessa: History and Place in Contemporary Ukraine.* Toronto: University of Toronto Press, 2008.

———. "Odessa, Ukraine: History, Place and Nation-Building in a Post-Soviet City." Ph.D. dissertation, University of Cambridge, 2004.

Riffaterre, Michael. *Fictional Truth.* Baltimore: Johns Hopkins University Press, 1990.

Rosengrant, Judson, trans. and intro. *No Day Without a Line,* by Yury Olesha. Ann Arbor, Mich.: Ardis, 1979.

Rosenshield, Gary. *The Ridiculous Jew: The Exploitation and Transformation of a Stereotype in Gogol, Turgenev, and Dostoevsky.* Stanford, Calif.: Stanford University Press, 2008.

Rosenstone, Robert. *King of Odessa.* Evanston, Ill.: Northwestern University Press, 2003.

Rosslyn, Wendy. "The Path to Paradise: Recurrent Images in the Poetry of Eduard Bagritsky." *Modern Language Review* 71, no. 1 (January 1976): 97–105.

Rothstein, Robert A. "How It Was Sung in Odessa: At the Intersection of Russian and Yiddish Folk Culture." *Slavic Review* 60, no. 4 (2001): 782–85.

Rougle, Charles. "Isaak Emmanuilovich Babel." In *Russian Prose Writers Between the World Wars,* edited by Christine Rydel. *Dictionary of Literary Biography,* vol. 272. Detroit: Gale, 2003. 3–22.

Rubin, Rachel. *Jewish Gangsters of Modern Literature.* Urbana: University of Illinois Press, 2000.

Russell, Robert. "Oberon's Magic Horn: The Later Works of Valentin Kataev." In *Russian Literature and Criticism,* edited by Evelyn Bristol. Berkeley, Calif.: Berkeley Slavic Specialties, 1982.

———. "The Problem of Self-Expression in the Later Works of V. P. Kataev." *Forum for Modern Language Studies* 11 (October 1975): 366–79.

———. *Valentin Kataev.* Boston: Twayne, 1981.

Rzhevskii, L. D. "Babel'—stilist." In *Prochtenie tvorcheskogo slova: Literaturovedcheskie problemy i analizy.* New York: New York University Press, 1970.

Safran, Gabriella. "Isaak Babel's El'ia Isaakovich as a New Jewish Type." *Slavic Review* 61, no. 2 (2002): 253–72.

Scherr, Barry. "Synagogues, Synchrony, and the Sea: Babel's Odessa." In *And Meaning for a Life Entire: Festschrift for Charles A. Moser on the Occasion of His Sixtieth Birthday,* edited by Peter Rollberg. Columbus, Ohio: Slavica, 1997. 337–50.

Shitareva, O. G. "Ia vsegda byl na konchike lucha . . ." *Russkaia Rech'* 2 (March-April 1989): 32–36.

Shklovskii, V. B. *Gamburgskii schet: Stat'i—vospominaniia—esse (1914–1933).* Moscow: Sovetskii pisatel', 1990.

——— (Victor Shklovsky). "Isaac Babel: A Critical Romance." In *Major Soviet Writers: Essays in Criticism,* edited by Edward J. Brown. Oxford: Oxford University Press, 1973. 295–300.

———. "Pis'mo redaktoru." *Literaturnaya gazeta,* April 29, 1933.

———. "Predislovie." In *Ni dnia bez strochki,* by Iurii Olesha. Moscow: Sovetskaia Rossiia, 1965.

———. "Struna zvenit v tumane." *Znamia* 12 (1973): 194–205.

Shneer, David. "The Path of a Russian Jewish Writer." "H-Russia" electronic discussion list, February 2002. http://www2.h-net.msu.edu/reviews/show rev.cgi?path=22751015344845.

Shneidman, N. N. "Valentin Kataev in His Eighties." *Slavic and East European Journal* 29, no. 1 (Spring 1985): 52–62.

Shrayer, Maxim. *Russian Poet/Soviet Jew: The Legacy of Eduard Bagritskii.* Lanham, Md.: Rowman and Littlefield, 2000.

Sicher, Ephraim. *Jews in Russian Literature After the Revolution.* Cambridge, Eng.: Cambridge University Press, 1995.

———. *Style and Structure in the Prose of Isaac Babel'.* Columbus, Ohio: Slavica, 1985.

Sinyavsky, Andrey. "Isaac Babel." In *Major Soviet Writers: Essays in Criticism,* edited by Edward J. Brown. Oxford: Oxford University Press, 1973. 301–9.

Skorino, L. I. *Pisatel' i ego vremia: Zhizn' i tvorchestva V. Kataeva.* Moscow: Sovetskii pisatel', 1965.

Slavic Review 53, no. 3 (Fall 1994). A special issue commemorating Babel's centenary, with articles by Scheglov, Avins, and others.

Slonim, Marc. *Soviet Russian Literature: Writers and Problems.* New York: Oxford University Press, 1964.

Smirnov, Valerii. *Bol'shoi polutolkovyi slovar' odesskogo iazyka.* Odessa: Druk, 2003.

Smith, Alexandra. "Valentin Petrovich Kataev." In *Russian Prose Writers Between the World Wars,* edited by Christine Rydel. *Dictionary of Literary Biography,* vol. 272. Detroit: Gale, 2003. 174–86.

Smith, Sidonie, and Julia Watson. *Reading Autobiography: A Guide for Interpreting Life Narratives.* Minneapolis: University of Minnesota Press, 2001.

Sobolev, Vladimir. "Izgnanie metafory: Beseda s V. Kataevym." *Literaturnaia gazeta,* May 17, 1933.

Spearman, Diana. *The Novel and Society.* London: Routledge and Kegan Paul, 1966.

Spengemann, William. *The Forms of Autobiography: Episodes in the History of a Literary Genre.* New Haven, Conn.: Yale University Press, 1980.

Stalin, J. V. "Speech to the 18th Party Congress" (February 1931). In *Problems of Leninism.* Moscow: Foreign Languages Publishing House, 1953. 454–55.

Struve, Gleb. *Soviet Russian Literature 1917–1950.* Norman: University of Oklahoma Press, 1951.

Suok-Olesha, Ol'ga, and and E. Pel'son, eds. *Vospominaniia o Iurii Oleshe.* Moscow: Sovetskii pisatel', 1975.

Sylvester, Roshanna P. *Tales of Old Odessa: Crime and Civility in a City of Thieves.* De Kalb: Northern Illinois University Press, 2005.

Tanny, Jarrod. "City of Rogues and Schnorrers: The Myth of Old Odessa in Russian and Jewish Culture." Ph.D. dissertation. University of California at Berkeley, 2008.

———. "The Many Ends of Old Odessa: Memories of the Gilded Age in Russia's City of Sin." University of California at Berkeley: Berkeley Program in Soviet and Post-Soviet Studies, 2007. http://www.escholarship.org/uc/item/2p3674pw.

Tarostschin, S., and Jürgen Schlenker. "Gespräch mit Valentin Katajew." *Sinn und Form: Beitrage zur Literatur* 37, no. 4 (July-August 1985): 692–701.

Tertz, Abram (Andrei Siniavskii). "On Socialist Realism." In *The Trial Begins and On Socialist Realism,* translated by Max Hayward. Berkeley: University of California Press, 1960.

———. "Otechestvo, blatnaia pesnia. . . ." *Sintaksis* 4 (1979): 72–118.

Toporkova, I., ed. *Tsyplenok zharenyi: Blatnye pesni.* Moscow: EKSMO, 2004.

Toporov, V. N. "Peterburg i peterburgskii tekst russkoi literatury." In *Semiotika goroda i gorodskoi kul'tury: Peterburg.* Tartu, Estonia: Uchenye zapiski tartuskogo gorodskogo universiteta, 1984.

———. "Prostranstvo i tekst." In *Tekst: semantika i struktura,* edited by Tatiana Tsiv'ian. Moscow: Nauka, 1983. 227–84.

Trilling, Lionel. Introductory essay to Isaac Babel, *Collected Stories,* translated and edited by Walter Morison. New York: Criterion Books, 1955.

Tucker, Janet G. *Revolution Betrayed: Jurij Olesa's "Envy."* Columbus, Ohio: Slavica, 1996.

Turgenev, I. S. *First Love and Other Stories.* Translated by Richard Freeborn. Oxford: Oxford University Press, 1989.

Twain, Mark. *The Innocents Abroad; Roughing It.* New York: Library of America, 1984.

Van de Stadt, Janneke. "A Question of Place: Situating *Old Shloime* in Isaac Babel's Oeuvre." *Russian Review* 66, no. 1 (January 2007): 36–54.

Vatnikova-Prizel, Z. *O russkoi memuarnoi literature.* East Lansing, Mich.: Russian Language Journal, 1978.

Vatulescu, Cristina. *Police Aesthetics: Literature, Film, and the Secret Police in Soviet Times.* Stanford, Calif.: Stanford University Press, 2010.

Vickery, Walter. "Odessa—Watershed Year: Patterns in Puškin's Love Lyrics." In *Puškin Today,* edited by David M. Bethea. Bloomington: Indiana University Press, 1993.

Vladimirskii, Boris. *Venok siuzhetov.* Vinnitsa, Ukraine: Kontinent-PRIM, 1994.

Volkovinskii, A. S. "Fel'eton i pozdniaia proza V. Kataeva: Vnutrenniaia preemstvennost'." *Voprosy Russkoi Literatury* 1, no. 55 (1990): 110–17.

Wachtel, Andrew B. *The Battle for Childhood: Creation of a Russian Myth.* Stanford, Calif.: Stanford University Press, 1990.

Waten, Judah. *From Odessa to Odessa: The Journey of an Australian Writer.* Melbourne: Cheshire, 1969.

Watt, Ian. *The Rise of the Novel: Studies in Defoe, Richardson and Fielding.* Berkeley: University of California Press, 1957.

Weinberg, Robert. *The Revolution of 1905 in Odessa: Blood on the Steps.* Bloomington: Indiana University Press, 1993.

Zholkovskii, A. K. *Poltora rasskaza Babelia: "Giui de Mopassan" i "Spravka/Gonorar": Struktura, smysl, fon.* Moscow: Komkniga (URSS), 2006.

——— (Alexander Zholkovsky). "Isaac Babel, Author of Guy de Maupassant." *Canadian Slavonic Papers/Revue canadienne des slavistes* 36:1/2 (1994: Mar/June): 89-105.

Zholkovskii, A. K., and M. B. Iampol'skii. *Babel'/Babel.* Moscow: Carte Blanche, 1994.

Zipperstein, Steven J. *Imagining Russian Jewry: Memory, History, Identity.* Seattle: University of Washington Press, 1999.

———. *The Jews of Odessa: A Cultural History, 1794–1881.* Stanford, Calif.: Stanford University Press, 1991.

Index

Abramovitsh, S. Y., 23
Abrams, M. H., 160n27
abundance, 12, 27–28, 29, 30
Acmeism, 12
action, men of, 60, 71, 76, 88–89, 94, 157n87
Adams, Timothy Dow, 53
Adamson, Sydney, 25–26, 154n41
aesthetic coherence, 57–58
Akhmatova, Anna, 4
Aksyonov, Vasily, 111–12, 170n31
Aleichem, Sholem. *See* Sholem Aleichem
Alexandria, 12
All-Union Congress. *See* Congress of Soviet
    Writers
Alter, Robert, 164n9
Andrei Babichev (in Olesha's *Envy*), 33, 37
androgyny, 32, 33, 81–82, 156n66
Anglophilia, 95
animals. *See* dogs; doves
anti-Semitism, 65, 69, 70, 165n14. *See also*
    Jews
aphorisms (Babel's): autumn/spectacles,
    94, 97, 114, 115, 165n15, 166n31; "full
    stop" (punctuation/knife), 35, 76, 97–98,
    114–15
architecture, 17, 20, 21, 25
Armenian culture, 27, 28
army. *See* Red Army; Red Cavalry; White
    Army
Arye-Leib (in Babel's "How It Was Done"),
    94, 97, 114, 165n15
Arzhak, Nikolai (Yuly Daniel), 35
associativeness: in Kataev, 113–15, 117; in
    Olesha, 125–26
Augustine of Hippo, Saint: *Confessions*, 51
authenticity, 41, 144; and autobiography

theory, 52–53, 55, 161n35; and Babel,
    67, 68, 100, 116, 142; in Dante, 141–42;
    and Kataev, 111, 115–16, 117, 123, 124;
    and Olesha, 126, 141–42
autobiographical discourse: Babel's, 49–50,
    55–57, 63–64, 91–92, 101, 143; as cen-
    tral feature of Odessa school, 7–8, 13–
    16, 41–42, 105, 143–44; Dante's, 140–42;
    Kataev's, 105–6, 111, 124, 169n23; and
    Odessa rogue, 34–37; Olesha's, 119, 125,
    130–33, 139; Paustovsky's, 71–73, 100;
    readers misinterpret, 15–16, 44, 101. *See
    also* autobiography theory
autobiographical narratives: in 19th-century
    prose, 49, 75, 160n26; Gorky's, 94; Odys-
    seus's, 40; Platonic, 51; in Thaw vs. early
    Soviet period, 41; as used by Stalinist
    secret police, 52; Wordsworth's, 50–51,
    161n27. *See also* autobiography theory;
    childhood cycle of stories; Dante Ali-
    ghieri; *My Diamond Crown; No Day
    Without a Line;* Pushkin, Alexander;
    Time of Great Expectations
autobiographical pact, 7, 15; and Babel,
    49, 55, 143; and Dante, 142; and Kataev,
    106; Lejeune's theory of, 5–6, 54–55; and
    Odysseus, 40. *See also* autobiography
    theory
autobiographicity, 7
autobiography theory, 131, 161n29,
    161n35; and aesthetic coherence, 57;
    central principles of, 41, 50–55; Soviet
    vs. Western, 51–53; waves of, 50,
    160n24. *See also* autobiographical pact
autofiction, 49
autos (self), 50

Index

England, 85, 95
epithets. *See* nicknames
Erlich, Victor, 92
Esenin, Sergei, 110
Eulenspiegel, Till. *See* Till Eulenspiegel
exile, 23, 41, 107, 142; Odessa as site of, 20, 22, 26, 32, 33, 39, 143; Pushkin's, 21, 27, 29, 151n15
Exorcist, 165n14
exoticism, 8, 19, 20, 27; in Babel, 73, 85, 95; and Gogol, 11, 31, 154n41; and nostalgia, 38
eyes. *See* visual perception

fabrication. *See* lying
fabula, 51
facts. *See* fiction mixed with truth; "life into literature"; reality; truth
Fainzilberg, Ilya. *See* Ilf, Ilya
falsification. *See* lying
family (in Babel's childhood cycle), 62–69, 76–93, 162n53; ambiguity of, 60; associated with claustrophobic confinement, 59–60, 76, 82, 87–90; contrasted to Borgman's, 84–86; and Cossack story, 79–81; and gymnasium exams, 63–65; literature as means to escape from, 87–91; as storytellers, 60–62, 66–68, 100. *See also* father; Grandfather Levi-Itskhok; grandmother; Great-Uncle Shoyl; men; mother; women
fantasy: in Babel, 74, 78–82, 84, 89, 91, 94; and Bagritsky, 99–100; in Dante, 141; and Kataev, 105–6, 112; in Olesha, 140
father (in Babel's stories): as absent, 60; Babel's allowance from, 56, 96; contrasted with hearty physicality, 76; and Cossack story, 44, 79–81; gullibility of, 64–65, 68; promises dovecote, 63–64; as unreliable, 66; as violent, 94; and violin lessons, 59, 87–88, 90
father (in Olesha's *Envy*), 139–40, 142
femininity, 17, 33, 156n66
fictionality, 45, 61, 63, 68, 99
fictionality markers, 45, 159n5
fictional pact, 5–6, 7, 44
fiction mixed with truth (in Babel): contrasted with domesticity, 82; and emphasis on storytelling, 61–62, 63, 66, 68; and literature's link to lies, 83–84; readers'

misinterpretations of, 15, 44–50, 96; and roguery, 34; strategies for, 55, 57, 74; as superior to reality, 85, 89, 101. *See also* fantasy; lying; storytelling; truth
fiction mixed with truth (in general): Bagritsky as symbol of, 99–100, 122; critical theory on, 44–45, 50–51, 53–55; in Dante, 140–42; in Kataev, 112, 124; and Odessa myth, 26; and Odysseus, 40; in Olesha, 125, 139–40, 142; in Paustovsky, 71–72, 97; in Pushkin, 3, 160n26; and roguery, 34–35, 42; as salient feature of Odessa school, 8, 33, 143–44. *See also* "life into literature"; "stories that come true"; truth
fiddlers: in Kuprin and Chekhov, 69–72, 80, 85–86, 143, 157n87; as symbol of Odessa, 20, 32. *See also* violins; violin teachers
First Cavalry, 48
fish, 28, 31, 36, 37, 66, 67, 75
Five-Year Plan (First, 1928), 28, 104
Flaubert, Gustave, 97, 115, 164n9
fog, 4, 11, 31, 32
food, 27–28, 31, 121, 136, 154n51. *See also* fish
Formalism, 13, 15, 51, 57, 158n101
Foucault, Michel, 18
fragments (*otryvki*): in Babel, 45, 59; in Kataev, 125, 138; in Olesha, 125–33, 136–38, 168n8, 173n64, 173n72
France. *See* French culture and literature; French language
Franko, Ivan, 152n30
freedom, 19, 35, 53, 87, 116; domesticity contrasted to, 59–60, 76, 82
Freidin, Gregory, 49, 92, 94–95, 96, 149n24, 155n64, 159n8, 166n30, 172n58
French culture and literature: and Babel, 9, 32, 95–98, 114, 148n15, 156n65; as central to Odessa text, 27, 30; and Mauvism, 116; and Odessa's political history, 20–21, 151n14
French language, 9, 24, 32, 156n65
French Revolution, 20, 21
freshness: in Babel, 31, 59, 82, 90; in Kataev, 120; in Olesha, 118, 135, 139
Freud, Sigmund, 47, 81, 96
Friedkin, William: *Exorcist,* 165n14
Frug, Shimon, 23
Futurism, 12, 158n101

195

Index

Inber, Vera, 6, 13, 136
indoors, 76, 78, 80, 91, 137. *See also* domestic sphere
innkeeper story, 62, 66, 67
intentional fallacy, 44
intentionality: and autobiographical pact, 5, 54; and Babel's blurring of fiction and lies, 44–45, 68; and St. Petersburg, 4, 17
invention: Babel's, 44, 56, 84–85, 96; Kataev's, 105; Olesha's, 139–40, 142; as salient feature of Odessan modernism, 7, 40–41, 42, 144–45; Shklovsky's, 120
inversion: in Babel, 65; and Mauvism, 116; and Odessa as looking-glass world, 17, 18, 19; in Olesha, 133, 134; as salient feature of Odessan modernism, 33, 41, 143
irony, 115, 135, 144; in Babel, 61, 65, 78, 94
Isocrates: *Antidosis*, 51
istina (truth), 85
Italian culture and Italians, 21, 24; and architecture, 17, 20, 25; in Babel, 30, 32, 92, 95; in Kataev, 120, 122–23; in Olesha, 140–42, 143–44; in Pushkin, 27, 30
Ivan Babichev (in Olesha's *Envy*), 33, 36, 139–40, 142, 156n76

Jabotinsky, Vladimir, 5, 6, 9
Jesus Christ, 141
Jewish Enlightenment, 23
Jewish Literary Society, 23
Jewish Pale of Settlement, 21
Jews, 16, 62, 67, 155n61, 164n4; Babel associates with claustrophobic domesticity, 59–60, 88, 91; Babel's contrasting versions of, 93, 95; and Babel's upbringing, 148n15; choose Russian identity, 9, 148n16; cuisine of, 28; demographic and cultural role of in Odessa, 12, 19, 22, 23, 24, 30–32, 153n31; as fiddlers, 69, 85–86, 157n87; as gangsters, 17, 20, 36, 157n83; and grandmother tales, 68; as men of contemplation, 71, 157n87; and misinterpretations of Babel, 47, 48; as New Men, 36; during Polish demonstrations (1861), 163n58; quotas and restrictions on, 23, 56, 64, 102; as red-headed, 80, 165n13; and roguery, 34; and sexuality, 36, 81, 156n66, 165n15; as victims, 69–71, 93; and weakness stereotypes

(small, bent, pathetic), 36, 37, 71, 80, 89, 91. *See also* anti-Semitism; ghetto; pogroms
jokes, 30–31, 34, 152, 152n30. *See also* humor

Kamennoostrovsky Prospekt, 30, 31
Kapnist, Vasily, 11
Karakina, Elena, 7
Karamzin, Nikolai: "Poor Liza," 86
Kataev, Evgeny. *See* Petrov, Evgeny
Kataev, Valentin Petrovich, 6, 14, 23, 33, 42, 102–26, 144, 169n19, 173n61; advocates Mauvism, 115–20, 171n40; and Babel, 113–17, 124, 169n17; and Bagritsky, 120–24, 143, 171n54; biographical background of, 7, 9–10, 102–3, 149n17; and Blok's death, 121–22; and Bunin, 103, 167n4; crown imagery in, 108–10, 112, 170n32; longevity of, 106–7; as Lord of Misrule, 116, 124; and Olesha, 118–20, 122, 124–26, 129, 138–39, 142, 170n32, 173n63, 174n74, 175n81; and Paustovsky, 120–22; and production novel, 36, 117, 118, 126; protégés of, 111–12, 170n31; and Pushkin, 107–12, 116, 124, 169n23, 170n25; and sculpture, 109, 111–13, 118, 170n32; and Socialist Realism, 104–5, 106, 117–19, 126, 168n13; and "South-West," 120–24, 171n45. *See also* nicknames
   WORKS: *Catacombs (Katakomby)*, 167n5, 168n13; "Eclipse of the Sun" ("Zatmenia solntsa"), 175n90; *Embezzlers (Rastratchiki)*, 103, 111, 126; *Erendorf Island (Ostrov Erendorf)*, 103; *Grass of Oblivion*, 173n61; *Holy Well*, 173n61; *I, Son of the Working People (Ia, syn trudovogo naroda)*, 104; *Little Iron Door in the Wall (Malen'kaia zheleznaia dver' v stene)*, 119–20; *Master of Iron (Povelitel' zheleza)*, 103; *My Diamond Crown* (see *My Diamond Crown*); *For the Power of the Soviets (Za vlast' sovetov)*, 168n13; *Shattered Life (Razbitaia zhizn')*, 125, 170n32, 175n90; *Son of the Regiment (Syn polka)*, 104; *Squaring the Circle (Kvadratura kruga)*, 103; *Time, Forward! (Vremia, vpered!)*, 36, 104, 106, 117, 119, 126; *Waves of the Black Sea*

About the Author

Rebecca Jane Stanton is an assistant professor of Russian at Barnard College.